Building Tribal Economies:
A Comprehensive Guide to Native American Economic Development, Business Structures, and Federal Programs

Building Tribal Economies:
A Comprehensive Guide to Native American Economic Development, Business Structures, and Federal Programs

PREPARED AND AUTHORED BY
Dante Desiderio and Max Muller, JD

Copyright Notice

First Edition
ISBN: 979-8-9987802-0-2

Published by Hyco River Development, Inc., Arlington, Virginia and Max Muller & Associates, LLC, Native American Interests Section, Overland Park, Kansas
ddesiderio@hyco-river.com / max@maxmullerassociates.com

Printed in the United States of America

About the Cover

Why The Catawba Map Graces Our Cover

The Catawba Deerskin Map, drawn around 1721 and presented to South Carolina's colonial governor Francis Nicholson, serves as the perfect visual metaphor for our exploration of Native American business structures. This rare example of indigenous North American cartography embodies the same principles that guide successful tribal economic development today: the power of networks, the importance of relationships, and the strategic navigation of complex jurisdictional landscapes.

Networks Over Geography

Like the most sophisticated tribal business strategies discussed in this book, the Catawba map prioritizes relationships over rigid boundaries. The connecting lines between tribal communities, represented as circles, illustrate the social, political, and trade networks that sustained indigenous economies for centuries before European contact. These pathways depict not just geographic routes, but the diplomatic and commercial relationships that enabled prosperity across vast territories.

This network thinking mirrors the modern tribal approach to business structure. Today's successful tribal enterprises, whether Section 17 corporations, tribally chartered LLCs, or complex joint ventures, succeed by building strategic relationships that transcend traditional jurisdictional boundaries. They create value through partnerships, alliances, and carefully constructed legal frameworks that honor sovereignty while enabling commerce.

Sovereignty Expressed Through Symbols

The map's visual language speaks to a fundamental theme of our book: the assertion of sovereignty through deliberate structural choices. The mapmaker's decision to represent Native communities as circles and European settlements as squares was no mere artistic preference. As archaeologist Gregory Waselkov suggests, this may have constituted a Native critique of European rigidity, circles representing the organic, interconnected nature of indigenous governance, while squares symbolized the foreign, inflexible boundaries imposed by colonial powers (Brown, Indigenous Cartography and Colonial Resistance, 2019, 45-52).

This symbolic distinction resonates powerfully with the modern tribal business landscape. Today's Native American business structures represent a sophisticated evolution of this same principle: maintaining the organic flexibility and cultural values of tribal governance while creating entities capable of engaging effectively with the often rigid requirements of modern commerce. A tribally chartered corporation or a carefully structured joint venture serves the same function as those circles on the deerskin, asserting indigenous identity and values while enabling productive engagement with external partners.

A Living Document for Modern Enterprise

The Catawba Deerskin Map transcends simple geographic representation to become a strategic document, a blueprint for navigating complex relationships while maintaining cultural identity. It demonstrates how indigenous leaders, even in the early colonial period, understood the necessity of engaging with external powers while preserving their own authority and values.

This same sophisticated thinking characterizes the most successful tribal business structures today. Whether creating a limited liability company to partner with external investors, establishing a holding company to manage diverse enterprises, or structuring a joint venture to access new markets, modern tribal business leaders employ the same strategic sophistication demonstrated by that unknown Catawba mapmaker three centuries ago.

Important Legal Disclaimer

NOT LEGAL OR TAX ADVICE

This document is provided SOLELY for general informational and educational purposes and does NOT constitute legal advice, tax advice, or professional consultation under any circumstances. Despite partial preparation by an attorney, no attorney-client relationship is established between the author(s) and any reader. The reader acknowledges and agrees that accessing, reading, or using any information in this document does not create any professional relationship whatsoever with the author(s).

NOT CERTIFIED PUBLIC ACCOUNTANTS

The author(s) are NOT Certified Public Accountants (CPAs), enrolled agents, or licensed tax professionals. Any tax-related information presented herein is strictly for general informational purposes only and should NOT be relied upon for tax planning, compliance, or decision-making of any kind.

COMPLEX LEGAL AND TAX LANDSCAPE

The information contained herein offers only general guidance regarding Native American business structures and related considerations. Native American law involves unique and complex intersections of tribal, federal, and state jurisdictions, which vary significantly across different tribal nations and geographic regions. The legal landscape governing tribal business entities, sovereign immunity, taxation, and regulatory compliance is extraordinarily complex and constantly evolving through legislation, treaty interpretation, court decisions, IRS rulings, and regulatory changes.

TAX MATTERS DISCLAIMER

Tax laws and regulations applicable to Native American business structures are particularly complex, involving federal tax law, tribal taxation authority, state tax considerations, and unique provisions under the Internal Revenue Code. Tax consequences vary dramatically based on tribal affiliation, business structure, location of operations, source of income, and numerous other factors. The IRS frequently issues new guidance, rulings, and interpretations that can materially affect tax treatment. Nothing in this document should be construed as tax advice or recommendations regarding tax strategies, deductions, elections, or compliance obligations.

NO WARRANTIES OR REPRESENTATIONS

The author(s) expressly disclaim all warranties, representations, and guarantees regarding the accuracy, completeness, timeliness, or applicability of any information presented, including but not limited to any tax-related information. Information is provided as-is, with all faults, and may quickly become outdated due to changing laws, regulations, IRS guidance, and policies. The author(s) make no representations whatsoever regarding the accuracy or applicability of any information to your specific situation, tribal affiliation, jurisdictional considerations, tax circumstances, or any other particular set of facts or circumstances.

MANDATORY INDEPENDENT PROFESSIONAL CONSULTATION

Readers MUST consult with qualified legal counsel specifically experienced in Federal Indian Law, tribal law, and business formation AND with qualified tax professionals (CPAs, enrolled agents, or tax attorneys) experienced in Native American taxation issues before taking any action based on information contained in this document. Such professionals should be licensed to practice in the relevant state jurisdiction and/or formally recognized by the appropriate tribal authority having jurisdiction over your matter.

LIMITATION OF LIABILITY

By accessing this document, you explicitly agree that the author(s) and any affiliated persons or entities shall not be liable for any direct, indirect, incidental, special, consequential, or exemplary damages (including but not limited to tax penalties, interest, legal fees, or adverse tax consequences) resulting from your use of or inability to use the information contained herein, regardless of whether such damages are based on warranty, contract, tort, or any other legal theory, and even if advised of the possibility of such damages.

READER ASSUMPTION OF RISK

Any reliance upon or application of information contained in this document is undertaken entirely at the reader's own risk. The reader assumes full responsibility for verifying all information through independent legal counsel and qualified tax professionals before making any decisions or taking any actions that may have legal or tax consequences.

IRS CIRCULAR 230 NOTICE

To ensure compliance with IRS requirements, any tax-related discussions in this document are not intended or written to be used, and cannot be used, for the purpose of avoiding penalties under the Internal Revenue Code or promoting, marketing, or recommending any tax-related matters addressed herein.

TABLE OF CONTENTS

Preface: How Native American Business Structures Differ from Non-Native Structures

Native American business structuring is uniquely rooted in the political and legal status of tribes as sovereign nations, distinct from state-chartered or federally regulated non-Native business entities. While non-Native businesses typically organize under state laws such as LLC or corporate statutes and operate within a uniform tax and regulatory framework, Native businesses must navigate an entirely different and layered landscape that blends tribal sovereignty, federal Indian law, and a growing body of tribal business codes.

Key Distinctions

Sovereign Status

Tribes are not just ethnic groups, they are sovereign governments with powers of self-governance (American Indian Law Deskbook 2021, Section 58). This means businesses operated directly by tribes or through tribal entities may enjoy sovereign immunity, meaning they cannot be sued without consent. Non-Native businesses never possess such protections. This immunity influences everything from risk management to how contracts are negotiated and enforced.

Legal Jurisdiction

Native businesses often operate under tribal law and within tribal court systems, especially if chartered under tribal codes. This autonomy allows tribes to create their own business regulations, dispute resolution mechanisms, and entity types. In contrast, non-Native businesses are subject to state jurisdiction, with limited flexibility in defining governance structures.

Entity Formation and Chartering Options

Tribes can structure businesses in ways not available to non-Native enterprises:

- **Section 17 corporations**, federally chartered under the Indian Reorganization Act, are unique to tribes and maintain tax-exempt status and immunity features (Bureau of Indian Affairs 2015, 8-12).

- **Oklahoma Indian Welfare Act corporations** formed by Oklahoma tribes under section 3 of this act are not subject to federal income tax. Oklahoma tribes are not eligible to incorporate under the Indian Reorganization Act of 1934.

- **Tribally chartered corporations and LLCs** are formed under tribal law and can blend cultural priorities with business needs.

- **State-chartered tribal entities** are used strategically when tribes need to operate in commercial settings where state laws offer advantages.

Non-Native businesses are limited to structures available under state or federal law and typically don't weigh legal sovereignty or government-to-government status in their formation.

Taxation

Tribes and tribally owned entities, especially those considered "arms of the tribe", may be exempt from federal income tax (Atkinson and Nilles 2008). Their income can also be shielded from certain state taxes, particularly for on-reservation activity. Non-Native businesses, regardless of their location or ownership, are generally subject to full federal and state taxation. Recent federal tax law changes have modified certain provisions affecting individual Native business owners and specific business structures, with comprehensive analysis provided in the detailed structural discussions that follow (U.S. Department of Treasury 2025).

Access to Specialized Federal Financing

The federal government's trust responsibility to tribes extends to economic development through specialized financing programs unavailable to non-Native businesses. Federal agencies including the Bureau of Indian Affairs, Indian Health Service, Department of Agriculture, Small Business Administration, and Department of Housing and Urban Development offer grant programs, loan guarantees, and direct lending specifically designed for tribal governments and Native-owned enterprises. These programs recognize both the unique capital challenges in Indian Country and the federal commitment to supporting tribal self-determination. Programs such as the Indian Loan Guaranty Program, USDA's Rural Business Development Grants for tribal areas, and SBA's 8(a) contracting advantages create financing pathways that acknowledge the distinctive legal and economic position of Native businesses within the federal system.

Direct Federal Appropriations and Grant Programs
Direct federal appropriations represent the most significant category of tribal financing, encompassing both formula-based allocations that tribes receive as a matter of federal obligation and competitive grant programs that support specific economic development and infrastructure initiatives. The constitutional foundation for federal appropriations to tribal governments derives from the federal trust responsibility and congressional plenary power over Indian affairs, establishing federal funding not as discretionary assistance but as fulfillment of governmental obligations arising from treaties, statutes, and the unique political relationship between tribal nations and the United States (Cherokee Nation v. Georgia 1831; Worcester v. Georgia 1832).

The Indian Self-Determination and Education Assistance Act of 1975 fundamentally transformed federal appropriations from paternalistic assistance administered by federal agencies into funding mechanisms that support tribal governmental operations and capacity building. Title I contracting provisions (25 U.S.C. §§ 5321-5348) enable tribes to redirect federal program funding toward tribally-determined priorities while building institutional capacity and generating program efficiencies that can support additional economic development activities. Title IV compacting provisions (25 U.S.C. §§ 5381-5423) provide even greater flexibility by enabling tribes to redesign federal programs and consolidate funding sources to achieve tribal strategic objectives while maintaining federal funding support.

The Tribal Self-Governance Act of 1994 (25 U.S.C. §§ 5381-5423) expanded these authorities by establishing permanent compacting mechanisms that enable qualifying tribes to assume responsibility for virtually all federal programs serving their communities, creating comprehensive funding mechanisms that support both governmental operations and economic development initiatives. Tribal compacts can include economic development components, infrastructure development, and business support activities that utilize federal appropriations to leverage additional private sector investment and generate sustainable revenue streams (National Congress of American Indians, Tribal Self-Governance Report, 2022, 12-18).

Cultural and Strategic Alignment

Tribal businesses may embed cultural values, language, and community goals into their organizational documents, governance, and economic strategies. For example, hiring preferences for tribal members, investment in cultural preservation, or stewardship of tribal lands may be foundational. These dimensions are not typically available or prioritized in standard non-Native business structures.

Economic Development Goals

For many tribes, business structuring is a tool of nation-building, meant to support long-term self-determination, diversify economies, and protect generational wealth. Non-Native businesses often prioritize shareholder returns and investor value. Native business structures are designed with broader community outcomes in mind.

Conclusion

Native American business structuring is not merely about forming a business entity, it is an expression of tribal sovereignty, legal self-determination, and cultural resilience. It operates within a legal and economic ecosystem that is uniquely tribal, often blending traditional governance with modern commercial needs. This approach allows for flexibility, protection, and strategic alignment that go beyond the norms of non-Native business formation.

Authors and Biographical Information

This book is a collaboration between Dante Desiderio, President, Hyco River Development, Inc. and Max Muller, Principal, Max Muller & Associates, LLC.

Dante Desiderio

Dante Desiderio, a citizen of the Sappony Tribe and its Executive Director, has emerged as one of Indian Country's most influential economic policy experts. Drawing from his tribal heritage, Dante has built a career focused on advancing tribal economic sovereignty and self-determination. His expertise in tribal finance, economic policy, taxation, and enterprise development has made him a trusted advisor to tribal leaders and federal policymakers alike.

Dante's influence on tribal economic development spans six critical areas:

1. Advocacy for Tribal Inclusion in Federal Economic Policy

He played a central role in ensuring tribal nations were included in major federal economic stimulus packages, including American Recovery and Reinvestment Act, the CARES Act, and the American Rescue Plan (Desiderio, Tribal Economic Policy During Federal Stimulus, 2016, 23-29). His advocacy at the highest levels of the federal government secured critical and historic funding for tribal governments during economic crises.

2. Improving Access to Capital

Recognizing capital access as a persistent barrier, Dante advocates for solutions like a development bank dedicated to Indian Country and reforms to help tribes access tax-exempt debt.

3. Building Sound Financial Frameworks

He helps tribes establish frameworks for sound financial systems, seek funding opportunities, and address complex financial challenges with data-driven solutions.

4. Modernizing Tax Policies

Dante champions pro-growth tax incentives and financing mechanisms, including the Indian Employment Tax Credit and accelerated depreciation, to stimulate business growth and infrastructure development in tribal communities.

5. Promoting Economic Diversification

He supports tribes in diversifying beyond gaming into commercial enterprises, infrastructure, and environmental projects, contributing to greater economic self-sufficiency.

6. Strengthening Tribal Sovereignty

By championing tribal control over economic decisions, Dante's work has empowered tribes to pursue development on their own terms.

Professional Experience

Dante left a successful career as a Certified Financial Planner (CFP) to become the Executive Director of the Native American Finance Officers Association (NAFOA), where he increased the organization's commitment to its members and elevated its national profile as a steward for tribal economic development. He spent over a decade bringing capital markets and the financial sector into Indian Country and creating leading professional development classes aimed at building financial capacity for tribal leaders at major universities including a leadership and sovereign fund oversight program at the Harvard Business School.

He also served as the Chief Executive Officer of the National Congress of American Indians and Alaska Natives (NCAI) and the NCAI Fund.

During the COVID-19 pandemic, Dante emerged as a powerful advocate ensuring tribal governments and businesses were not overlooked in federal relief efforts. His work was instrumental in securing tribal access to the Paycheck Protection Program and the $8 billion Coronavirus Relief Fund established by the CARES Act and the historic $32 billion in relief under the American Recovery Act.

Today, Dante operates Hyco River Development, Inc, a consultancy providing economic guidance to Native American tribes and enterprises, as well as Native American nonprofits, continuing his commitment to tribal economic sovereignty. His career exemplifies the power of combining cultural understanding with technical expertise and strategic advocacy to create pathways for tribal prosperity while honoring the fundamental principles of tribal sovereignty.

Dante lives in Virginia with his two beautiful daughters.

Contact: ddesiderio@hyco-river.com

Max Muller, JD, THRP

Max Muller brings more than 50 years of expertise as an attorney, business executive, author, consultant, professional speaker, OSHA Authorized General Industry Outreach Trainer, real estate agent, and U.S. Army veteran to his work with Native American governments and enterprises. With a Juris Doctor degree from the University of Kansas School of Law and a Bachelor of Arts in Sociology from the University of Kansas, Max has established himself as a respected authority in developing customized training programs for tribal organizations across the United States.

As founder and principal of Max Muller & Associates, LLC he has specialized in providing practical and culturally relevant solutions to Native American tribal governments and enterprises, focusing on workplace legalities, regulatory compliance, and organizational development. His firm works closely with tribal leadership to eliminate guesswork in program development by providing tailored recommendations that address the unique governance and regulatory challenges faced by Native communities. Max has also served as an independent investigator for various tribes related to confidential internal investigations of noncriminal employee misconduct.

Max has presented more than 3,000 seminars, keynote speeches, and professional development programs worldwide, with significant experience delivering specialized training for tribal organizations on topics ranging from employment law to operational excellence. His approach emphasizes respect for tribal sovereignty while providing the same high-quality legal and business expertise demanded by other sophisticated enterprises.

As the primary instructional designer and author of the National Native American Human Resources Association's (NNAHRA) Tribal Management Professional Certification Program (TMP), Max has made significant contributions to professional development in Indian Country[1]. He holds the Tribal Human Resource Professional (THRP) certification from the NNAHRA Foundation, demonstrating his commitment to understanding and addressing the unique human resource challenges in tribal organizations.

Prior to establishing his consulting practice in 1990, Max held various executive positions in distribution and information technology companies. This diverse operational background informs his practical approach to addressing the complex challenges facing tribal governments and businesses.

Max has provided General Counsel services to the Native American Finance Officers Association (NAFOA) and the National Congress of American Indians and Alaska Natives (NCAI).

Max is the author of a number of business books including "The Manager's Guide to HR: Hiring, Firing, Performance Evaluations, Documentation, Benefits, and Everything Else You Need to Know" (Second Edition, AMACOM Books, now HarperCollins Publishing, and SHRM); "The Fundamentals of Inventory Control and Management" Self-Study (4th Edition, AMACOM Books); "The Legal Side of HR Practice" (AMACOM Books); "Essentials of Inventory Management" (4th Edition, Harper Collins Publishing) [Edition One published in Spanish as "Fundamentos De Administracion De Inventarios"]; and "The Essential OSHA Self-Study Guide" (Sound Learning Solutions).

....

[1] In developing the TMP Certification Program, Max had the honor of working with the late Tal D. Moore, Director, NNAHRA Foundation. Tal was a nationally known and highly respected educator throughout Indian Country.

Max's commitment to understanding the distinct needs of Native American communities has established him as a trusted advisor who bridges traditional business expertise with the cultural and governance realities of Indian Country.

Max lives in Overland Park, Kansas with his wife of more than 56 years. He has three children and five grandchildren.

Contact: max@maxmullerassociates.com

Acknowledgment

Portions of this book were developed with the assistance of artificial intelligence tools, including ChatGPT (OpenAI), Claude (Anthropic PBC), and Perplexity (Perplexity AI, Inc.). These tools were used to support the authors in conducting research, drafting initial content, refining language, brainstorming, and enhancing the clarity of complex topics. At no point did these tools replace the authors' own judgment, interpretation, or analytical framework. Their use was carefully managed to maintain the integrity, originality, and scholarly rigor of the work.

The legal documents in this book and its supplements incorporate standard legal language and commonly used contractual terms that are part of established legal practice.

Introduction

Building Tribal Economies: A Comprehensive Guide to Native American Economic Development, Business Structures, and Federal Programs

Native American tribes engage in economic development through a complex intersection of sovereign authority, business structures, and federal programs that creates both unique opportunities and distinct challenges not found in any other sector of the American economy. This comprehensive guide addresses three fundamental components that drive successful tribal economic development: the federal legal authority that establishes specialized financing and support programs for tribal governments, the diverse array of business structures available for tribal enterprises, and the detailed implementation strategies necessary to effectively coordinate federal programs with appropriate business structures to achieve sustainable economic growth.

Federal Legal Authority and Tribal Financing Programs

The federal government's authority to establish specialized financing programs for tribal governments stems from the unique constitutional relationship between the United States and federally recognized tribal nations, representing one of the most significant expressions of the federal trust responsibility in the modern era. This authority encompasses both the plenary power doctrine established in federal Indian law and the specific constitutional mandate to regulate commerce with Indian tribes, creating comprehensive frameworks for federal financial assistance that distinguish tribal financing programs from general federal economic development initiatives.

This book provides detailed analysis of federal legal authority across eleven major categories of financing sources, from Treasury Department programs and Economic Development Administration grants to specialized environmental and energy development initiatives. Each program analysis includes comprehensive coverage of eligibility requirements, application procedures, compliance obligations, and strategic coordination opportunities that enable tribal governments to make informed decisions about program participation and integration strategies.

Business Structures: Traditional to Modern

Recognizing significant developments in law, taxation, and tribal economic strategy following an IRS presentation in 2013 and subsequent federal tax law changes in 2025 that have significantly enhanced tax incentives and opportunities for tribal economic development on tribal business structures (Economic Innovation Group 2025; U.S. Department of Treasury 2025), this guide provides updated analysis of both traditional structures (unincorporated enterprises, sole proprietorships, partnerships) and modern legal entities (corporations, especially Section 17 corporations, tribal LLCs, state-chartered entities), including emerging hybrid models and complex joint venture arrangements.

Critically, the business structure analysis in this book addresses **all types of business structures available to tribal governments and enterprises, not merely those related to federal programs.** Whether a tribe is considering a simple unincorporated enterprise for local community services, a sophisticated holding company structure for diversified business operations, or a joint venture with private sector partners, this guide provides comprehensive coverage of structural options, advantages, limitations, and strategic considerations that apply regardless of federal program participation.

However, the guide also provides detailed analysis of how various business structures interface with federal programs, recognizing that optimal economic development often requires strategic coordination between appropriate business structures and federal financing opportunities. This integration analysis helps tribal governments understand

how structure selection affects program eligibility, compliance requirements, tax implications, and strategic implementation approaches.

Sovereignty and Business Integration

Federally recognized tribes are sovereign governments predating the
United States, and their business activities carry unique legal considerations that fundamentally distinguish tribal economic development from
other forms of business and economic development. Key factors include
sovereign immunity protections that can shield tribal assets while requiring strategic navigation in commercial settings, specialized tax treatment
where tribes themselves are not subject to federal income tax while the
tax status of tribal business entities depends on their structure and charter, and regulatory frameworks that recognize tribal sovereignty while enabling participation in federal programs and commercial markets.

The analysis incorporates sovereign immunity considerations, federal
tax implications, and regulatory requirements to ensure that both business structure selection and federal program participation align with
appropriate governance frameworks while preserving tribal sovereignty
and self-determination. Since 2013, federal policy has increasingly recognized tribally formed entities as extensions of tribal governments for
tax purposes, creating new opportunities for strategic structure selection
that this guide addresses comprehensively. Recent federal legislation has
further enhanced these opportunities through permanent extensions of
key tax incentives and expanded benefits for rural and tribal economic
development initiatives while preserving the fundamental sovereignty
advantages that distinguish tribal economic development from conventional business development (Economic Innovation Group 2025; U.S.
Department of Treasury 2025).

Strategic Framework and Coordination

This guide develops systematic decision-making methodologies that
parallel strategic business planning while addressing the unique complexities of federal program coordination and multi-source financing
strategies. The strategic framework enables tribal governments to evaluate program opportunities against their development priorities, organizational capacity, and strategic objectives while ensuring that program

selections support rather than compete with community priorities and governance arrangements.

The coordination framework addresses timing and sequencing considerations, matching fund strategies, administrative capacity requirements, and performance measurement systems that enable effective multi-program implementation while building sustainable institutional capacity for ongoing economic development activities.

Scope and Organization

This book is organized to provide both comprehensive reference material and strategic guidance for implementation. Traditional and modern business structures are analyzed systematically, from unincorporated enterprises through complex holding company arrangements, with detailed attention to advantages, limitations, recent legal and regulatory developments, and strategic applications. Federal programs are presented through both categorical analysis and strategic coordination frameworks that enable effective program selection and implementation.

The guide concludes with best practices for choosing and structuring tribal businesses that integrate business structure selection with federal program coordination and long-term strategic planning, providing practical frameworks that tribes, Native entrepreneurs, and their professional advisors can utilize to make informed decisions that protect tribal assets, optimize federal program benefits, and foster sustainable economic development.

Note on Scope: While this book provides comprehensive coverage of tribally owned businesses and tribal government economic development activities, individual Native American entrepreneurs generally follow business structure approaches similar to other small businesses, though special rules can apply when operating on-reservation. The authors applaud and encourage all existing and future individual Native American entrepreneurs while focusing this guide on the unique considerations that affect tribal governments and tribally owned enterprises.

However, the intersection between tribal governmental programs and individual business development creates important opportunities that warrant specific attention. (See Supplement O: Tribal General

Welfare Exclusion (GWE): Key Concepts) Supplement O addresses the Tribal General Welfare Exclusion (GWE), which provides tribal governments with significant tools for supporting individual tribal members, including potential business development assistance, through programs that maintain favorable tax treatment for recipients. While GWE programs cannot directly support business entities, they represent powerful mechanisms for tribal governments to provide individual support that may facilitate business development while serving broader community welfare objectives.

The book's goal is to help tribal governments, Native entrepreneurs, and their professional advisors, including attorneys, financial professionals, and consultants serving Indian Country, make informed decisions that advance tribal economic self-determination while capitalizing on the unique opportunities created by tribal sovereignty, federal program access, innovative business structure selection, and strategic individual support programs that complement business development initiatives.

Chapter 1: Federal Legal Authority and Program Foundation

While this book's primary focus is a comprehensive analysis of Native American business structures, from traditional unincorporated enterprises to sophisticated modern entities, understanding the federal legal framework and program landscape provides essential context for informed structural decision-making. The federal government's unique trust responsibility to tribes, established through treaties, statutes, and case law, has created both opportunities and complexities that influence how tribal businesses are conceived, structured, and operated.

Federal economic development programs, while not required for tribal business formation, often present strategic advantages that can inform structural choices. A tribe considering whether to organize as a Section 17 corporation, a tribally chartered LLC, or a state-chartered entity benefits from understanding not only the inherent characteristics of each structure, but also how those structures interact with available federal resources. Similarly, tribes evaluating partnership arrangements, joint ventures, or holding company models gain strategic insight by understanding the federal policy environment that shapes Indian Country economics.

This foundational understanding of federal authority and programs does not suggest that tribal business success depends on federal participation. Rather, it recognizes that informed structural decisions, whether pursued entirely through tribal resources or in combination with federal programs, require knowledge of the full legal and economic landscape in which Native businesses operate. The structural analysis that follows in subsequent chapters applies universally, empowering tribes to make strategic choices that align with their sovereignty, cultural values, and economic objectives, regardless of their relationship with federal programs.

The federal government's authority to establish financing programs for Native American tribes derives from the unique constitutional relationship between the United States and federally recognized tribal nations, representing one of the most significant expressions of the federal trust responsibility in the modern era. This authority encompasses both the plenary power doctrine established in federal Indian law and the specific constitutional mandate to regulate commerce with Indian tribes, creating a comprehensive framework for federal financial assistance that distinguishes tribal financing programs from general federal economic development initiatives (Cohen's Handbook of Federal Indian Law 2012, § 5.04[1]).

The constitutional foundation for federal tribal financing programs reflects the government-to-government relationship between the United States and tribal nations, emphasizing that such programs serve not merely social welfare objectives but fundamental governmental obligations arising from treaties, statutes, and the federal trust responsibility. This governmental foundation connects federal financing programs to the broader themes of tribal sovereignty and self-determination that characterize modern federal Indian policy, positioning financial assistance as a tool for enhancing tribal governmental capacity rather than creating dependency relationships (National Congress of American Indians 2019).

Understanding the legal framework for federal tribal financing requires integration with the constitutional principles, statutory authorities, and policy developments that have shaped federal Indian law since the founding of the Republic. The evolution of federal tribal financing policy reflects broader changes in federal Indian policy, from the termination era's emphasis on assimilation through the self-determination era's focus on tribal governmental capacity building, culminating in the current emphasis on tribal economic sovereignty and nation-building (Harvard Project on American Indian Economic Development, Policy Brief, 2021).

Section I: Constitutional Foundation for Federal Tribal Financing Programs

Commerce Clause Authority and Plenary Power Doctrine

The constitutional authority for federal tribal financing programs derives primarily from the Commerce Clause power "to regulate Commerce with foreign Nations, and among the several States, and with the Indian Tribes" (U.S. Constitution, Article I, Section 8, Clause 3). The Supreme Court's interpretation of this clause has established that Congress possesses plenary power over Indian affairs, including broad authority to establish programs and policies affecting tribal governments and their economic development (*United States v. Lara* 2004).

This plenary power encompasses not only regulatory authority but also the affirmative power to provide financial assistance and create specialized financing mechanisms that support tribal governmental functions and economic development objectives.

The plenary power doctrine, while controversial in its historical applications, provides the constitutional foundation for comprehensive federal financing programs that recognize tribes' unique status as domestic dependent nations requiring federal support to exercise their inherent sovereignty effectively. In *Morton v. Mancari* (1974), the Supreme Court established that federal programs providing benefits to Indians as members of quasi-sovereign tribal entities constitute political rather than racial classifications, thereby satisfying constitutional equal protection requirements while enabling specialized federal assistance. This constitutional framework enables federal financing programs that would be impermissible if directed toward racial or ethnic groups lacking governmental status.

Trust Responsibility and Federal Obligations

The federal trust responsibility provides additional constitutional foundation for tribal financing programs, establishing affirmative federal obligations to protect and promote tribal interests that extend beyond mere regulatory authority. The Supreme Court has recognized that the trust relationship "has been deemed to impose upon the United States extensive responsibilities that it might not otherwise bear" (*Nevada v. United States* 1983). This trust responsibility encompasses economic development assistance as a means of fulfilling federal obligations to promote tribal self-sufficiency and governmental capacity.

Federal courts have established that the trust responsibility includes obligations to provide tribes with the tools and resources necessary to exercise their inherent sovereignty effectively, including access to capital and financing mechanisms that enable tribal governments to provide essential services and pursue economic development objectives (*United States v. Mitchell* 1983). The trust responsibility thus provides both constitutional authority and federal obligation to establish financing programs that support tribal governmental functions and economic development initiatives, distinguishing such programs from discretionary federal spending and establishing them as fulfillment of federal legal obligations.

The integration of plenary power authority with trust responsibility obligations creates a unique constitutional framework for federal tribal financing that combines broad congressional authority with specific federal duties to support tribal self-determination and economic development. This framework enables comprehensive federal financing programs while establishing legal standards for program design and implementation that must serve tribal governmental interests rather than federal assimilationist objectives (Bureau of Indian Affairs 2023).

Section II: Key Federal Statutes Creating Financing Authorities

Indian Financing Act of 1974

The Indian Financing Act of 1974 represents the foundational federal statute establishing comprehensive financing assistance for tribal governments and individual Indians, creating the legal framework for most subsequent federal tribal financing initiatives (25 U.S.C. §§ 1451-1543). The Act established multiple financing mechanisms, including the Indian Loan Guarantee and Insurance Fund, revolving loan funds for tribes, and interest subsidy programs designed to improve tribal and individual Indian access to private capital markets (25 U.S.C. § 1481). The statute's findings emphasize that "the lack of access to capital is one of the most serious impediments to the economic development of Indian reservations" and that federal assistance in obtaining financing is essential for promoting tribal economic self-sufficiency (25 U.S.C. § 1451).

The Indian Financing Act's comprehensive approach includes both direct federal lending and loan guarantee mechanisms designed to leverage private sector capital while reducing risk through federal backing. The Act authorizes the Secretary of the Interior to make direct loans to tribal governments and individual Indians for economic development purposes, including business enterprises, land acquisition, and infrastructure development (25 U.S.C. § 1484). Additionally, the loan guarantee provisions enable the federal government to guarantee up to 90% of private loans to qualified borrowers, significantly expanding access to conventional financing sources while limiting federal fiscal exposure (25 U.S.C. § 1481(b)).

The Act's revolving loan fund provisions (25 U.S.C. § 1485) established a mechanism for tribes to receive federal grants that capitalize tribal lending programs, creating sustainable financing mechanisms that operate under tribal control while serving tribal economic development objectives. These revolving funds have proven particularly significant because they enable tribes to develop internal lending capacity and expertise while serving local economic development needs more effectively than centralized federal programs (Economic Development Administration 2019).

Native American Programs Act of 1974
The Native American Programs Act of 1974 (42 U.S.C. §§ 2991-2992d) created the Administration for Native Americans (ANA) within the Department of Health and Human Services and established grant programs specifically designed to support tribal governmental capacity building and economic development initiatives. The Act's purpose is "to promote the goal of economic and social self-sufficiency for American Indians, Native Hawaiians, and Alaska Natives" through grants that "support projects that increase economic opportunity" and "strengthen tribal governments" (42 U.S.C. § 2991(a)). Unlike loan programs that require repayment, ANA grants provide direct federal financial assistance for capacity building and development activities that lay the foundation for sustainable economic development.

The Native American Programs Act emphasizes community-controlled development approaches that respect tribal sovereignty and cultural values while building institutional capacity for long-term economic success. Grant programs under the Act support tribal governments in developing strategic plans, improving administrative systems, and building the institutional infrastructure necessary for effective economic development programming. This focus on governmental capacity building complements loan and financing programs by ensuring that tribes possess the institutional capabilities necessary to utilize capital effectively and manage complex development projects successfully.

Indian Self-Determination and Education Assistance Act of 1975
The Indian Self-Determination and Education Assistance Act of 1975 (25 U.S.C. §§ 5321-5423) revolutionized federal tribal financing by establishing mechanisms for tribes to assume responsibility for federal programs and services while maintaining federal funding support. While not primarily a financing statute, the Act's contracting and compacting provisions have created significant opportunities for tribal economic development by enabling tribes to redirect federal program funds toward economic development objectives while building institutional capacity and generating program savings that can support additional development activities (25 U.S.C. § 5325).

Community Development Financial Institutions Fund Act of 1994
The Community Development Financial Institutions Fund Act of 1994 (12 U.S.C. §§ 4701-4718) created specialized financing mechanisms that have proven particularly valuable for tribal economic development, establishing the CDFI Fund within the Treasury Department to support community development financial institutions serving low-income communities, including tribal communities. The CDFI Fund provides grants, loans, and other financial assistance to certified CDFIs that demonstrate capacity to serve low-income communities with appropriate lending products and technical assistance services. Tribal CDFIs have utilized these resources to establish lending programs, provide technical assistance to tribal businesses, and support economic development initiatives that might not qualify for conventional financing (CDFI Fund 2023).

Section III: Federal Agency Programs and Authorities

Department of the Interior and Bureau of Indian Affairs

The Department of the Interior, through the Bureau of Indian Affairs, maintains primary responsibility for implementing federal tribal financing programs based on the Department's general trust responsibility for Indian affairs and specific statutory authorities governing tribal economic development. The BIA's economic development programs operate under multiple statutory authorities, including the Indian Financing Act, the Buy Indian Act, and various appropriations measures that provide funding for tribal business development and technical assistance activities.

BIA economic development appropriations support both direct tribal governmental economic development activities and comprehensive technical assistance programs that build tribal capacity to access additional financing sources and manage complex development projects. The Indian Business Development Program, funded through annual appropriations, provides grants for feasibility studies, business planning, and technical assistance that enable tribal governments and tribal members to develop bankable projects and access private sector financing (25 C.F.R. Part 286).

This approach emphasizes that effective economic development requires both capital and technical capacity, with federal appropriations serving as catalysts for additional investment rather than sole funding sources. The program reflects lessons learned from earlier federal programs that provided capital without adequate technical assistance, resulting in high failure rates and limited long-term impact.

The BIA's Division of Economic Development coordinates with other federal agencies to leverage tribal access to specialized financing programs and avoid duplication of federal efforts. This coordination includes referrals to SBA programs, USDA rural development initiatives, and other federal financing sources that may provide more appropriate assistance for specific tribal projects. The BIA's coordinating role reflects the complex landscape of federal tribal financing and the need for systematic approaches to helping tribes navigate multiple federal programs and agencies.

Small Business Administration

The Small Business Administration's tribal programs recognize both the unique needs of tribal businesses and the potential for tribal enterprises to contribute to broader economic development objectives in tribal communities. SBA programs serve tribal communities through general small business assistance programs and specialized initiatives that address the unique legal and economic circumstances of tribal enterprises (Small Business Administration 2023).

The SBA's 8(a) Business Development Program has proven particularly valuable for tribal enterprises, providing access to federal contracting opportunities and business development assistance that can generate revenue and build institutional capacity for tribal businesses. The SBA's Loan Guarantee Programs provide tribal businesses with access to conventional small business financing through federal guarantee mechanisms that reduce lender risk while maintaining private sector lending standards.

Department of Agriculture Rural Development

The Department of Agriculture's Rural Development mission includes significant focus on tribal communities, reflecting the rural location of most tribal lands and the alignment between USDA programs and tribal infrastructure and economic development needs. USDA financing programs serve tribal communities through both general rural development authorities and specific tribal provisions that recognize the unique legal and economic circumstances of tribal governments (USDA Rural Development 2023).

Department of Housing and Urban Development

HUD's tribal programs focus primarily on housing development but include significant economic development components that increasingly recognize the interconnection between housing, community development, and economic opportunity in tribal communities. The Indian Community Development Block Grant (ICDBG) program, funded through HUD appropriations, provides flexible funding that tribes can utilize for economic development projects, infrastructure development, and other community development activities that support both housing and economic development objectives (24 C.F.R. Part 1003; HUD ONAP 2022).

HUD's Section 184 Indian Housing Loan Guarantee Program, while primarily focused on homeownership, includes provisions that support mixed-use development and community development activities that combine housing with economic development components. The program's loan guarantee mechanism reduces lender risk and improves tribal access to conventional financing sources for development projects that serve both housing and economic development objectives (12 U.S.C. § 1715z-13a; HUD Office of Native American Programs 2023).

Section IV: Federal Tax Incentives and Economic Development Programs

Federal tax incentives represent a critical component of the economic development landscape that influences tribal business structure decisions and investment opportunities. These programs, while not specific to tribal communities, often provide significant advantages for tribal economic development when properly structured and implemented through appropriate business entities.

New Markets Tax Credit Program

The New Markets Tax Credit (NMTC) program, authorized under Section 45D of the Internal Revenue Code (26 U.S.C. § 45D), provides tax credits to investors who make qualified investments in designated Community Development Entities (CDEs) that serve low-income communities, including many tribal communities. The program has proven particularly valuable for tribal economic development because it enables tribes to access patient capital at below-market rates while maintaining control over development projects and priorities (Community Development Financial Institutions Fund 2024). NMTC investments often support larger-scale tribal development projects that require substantial capital and extended development periods.

The program's structure, providing tax credits to private investors who invest in certified CDEs, creates incentives for private sector investment in tribal communities while requiring that investments support genuine community development objectives rather than investor profit maximization. Many tribal organizations have obtained CDE certification to access NMTC funding directly, while others have partnered with established CDEs to access program benefits while maintaining tribal control over project implementation (Internal Revenue Service 2022).

NMTC investments in tribal communities have supported diverse projects including healthcare facilities, educational institutions, manufacturing facilities, and mixed-use developments that combine commercial, residential, and community facility components. The program's flexibility enables tribes to structure complex development projects that serve multiple community objectives while accessing substantial private sector investment through the tax credit incentive mechanism (Community Development Financial Institutions Fund 2024).

Opportunity Zones and Qualified Opportunity Funds

The Opportunity Zones program underwent significant transformation with the enactment of the One Big Beautiful Bill Act (OBBBA) in July 2025, which made the program permanent and introduced substantial enhancements particularly beneficial to rural and tribal communities. The program provides tax incentives for private investment in designated distressed communities, including many tribal communities that qualify as low-income census tracts, creating incentives for long-term private sector investment in tribal economic development (U.S. Department of Treasury 2025).

The OBBBA eliminated the original program's 2026 expiration date and established a rolling 10-year redesignation process beginning January 1, 2027. Under this new framework, governors will nominate new Opportunity Zones every decade, with at least 33% of designations required to be in rural areas. This rural focus significantly benefits tribal communities, as many tribal lands qualify as rural under the program's definitions (Economic Innovation Group 2025).

The legislation created a new category of "Qualified Rural Opportunity Funds" (QROFs) that provide enhanced tax benefits for investments in rural areas, including many tribal communities. Investors in QROFs receive a 30% basis step-up after five years, compared to the standard 10% step-up for non-rural investments. Additionally, the substantial improvement requirement for rural investments is reduced to 50% of adjusted basis, compared to 100% for standard Opportunity Zone investments (U.S. Department of Treasury 2025).

Tribal communities have approached Opportunity Zone investments through multiple strategies, including establishing tribal-controlled QOFs that can attract external investment while maintaining tribal oversight of development activities, partnering with external QOFs that invest in tribal projects, and developing projects that attract QOF investment from private sector funds seeking tax benefits. The program's emphasis on long-term investment (minimum 10-year holding periods for maximum tax benefits) aligns well with tribal development priorities for sustainable, community-controlled economic development.

The integration of Opportunity Zone investments with tribal sovereignty requires careful attention to program structure and governance arrangements that preserve tribal control while accessing private sector capital. Many tribes have utilized existing tribal business structures, such as Section 17 corporations or tribally chartered LLCs, as vehicles for Opportunity Zone investments while maintaining compliance with both federal tax requirements and tribal governmental authority.

Historic Tax Credits and Cultural Resource Development
The Historic Preservation Tax Credit program (26 U.S.C. § 47) provides tax credits for qualified rehabilitation of historic structures that can support tribal economic development through adaptive reuse of historic buildings for economic development purposes. Many tribal communities possess historic structures that can be rehabilitated for tourism, cultural enterprises, or other economic development activities while preserving cultural and historical significance (National Park Service 2023).

The program's requirements for historic preservation compliance align well with tribal cultural preservation priorities while providing tax incentives that can attract private sector investment in rehabilitation projects. Tribal historic preservation offices often coordinate with economic development officials to identify rehabilitation opportunities that serve both cultural preservation and economic development objectives, creating integrated approaches to community development that honor tribal heritage while generating economic benefits (Advisory Council on Historic Preservation 2022).

Cultural resource development through historic tax credits can support tourism development, cultural enterprises, and adaptive reuse projects that generate ongoing revenue while preserving tribal cultural assets. The tax credit mechanism enables tribes to attract private sector investment for preservation and development activities that might not otherwise be financially viable, creating sustainable approaches to cultural resource management that support economic development objectives (National Trust for Historic Preservation 2023).

Renewable Energy Tax Credits and Tribal Energy Development

Federal renewable energy tax credits, including the Production Tax Credit (26 U.S.C. § 45) and Investment Tax Credit (26 U.S.C. § 48), have become increasingly important for tribal energy development projects that can generate substantial revenue while supporting tribal energy sovereignty objectives. The Inflation Reduction Act of 2022 included significant enhancements to renewable energy tax credits, including provisions for direct payment of tax credits to tax-exempt entities, including tribal governments, eliminating the need for complex tax equity partnerships that could compromise tribal control over energy projects (26 U.S.C. § 6417).

The direct payment provisions represent a significant improvement in federal tax policy for tribal energy development, enabling tribal governments to capture the full value of renewable energy tax credits directly rather than partnering with private investors primarily for their tax capacity. This policy change enables tribes to maintain greater control over energy projects while accessing the same federal tax incentives available to private sector developers (U.S. Department of Treasury 2024).

Tribal energy development utilizing federal tax credits can serve multiple objectives, including revenue generation for tribal governmental operations, energy cost reduction for tribal facilities and enterprises, and energy independence that reduces tribal dependence on external energy sources. The combination of federal tax credits with tribal sovereignty over natural resources creates opportunities for substantial energy development projects that can transform tribal economic development capacity while supporting broader objectives of energy independence and environmental stewardship (U.S. Department of Energy 2023).

Section V: Relationship to Tribal Sovereignty and Self-Determination Policies

Integration with Self-Determination Policy Framework

Federal tribal financing programs operate within the broader policy framework of tribal self-determination that has guided federal Indian policy since the 1970s, emphasizing tribal control over development priorities and implementation approaches rather than federal direction of tribal activities. The Indian Self-Determination and Education Assistance Act of 1975 established the policy foundation that tribal governments should assume primary responsibility for programs serving their communities, with federal agencies providing funding and technical assistance rather than direct program administration (25 U.S.C. § 5321).

Self-determination principles require that federal financing programs respect tribal sovereignty while providing assistance, avoiding paternalistic approaches that substitute federal judgment for tribal decision-making. Effective federal financing programs provide tribes with resources and technical assistance to pursue their own development priorities rather than directing tribes toward federally-preferred activities or outcomes (National Congress of American Indians 2018).

Sovereignty Preservation and Program Design

Federal financing programs must be designed and implemented in ways that strengthen rather than undermine tribal sovereignty, requiring careful attention to program requirements, compliance mechanisms, and accountability systems that respect tribal governmental authority. Effective program design recognizes tribes as governments rather than beneficiaries, providing assistance that enhances tribal capacity to exercise sovereign authority rather than creating dependency relationships or external control over tribal activities (Harvard Project on American Indian Economic Development 2019).

Cultural Integration and Traditional Economic Systems

Federal financing programs increasingly recognize the importance of integrating traditional tribal economic systems and cultural values with modern economic development approaches, acknowledging that sustainable tribal economic development must build upon rather than replace traditional economic relationships and values. This integration requires program flexibility that accommodates traditional tribal decision-making processes, collective ownership concepts, and cultural priorities that may differ from mainstream economic development approaches.

Section VI: Evolution of Federal Tribal Financing Policy Since 1975

From Assimilation to Self-Determination

The evolution of federal tribal financing policy since 1975 reflects the broader transformation of federal Indian policy from assimilationist approaches that sought to integrate Indians into mainstream society toward self-determination policies that support tribal sovereignty and cultural preservation. The Indian Self-Determination and Education Assistance Act of 1975 marked the beginning of this policy transformation, establishing tribal control over federal programs as a policy objective and creating mechanisms for tribes to assume responsibility for their own development initiatives (25 U.S.C. § 5321).

Legislative Milestones and Policy Development

The Indian Gaming Regulatory Act of 1988 (25 U.S.C. §§ 2701-2721) created new opportunities for tribal economic development while establishing federal regulatory frameworks that balance tribal sovereignty with state interests and federal oversight. Gaming revenues have provided many tribes with capital for economic diversification and infrastructure development, reducing dependence on federal financing programs while creating new opportunities for tribal investment in economic development initiatives.

Contemporary Policy Challenges and Opportunities

Contemporary federal tribal financing policy faces ongoing challenges in balancing federal accountability requirements with tribal sovereignty rights, ensuring program effectiveness while respecting tribal self-determination, and adapting programs to changing economic conditions and tribal development priorities. Opportunities for policy development include expanding tribal access to mainstream federal programs, improving coordination among federal agencies, and developing innovative financing mechanisms that leverage private sector capital while maintaining tribal control over development activities .

Chapter 2: Traditional Business Structures

Unincorporated Tribal Enterprises (Tribal Government Entities)

Traditionally, many tribes conducted business directly as an extension of the tribal government without forming a separate legal entity. These are often called unincorporated enterprises or tribal government entities. In this model, a business is operated by a tribal department, economic committee, or the tribal council itself. All assets and liabilities belong to the tribe, and there is no legal distinction between the tribal government and the enterprise (American Indian Law Deskbook 2021, Section 58).

Advantages

Advantages of unincorporated tribal enterprises include:

- Full sovereign immunity protection - cannot be sued or taxed as separate entities
- Asset protection - creditors cannot reach tribal government assets without consent
- Tax exemption - treated as tribal income, not subject to federal income tax (Atkinson and Nilles 2008)
- Simplicity - no incorporation process required
- Direct tribal control over operations

Limitations

Because the enterprise and the tribe are the same legal entity, the tribe's assets are fully at risk for business obligations. Sovereign immunity, while protecting the tribe, can become a barrier in commercial dealings: lenders or partners often insist on a waiver of immunity or other dispute resolution mechanism before doing business. Additionally, since the enterprise has no separate legal persona, it cannot easily enter contracts or sue/be sued in its own name (everything is in the tribe's name). This close connection between business and tribal politics can sometimes hamper efficient decision-making. Best practice in modern tribal governance is to separate day-to-day business management from tribal council politics to ensure stability and investor confidence (Federal Reserve Bank of Minneapolis 2024). The unincorporated model makes such separation difficult, as the council typically oversees the enterprise directly.

Sovereign Immunity

Any contract or agreement entered into by a tribe or its unincorporated arm implicates sovereign immunity, a partner or customer cannot sue the enterprise unless the tribe clearly waives immunity in that agreement (*Michigan v. Bay Mills Indian Community* 2014). Many tribes address this by enacting ordinances specifying how and when immunity may be waived (for example, requiring a tribal council resolution to authorize a limited waiver for a particular contract). (See Supplement B: Sample Sovereign Immunity Waiver Language for Commercial Contracts.) Without a waiver, tribes may find it hard to access credit, since lenders have no judicial recourse if the tribe defaults. Congress understood these challenges long ago, which led to the creation of federally chartered tribal corporations (Section 17 corporations) to provide a separate business entity that could waive immunity for business purposes while protecting the main tribal government, a point discussed more under the Modern Business Structures section.

Taxation

As noted, income of the tribe (including from an unincorporated enterprise) is not subject to federal income tax. Tribes are also exempt from many state taxes for on-reservation activities. For example, states cannot tax a tribe's on-reservation business revenues absent clear congressional authorization. However, if the tribal enterprise operates off reservation, states may impose taxes as they would on any non-Indian business. In *Mescalero Apache Tribe v. Jones* (1973), the U.S. Supreme Court held that when a tribe operates a business off Indian lands, it does so "as any other" and can be subject to state taxes. Tribes are generally immune from state suit as sovereigns (even for off-reservation commercial activity), but that immunity will not stop a state from taxing off-reservation operations unless a federal law preempts the tax. In short, unincorporated status gives no special tax benefits beyond those the tribe already has; it mostly affects liability and governance.

Individually Owned Businesses (Sole Proprietorships)

Not all Native American businesses are owned by tribal governments; many are owned by individual tribal members. Traditional small businesses, a single owner (sole proprietorship) or a family partnership, remain common in Indian Country. In legal terms, an individual Native American operating a business is subject to the same general rules as any U.S. citizen, with a few important distinctions when the business is on tribal land.

Sole Proprietorships

A sole proprietorship is simply an individual operating a business for profit, without any separate legal entity. Many Native artisans, tradespeople, or merchants use this structure by default.

- **Advantages:** It is easy to set up (no formal filing required) and the owner has complete control.

- **Limitations:** The owner has personal liability for all business debts, there is no liability shield. Moreover, a private individual does not have sovereign immunity, even if they are a tribal member. Sovereign immunity belongs to the tribe as a government, not to individual citizens. Thus, a Native American sole proprietor can be sued in state or federal court on business obligations just like any other person.

Note: If a tribe has enacted business codes, a tribal member may be able to incorporate a sole proprietorship under tribal law, potentially gaining access to modest benefits such as tribal business licensing, participation in tribal procurement programs, or eligibility for tribal business development resources.

Taxation

Income earned by individual tribal members from business activities is generally subject to federal income tax. There is no blanket exemption for Native Americans operating private businesses. For instance, if a Navajo artisan sells jewelry online or a Choctaw rancher sells cattle, they must report that income to the IRS and pay taxes just as any other sole proprietor would. One notable exception is if an individual's income is derived directly from their allotment or a treaty-protected source, but those are narrow cases (e.g., certain fishing or farming rights). Generally, individually owned businesses are taxable at the federal level.

At the state level, however, if the business is conducted by an enrolled tribal member on their own reservation, many states cannot tax the income. Under the Supreme Court's *McClanahan* precedent (*McClanahan v. Arizona State Tax Commission* 1973), states are barred from taxing on-reservation income of tribal members absent congressional authorization.[2] For example, Arizona could not tax the on-reservation earnings of a Navajo craftsperson. This state tax immunity for on-reservation income can be a modest advantage for individual Native business owners, but it does not apply off-reservation.

Partnerships

Partnerships involve two or more co-owners. In Indian Country, a partnership might consist of multiple tribal members or a mix of a tribe and outside investors in a joint venture. A partnership can be general (all partners manage and are liable) or limited (some investors are passive and have limited liability). Historically, tribes might not often use a general partnership as a formal structure for tribal enterprises because it doesn't shield liability, if a tribe were a general partner, it could actually increase exposure by making the tribe liable for partnership debts. More commonly, tribes enter partnerships by using an LLC or corporation (e.g., the

---

[2] The McClanahan precedent refers to the landmark U.S. Supreme Court case *McClanahan v. Arizona State Tax Commission*, 411 U.S. 164 (1973) that established crucial principles regarding state taxation of tribal members on reservations.

tribe's corporation partners with a private company's LLC). Still, understanding partnerships is important:

- **Advantages:** Flexibility and pass-through taxation. A partnership itself usually doesn't pay income tax (it passes income to partners). If a tribe is a partner, the tribe's share of income is not taxed (tribal immunity from federal tax extends to its share of partnership earnings). If an individual tribal member is a partner, their share is taxed to them. Partnerships allow pooling resources without formal incorporation, which can be useful for short-term projects or joint ventures.

- **Limitations:** Unless structured as a limited partnership or LLP, at least one partner (and in a general partnership, all partners) have unlimited personal liability. Sovereign immunity does not automatically extend to a partnership that includes a tribe, especially if the partnership is not under tribal law. In practice, if a tribe participates in a business venture, it often uses an LLC or corporate subsidiary rather than being a partner in name, to avoid legal entanglements. For example, some tribes create a wholly owned LLC, and that LLC enters a joint venture partnership with a private company, this preserves the tribe's immunity for itself while the LLC takes on the business liabilities.

- **Sovereign immunity:** A partnership itself is not a sovereign entity. If a tribe is one of the partners, the partnership's obligations typically cannot be enforced directly against the tribe's assets (absent the tribe's consent), but the non-tribal partners and partnership assets could be at risk. Lenders may still insist on the tribe guaranteeing or waiving immunity for the partnership's dealings. Thus, partnerships are usually supplemented by explicit agreements on dispute resolution.

In summary, individually owned businesses (sole proprietorships or partnerships of individuals) follow mainstream rules: no built-in sovereign immunity or tax exemption, except for certain state tax protections on reservations. Many tribes encourage Native entrepreneurs through their laws (small business codes, lending programs, etc.), but legally these businesses must plan like any other business for liability and taxes.

Note: One unique type of partnership in Indian Country is when multiple tribes form a consortium or inter-tribal partnership for a joint enterprise. In such cases, often a separate entity (like a new corporation owned by the tribes collectively) is formed to carry out the business, rather than using a pure common-law partnership. This is discussed under the Emerging Models section.

Chapter 3: Modern Business Structures

Modern legal entities allow tribes to compartmentalize business activities, attract investment, and clarify tax status. Key modern structures include corporations (formed under federal, tribal, or state law) and limited liability companies. These entities create a "separate legal person" for the business, distinct from the tribal government. The separate entity ("person") can sue and be sued, enter contracts, and hold property in its own name.[3] This separation can protect the tribe's treasury from business liabilities and vice versa. Below we discuss the primary modern structures and their updated status.

Section 17 Corporations (Federally Chartered Tribal Corporations)

A Section 17 corporation is a business entity chartered under Section 17 of the Indian Reorganization Act of 1934 (IRA). Congress added Section 17 to give tribes a mechanism to engage in commerce using "the devices of modern business organization" (Bureau of Indian Affairs 2015, 8-12). A Section 17 corporation is wholly owned by the tribe but legally separate from the tribal government.

Despite the administrative complexities and federal oversight requirements of Section 17 corporations, explained in subparagraphs be-

---

[3] A "sue and be sued" clause is a provision in a charter, statute, or contract that waves sovereign immunity by explicitly granting an entity such as a tribal government, government agency, or corporation) the capacity to sue others and be sued in court.

low, they can effectively serve as holding companies for tribal business enterprises. The federal charter structure allows the Section 17 corporation to own subsidiaries organized under tribal, state, or other federal law, creating a diversified business portfolio while maintaining the tax advantages and sovereign immunity protections of the parent entity.

Hypothetical **Examples of Section 17 Corporation Holding Company Structures**

Hypothetical Example 1: The Mountain Vista Tribe's Integrated Business Model
The Mountain Vista Tribe provides an illustrative example of how a Section 17 corporation can effectively serve as a holding company for diversified tribal enterprises. The tribe established Mountain Vista Development Corporation (MVDC) as a Section 17 corporation in 2010 to act as the parent entity for multiple subsidiary businesses.

Structure Details:
- **Parent Entity:** MVDC operates as the Section 17 federal corporation, maintaining the tribe's sovereign immunity protections and federal tax-exempt status
- **Subsidiaries:** The corporation owns and oversees multiple LLCs and other business entities, including:
  - Mountain Vista Gaming LLC (casino and entertainment operations)
  - Vista Construction Services LLC (general contracting and infrastructure)
  - Mountain Vista Energy LLC (renewable energy development)
  - Vista Tech Solutions LLC (IT services and federal contracting)
  - Mountain Vista Real Estate Holdings LLC (commercial property development)

Key Benefits Demonstrated:

1. **Asset Protection:** The Section 17 structure shields tribal government assets from business liabilities while allowing each subsidiary to operate independently

2. **Tax Efficiency:** Federal tax immunity flows through the holding company structure, maximizing revenue available for tribal programs

3. **Operational Flexibility:** Individual subsidiaries can enter contracts, hire non-tribal employees, and compete in specialized markets while maintaining connection to tribal sovereign benefits

4. **Strategic Coordination:** The holding company structure allows for coordinated business strategy and shared administrative services across diverse industries

Hypothetical Example 2: The Riverside Nation's Federal Contracting Focus

The Riverside Nation demonstrates another approach, using their Section 17 corporation, Riverside Federal Solutions Corporation (RFSC), as a specialized holding company for government contracting ventures.

Structure Details:

- **Parent Entity:** RFSC serves as the Section 17 corporation focused specifically on federal contracting opportunities

- **Subsidiaries:** The corporation owns multiple specialized contracting entities:

    - Riverside Defense Systems LLC (8(a) certified defense contractor)

    - Riverside Environmental Services LLC (environmental remediation and consulting)

    - Riverside Healthcare Solutions LLC (healthcare IT and management services)

    - Riverside Infrastructure LLC (construction and engineering services)

Strategic Advantages:

1. **Federal Contracting Benefits:** The Section 17 structure enables access to 8(a) Program benefits, HUBZone preferences, and Buy Indian Act opportunities across multiple subsidiary companies

2. **Liability Separation:** Each contracting subsidiary operates independently, limiting cross-liability while maintaining sovereign immunity protections

3. **Scalability and Efficiency:**
   - New subsidiaries can be easily established under the holding company structure as contracting opportunities emerge
   - Administrative efficiencies can be established with like businesses

4. **Compliance Management:** Centralized compliance and administrative functions through the parent corporation while allowing operational independence for each subsidiary

These hypothetical examples illustrate how Section 17 corporations can serve as effective holding company structures, providing tribes with sophisticated business organization tools while preserving the unique benefits of tribal sovereignty and federal recognition.

Formation

To create a Section 17 corporation, a tribe petitions the U.S. Secretary of the Interior for a federal corporate charter through the Bureau of Indian Affairs. (See Supplement C: Sample Section 17 Petition to the Secretary of the Interior.) The charter, once approved and ratified by the tribe, constitutes a federally chartered corporation wholly owned by the tribe but separate and distinct from the tribal government. (See Supplement D: Sample Tribal Corporate Charter) This process can be time-consuming and involves extensive federal oversight, traditionally requiring several steps (tribal resolution, drafting a charter, Bureau of Indian Affairs (BIA) review, tribal ratification). The IRA originally required that a tribe have an IRA government (Section 16 constitution) to form a Section 17 company, but amendments in 1990 opened Section 17 incorporation to tribes without IRA constitutions as well.

Notably, Oklahoma tribes are not eligible to incorporate under Section 17 and must instead use Section 3 of the Oklahoma Indian Welfare Act (OIWA), which provides a more streamlined process specifically designed for Oklahoma's unique post-allotment circumstances.[4] In both cases, the result is a federally chartered corporation that enjoys favorable tax treatment under the Internal Revenue Code. (See Supplement E: A Comparative Analysis of Section 17 IRA, OIWA, and Tax Implications.)

Organizational Features: A Section 17 corporation's ownership is held by the tribe (often the tribal council holds the voting stock on behalf of the tribe). The corporation can only be dissolved or amended with federal approval. Unlike a typical state corporation code with extensive provisions, Section 17 provides only a skeletal framework (25 U.S.C. § 5124, formerly § 477, is just one paragraph of law). This means tribal leaders have flexibility in charter terms, but also that the charters may lack detail -- "the absence of comprehensive corporate statutes may increase litigation risk" for Section 17 companies. The charter usually contains a "sue and be sued" clause, which has important implications for sovereign immunity.

Advantages

Section 17 corporations are often considered the "gold standard" for tribal economic development entities in terms of legal status:

Protects Tribal Assets: The Section 17 corporation is separate from the tribe. If the corporation incurs debts or gets sued, only its assets (the business assets) are at risk, not the tribe's government assets. This was a key reason Congress created them, to let tribes waive immunity for business dealings and risk corporate assets, while keeping core tribal assets immune.

No Federal Income Tax: Section 17 corporations have the same federal tax status as the tribe itself (Atkinson and Nilles 2008). Both IRS rulings and regulations have confirmed that a federally chartered Section 17 corporation is not a separate taxable entity. In effect, its income is treated as the tribe's income, which is exempt from federal tax.

---

[4] Oklahoma Indian Welfare Act (OIWA) of 1936; also known as Thomas-Rogers Act, extended many provisions of the 1934 Indian Reorganization Act (IRA) to tribes in Oklahoma who had been initially excluded from the legislation.

This holds true whether the business operates on or off the reservation. Courts have upheld that Section 17 companies enjoy the tribe's immunity from federal income tax (e.g., Mescalero Apache Tribe v. Jones 1973).

Update: This tax treatment has been consistently applied; in 2024, the IRS proposed regulations to formally codify that entities wholly owned by a tribe and chartered under Section 17 (or tribal law) are not recognized as separate taxpayers (Department of the Treasury 2024).

Access to Tax-Exempt Financing: Section 17 corporations qualify as instrumentalities of the tribe for certain financing benefits. For example, they can issue tax-exempt bonds to fund essential governmental functions. Under 26 U.S.C. § 7871, tribes (and by extension Section 17 corporations) can issue tax-exempt debt similar to states, though with some limitations (tribal bonds must finance "essential government" projects). This can lower borrowing costs for infrastructure and development projects.

Sovereign Immunity (Conditional): By default, a Section 17 corporation shares the tribe's sovereign immunity unless explicitly waived (American Indian Law Deskbook 2021, Section 58). The IRA requires that the corporate charter include a "sue and be sued" clause, which some courts interpret as a limited waiver of immunity. However, other courts have held that this language is not a blanket waiver, it simply empowers the entity to sue/be sued if the tribe or corporation consents. In practice, absent a clear waiver, most authorities treat Section 17 corporations as having sovereign immunity coextensive with the tribe's immunity.

Federal Recognition and Stability: Being federally chartered, Section 17 corporations may enjoy easier recognition by outside entities. For instance, some federal programs and grants treat Section 17 corporations akin to tribal governments for eligibility. Also, since the charter is federal, its validity is not subject to state law or even changes in tribal law, providing a stable legal existence that investors might appreciate.

Enhanced Tax Benefits from Recent Federal Legislation

The One Big Beautiful Bill Act (OBBBA) of 2025 has significantly enhanced the tax advantages available to Section 17 corporations through several key provisions. The permanent extension of 100% bonus depreciation enables Section 17 corporations to immediately expense the full cost of qualifying equipment and property placed in service, creating substantial cash flow advantages for tribal businesses investing in manufacturing equipment, technology infrastructure, or other qualifying assets (Economic Innovation Group 2025).

The permanent reinstatement of research and development expense deductions, made permanent for domestic R&E activities, particularly benefits Section 17 corporations engaged in technology development, innovation activities, or business process improvements. Small businesses with average annual gross receipts of $31 million or less can retroactively claim these deductions back to 2022, while larger tribal enterprises benefit from immediate expensing of domestic R&E costs starting in 2025 (U.S. Department of Treasury 2025).

Note: Alaska Native Corporations (ANCs) created under the Alaska Native Claims Settlement Act (ANCSA) in 1971 are a dominant business structure in Alaska, which might reduce reliance on Section 17 (in Alaska).

ANCSA was landmark federal legislation that resolved Alaska Native land claims by transferring approximately 44 million acres of land and $962.5 million to Alaska Native ownership.

Rather than creating reservations, ANCSA established a unique corporate model:

- 12 Regional Corporations (plus a 13th for non-resident Alaska Natives)
- Over 200 Village Corporations
- Alaska Natives became shareholders in these corporations

These ANCs operate as for-profit businesses under state law, engaging in everything from natural resource development to federal contracting, and have become major economic forces.

Disadvantages

Despite the benefits, Section 17 corporations have some downsides that have made them "inflexible" in the eyes of many tribes:

- **Inflexibility and Control:** Once granted, a Section 17 charter cannot be easily amended or revoked without approval from the Secretary of the Interior. Tribes cannot unilaterally dissolve a Section 17 corporation except by an act of Congress or with federal consent. This rigidity can be problematic if the tribe wants to change the business structure or update its governance. Therefore, charters should be carefully crafted so as to allow the tribe significant flexibility in formulating, developing, and implementing future endeavors.

By contrast with the dissolution requirements of Section 17, a corporation under tribal or state law can usually be dissolved or changed by the owners' decision.

- **Minimal Statutory Guidance:** The IRA's Section 17 is very brief (originally just one paragraph of law). There is no comprehensive federal corporate code for Section 17 entities. As a result, there is variation in charters and sometimes uncertainty in corporate governance rules. Basic issues -- like how meetings are conducted, fiduciary duties of directors, minority shareholder (in this case, the tribe is sole shareholder) rights -- must all be addressed in the charter or depend on common law.[5] Some tribes may find this lack of a built-in code a disadvantage when compared to using a well-developed state incorporation statute.

- **Perception by Lenders/Partners:** Because of the above two points (immunity and lack of public disclosure requirements), some business partners are cautious about Section 17 corporations. The BIA notes that the sparse statutory framework could "make prospective business partners hesitant" to enter contracts with Section 17 entities. Often, any concerns are addressed through careful charter provisions or waivers for specific deals.

Tribally Chartered Corporations (Tribal Law Corporations)

Apart from federal charters, tribes can charter corporations under their own tribal laws. A tribally chartered corporation is formed pursuant to a tribal code or ordinance, rather than under state or federal incorporation

---

[5] Common law refers to the body of legal principles developed through court decisions and judicial precedents rather than written statutes or regulations. In the corporate context, common law provides default rules for governance issues like director duties and shareholder rights when specific statutes or corporate documents do not address these matters.

laws (Moyer 2021, 12-15). (See Supplement G: Sample Tribal Economic Development Ordinance) Essentially, the tribe acts as the incorporating sovereign. Many tribes have adopted business corporation codes modeled on state laws to enable this. In other cases, a tribal council may simply pass a resolution creating a single corporation and approving its articles of incorporation.

Example One: The Citizen Potawatomi Nation's Tribally Chartered Corporation Approach

The Citizen Potawatomi Nation (CPN) in Oklahoma provides an excellent real-world example of how tribes can effectively utilize tribally chartered corporations for economic development. CPN chose to charter the Citizen Potawatomi Community Development Corporation (CPCDC) under its own tribal laws. CPN established CPCDC as a tribally chartered corporation, demonstrating how tribes can utilize their inherent sovereignty for economic development (Harvard Project on American Indian Economic Development 2006); (Native CDFI Network 2022)

Structure Details:

- **Corporate Formation:** CPCDC operates as a tribally authorized nonprofit corporation, deriving its authority from CPN's own laws of incorporation rather than federal chartering mechanisms (Citizen Potawatomi Nation 2025)

- **CDFI Certification:** The corporation is certified as a Community Development Financial Institution (CDFI) by the U.S. Department of Treasury, enabling it to access federal funding and lending programs

- **Operational Focus:** CPCDC provides capital and technical assistance to support economic development for CPN citizens and other Native populations through:
  - Microloans and commercial lending ($5,000 to $8 million range)
  - Financial education and credit counseling services
  - Business development assistance and entrepreneurship support
    - Employee loan programs for tribal citizens

Key Benefits Demonstrated:

1. **Tribal Sovereignty:** The tribally authorized structure maintains full tribal control without federal oversight requirements of Section 3 corporations

2. **Operational Flexibility:** CPN can modify the corporation's structure, governance, and operations through tribal law without seeking federal approval

3. **Strategic Focus:** The nonprofit structure allows CPCDC to concentrate on community development rather than profit generation, supporting broader tribal economic goals

4. **Federal Program Access:** CDFI certification provides access to federal funding while maintaining tribal charter benefits

This example illustrates how tribes can leverage their inherent sovereignty to create specialized corporate entities that serve specific economic development needs while avoiding the administrative complexities of federal incorporation processes. CPN's approach demonstrates that tribally chartered corporations can effectively access federal programs and funding while maintaining complete tribal control over corporate governance and operations.

Example Two: Ho-Chunk, Inc. (Winnebago Tribe of Nebraska)

Ho-Chunk, Inc., the economic development arm of the Winnebago Tribe of Nebraska, exemplifies the strategic use of tribally chartered corporations for large-scale business operations. Rather than organizing as an IRA Section 17 corporation, the Winnebago Tribe deliberately chose to establish Ho-Chunk, Inc. as a tribally chartered corporation under its own tribal laws, creating a wholly owned subsidiary that operates with significant autonomy from tribal government functions (Ho-Chunk, Inc. 2024).

Strategic Corporate Structure:

- **Tribal Charter Foundation:** Ho-Chunk, Inc. derives its corporate authority from Winnebago Tribal law rather than federal incorporation mechanisms, providing maximum flexibility in governance and operations (Ho-Chunk, Inc. 2024)

- **Separation of Powers:** The structure intentionally creates institutional separation between business operations and tribal government, allowing commercial enterprises to operate according to market principles rather than political considerations (Ho-Chunk, Inc. 2024)

- **Board Governance:** While the Winnebago Tribal Council appoints the board of directors, Ho-Chunk, Inc. operates with independent management authority, insulating business decisions from day-to-day tribal political processes (Ho-Chunk, Inc. 2024)

Holding Company Operations: Ho-Chunk, Inc. functions as a sophisticated holding company managing a diverse portfolio of enterprises across multiple industries (Ho-Chunk, Inc. 2024):

- **Hospitality Sector:** Hotel operations and related services

- **Retail Operations:** Convenience stores and consumer-facing businesses

- **Distribution Networks:** Supply chain and logistics companies

- **E-commerce Ventures:** Digital marketplace and online retail platforms

- **Strategic Joint Ventures:** Partnerships with non-tribal entities for expanded market access

Key Advantages of the Tribal Charter Approach:

1. **Operational Flexibility:** The tribally chartered structure allows Ho-Chunk, Inc. to adapt quickly to market conditions without federal oversight or approval requirements that would apply to Section 17 corporations

2. **Political Insulation:** Independent management structure protects business operations from potential political volatility within tribal governance while maintaining tribal ownership

3. **Strategic Agility:** The holding company can acquire, divest, or restructure subsidiary businesses based on market opportunities rather than bureaucratic constraints

4. **Cultural Alignment:** Operating under tribal law ensures business practices can reflect tribal values while maintaining commercial competitiveness

Economic Impact and Success Metrics: Since its establishment in 1994, Ho-Chunk, Inc. has demonstrated the effectiveness of the tribally chartered holding company model by creating substantial employment opportunities for tribal members, generating significant revenue for tribal government operations, and establishing the Winnebago Tribe as a major economic force in rural Nebraska (Ho-Chunk, Inc. 2024). The corporation's success has enabled tribal investment in housing, education, and infrastructure development, illustrating how tribally chartered business structures can serve broader community development goals while maintaining commercial viability (Ho-Chunk, Inc. 2024).

This example demonstrates that tribes can achieve sophisticated business organization and significant economic success through tribally chartered corporations, often with greater operational efficiency than federally chartered alternatives, while maintaining the fundamental benefits of tribal ownership and control.

Formation

If a tribe has a corporate code, organizers follow the tribal law requirements (filing articles of incorporation with a tribal registrar, etc.). If no code exists, a tribal council resolution can directly charter a corporation and issue a "certificate of incorporation" to it. The resulting entity is governed by its tribal charter and bylaws, and by any default provisions in the tribal code.

Advantages

Tribally chartered corporations offer a middle ground between Section 17 and state entities:

- **Avoids State Oversight and Taxation (On-Reservation):** When a business is incorporated under tribal law and operates on Indian land, it is generally not subject to state corporate laws or state taxes (as long as its ownership is primarily tribal or tribal member). The tribe's sovereignty shields the entity from state company regulations and certain state taxes, similar to how the tribe itself is shielded.

- **Ease of Formation and Control:** No approval from the federal government or any state is needed, the tribe is the incorporating authority. This makes it much quicker and more flexible to create a corporation than going through the Section 17 process. The tribe can tailor the charter to its needs and can amend or dissolve the corporation by its own laws.

- **Tribal Sovereignty and Immunity:** A tribally chartered corporation can share in the tribe's sovereign immunity, provided it functions as an arm of the tribe. (See Supplement F: Checklist: Determining If An Entity Qualifies As An "Arm Of The Tribe") The extent of immunity might depend on how the entity is organized. The IRS noted that if a tribal corporation is an "integral part of the tribe" (fully owned and controlled by the tribe), the IRS (and by implication, others) will treat it as not separate from the tribe.

Disadvantages

1. **Transparency and Credibility Challenges:** One cited drawback is the "potential lack of transparency for lenders and partners." Outside investors can easily look up a state-chartered company's records in public databases, but a tribally chartered corporation might not have public filings accessible outside the tribe.

2. **Uncertain Tax Status (improving as of 2025):** The federal income tax status of tribally chartered corporations has historically been a gray area. Unlike Section 17 corporations (which are clearly tax-exempt as tribal entities), the IRS until recently had no official published guidance on whether a corporation chartered under tribal law is taxable or not.

Recent Update: In October 2024, the IRS proposed regulations to finally clarify this (Internal Revenue Service 2024). The proposed rule states that entities wholly owned by one or more federally recognized tribes and organized under tribal law will generally not be recognized as separate taxable entities.

Federal Tax Law Enhancements for Tribal Entities

The convergence of proposed IRS regulations clarifying tribal entity tax treatment with recent federal tax legislation creates powerful opportunities for tribally chartered corporations. Under the proposed regulations, wholly owned tribally chartered entities would gain tax-exempt status similar to Section 17 corporations, while simultaneously accessing enhanced tax benefits including permanent 100% bonus depreciation for qualifying investments and reinstated R&E expense deductions for innovation activities (Treasury Department 2024; Economic Innovation Group 2025).

This combination enables tribally chartered corporations to benefit from both tax exemption on operational income and accelerated tax benefits for qualifying investments, creating optimal conditions for tribal business development while maintaining complete tribal control over corporate governance and operations and preserving the sovereignty-based advantages that make tribal business structures unique.

State-Chartered Corporations (Including Alaska Native Corporations)

Tribes or Native groups may also form corporations under state law (e.g., incorporating under Delaware or state where they operate). In fact, American Indian tribes were initially not allowed to incorporate under IRA if they opted out of it (some did); those tribes often turned to state charters for their businesses. Also, Alaska Native regional and village corporations were created by federal law (ANCSA of 1971) but function as state-law corporations.

Formation and Characteristics

A state-chartered tribal corporation is simply a corporation organized under the law of some state, but owned (in whole or part) by a tribe or tribal members. For example, a tribe might form a corporation under Delaware law called "Tribe XYZ Enterprises, Inc." and be the sole shareholder (Birch Horton Bittner & Cherot 2021). These corporations are subject to that state's corporation code like any other corporation.

Advantages

1. **Familiarity and Transparency:** Using a state incorporation provides credibility and transparency to outside investors, banks, and partners. The entity looks and operates like any other corporation, which outsiders understand.

2. **Ease of Formation:** Incorporating in a business-friendly state (like Delaware, Nevada, etc.)[6] is quick and straightforward. Tribes don't need federal approval or to pass their own laws, they can use off-the-shelf legal infrastructure.

3. **Possibility of Outside Investment:** A state-chartered corporation can more readily issue stock, bring in outside shareholders, or go public, compared to a tribally chartered company.

Disadvantages

1. **Federal Taxation:** A state-chartered corporation owned by a tribe is regarded as a separate taxable entity by the IRS. It may not share the tribe's tax-exempt status (U.S. Government Accountability Office 2022, 45-48). Such a corporation is typically a C-corporation for tax purposes, meaning its income is taxed at corporate tax rates, and distributions (dividends) to the tribe could be taxed again (double taxation).

Recent Tax Law Changes Affecting Entity Selection
Recent modifications to Qualified Business Income (QBI) deduction provisions under the 2025 federal tax legislation have created additional considerations for tribal businesses evaluating state-chartered structures. While C-corporations face the double

---

[6] Delaware and Nevada are widely regarded as the most business-friendly jurisdictions due to several key features: (1) their specialized business courts provide predictable, sophisticated jurisprudence on corporate matters; (2) flexible corporate statutes that maximize board and management discretion while minimizing mandatory rules; (3) strong protection for directors and officers through broad indemnification provisions and the ability to limit or eliminate personal liability for breaches of fiduciary duty; (4) Nevada's lack of state corporate income tax and Delaware's franchise tax structure that favors large corporations; and (5) extensive privacy protections, with Nevada particularly notable for not requiring disclosure of shareholders or board members in public filings.

taxation described above, state-chartered tribal entities organized as pass-through entities like LLCs, partnerships, and S-corporations may be affected by changes to specified service trade or business (SSTB) entities and wage and income limitations that impact overall tax efficiency (U.S. Department of Treasury 2025). Tribal businesses considering state incorporation should evaluate these QBI changes alongside traditional corporate tax implications when assessing optimal structure selection.

2. **Minimal Sovereign Immunity:** When a tribe incorporates under state law, it is generally deemed to have waived sovereign immunity for that entity. The corporation is treated like any other state corporation, it can be sued in state or federal court, and cannot claim the tribe's immunity from suit.

Limited Liability Companies (LLCs and LLPs)

Limited Liability Companies (LLCs) have become one of the most common business structures for tribes in the 21st century. An LLC is a hybrid entity offering the liability protection of a corporation with the pass-through taxation of a partnership (Birch Horton Bittner & Cherot 2021). Most states and many tribes have LLC statutes, and tribes utilize both.

Tribal LLCs vs. State LLCs

A tribal LLC refers to an LLC organized under a tribal nation's laws. Many tribes have enacted LLC codes enabling the formation of LLCs by the tribe or tribal members. A tribe can form an LLC under tribal law and be the sole member (owner). Alternatively, a tribe might form an LLC under state law to own a business, especially if operating off-reservation.

Advantages of LLCs

1. **Liability Protection:** Regardless of jurisdiction, an LLC provides that members (owners) are not personally liable for the company's debts or liabilities beyond their investment. For a tribe, this means if the tribe owns an LLC that runs a business, claims from that business generally cannot reach the tribe's other assets.

2. **Pass-through Taxation:** By default, LLCs are not taxed as separate entities (unless they elect to be treated as a corporation). Single-member LLCs are "disregarded entities" for federal tax, the IRS ignores the LLC and treats the income as earned directly by the owner. Multi-member LLCs default to partnership taxation, the LLC files an informational return but pays no tax; profits pass through to members. This feature is extremely advantageous for tribes: If a tribe is the sole owner of an LLC and does not elect corporate taxation, the LLC's income is treated as the tribe's income, hence no federal income tax (Atkinson and Nilles 2008).

3. **Flexibility and Simplicity:** LLCs are very flexible in management and structure. Tribes like them because they can customize the LLC's operating agreement to fit the deal. They can also form and dissolve LLCs relatively easily.

Enhanced Tax Planning Opportunities Under Recent Legislation

The 2025 federal tax law changes have created additional strategic advantages for tribal LLCs across multiple areas. The permanent extension of 100% bonus depreciation enables tribal LLCs to immediately expense qualifying equipment purchases, providing significant cash flow benefits for businesses investing in technology, manufacturing equipment, or infrastructure improvements. This permanent provision eliminates the uncertainty of previous phaseout schedules and enables long-term strategic planning for capital investments (Economic Innovation Group 2025).

For tribal LLCs engaged in research and development activities, the permanent reinstatement of research and development expense deductions provides immediate tax benefits for innovation activities, software development, and business process improvements. Combined with the LLC's pass-through tax treatment, these deductions flow directly to tribal government owners without corporate-level taxation, maximizing the tax efficiency of innovation investments (U.S. Department of Treasury 2025).

The modified QBI deduction provisions create additional planning opportunities for tribal LLCs structured as pass-through entities, though tribes must carefully evaluate the interaction between QBI limitations and their specific operational characteristics to optimize tax benefits while maintaining compliance with tribal ownership requirements (see also enhanced tax planning discussions in Chapter 3, Supplement E, and Supplement J).

4. **Use in Layered Structures:** Tribes frequently incorporate LLCs as subsidiaries of corporations. For instance, a Section 17 or tribal chartered holding company might spawn LLCs for each casino, gas station, or federal contract.

5. **Partnering Tool:** LLCs are often the entity of choice for partnering with non-tribal businesses. They allow a mix of ownership while clearly delineating rights in the operating agreement.

Disadvantages of LLCs

1. **Not Permanently Tax-Exempt if Ownership Changes:** If a tribe brings in outside investors to an LLC, it loses the full pass-through exemption (though still better than corporation because only the non-tribal portions get taxed).

2. **State Law LLC Issues:** If formed under state law, the LLC must follow state requirements (annual reports, fees) and is subject to that state's jurisdiction.

3. **Sovereign immunity ambiguity:** There's been at least one instance where a court hinted that because an LLC shields the owner from liability by state law, perhaps a tribe as sole owner might not get immunity or might be subject to an "alter ego" theory if it abuses the LLC form.

Chapter 4: Emerging Models and Hybrid Structures

Beyond the standard structures above, tribal economic development continually innovates. Since 2013, LLCs have only grown in use. Tribes have gotten sophisticated with series LLCs (where allowed by law), holding LLC structures, and use of LLCs in financing deals. A very current development is in the renewable energy sector: The Inflation Reduction Act of 2022 allows tribes to get direct payment of certain tax credits (instead of partnering with tax equity investors).

While the traditional and modern structures discussed above, from unincorporated enterprises to Section 17 corporations to LLCs, form the foundation of tribal business organization, they represent only part of the current landscape. As tribal economies have grown more sophisticated and diversified, tribes have begun combining these basic structures in innovative ways and creating entirely new organizational approaches that better serve their unique economic development goals.

Joint Ventures and Partnerships with Non-Tribal Entities

Collaborative partnerships between Native American tribes and private companies have emerged as powerful vehicles for economic development, diversification, and mutual growth (First Nations Capital Partners 2025). These create significant economic benefits for tribal members while offering private companies unique advantages. (See Supplement H: Sample Joint Venture Agreement.)

The structures of these partnerships often involve multiple organizational layers to maximize benefits for all parties. For instance, a tribe may form a tribally chartered LLC, which then partners in a joint venture LLC with a private investor, sometimes creating another LLC beneath for actual operations. These multi-entity arrangements allow each party to leverage their unique strengths, the tribe contributes land, sovereignty, and potential tax advantages, while the private partner brings capital and industry expertise.

Gaming and Entertainment Partnerships

The gaming industry has witnessed some of the most prominent and profitable tribal-private joint ventures, with tribes strategically expanding beyond reservation boundaries into major markets.

Mohegan Sun's Strategic Expansion

The Mohegan Tribe established one of the earliest successful casino partnerships by collaborating with South African casino developer Sol Kerzner to create Mohegan Sun, which has become one of the largest gaming destinations in the United States. Building on this success, Mohegan extended their reach by becoming the first tribal entity to operate a casino in Las Vegas when they took over casino operations at Virgin Hotels Las Vegas (formerly Hard Rock).

San Manuel's Landmark Acquisition

In a groundbreaking move, the San Manuel Band of Mission Indians (operators of Yaamava' Resort) became the first tribal owners and operators of a full Las Vegas casino resort when they acquired The Palms for $650 million (Gaming America 2025). This strategic investment enables the tribe to service their existing California customers when they travel to Las Vegas while diversifying their revenue streams and holdings.

Hospitality Development Ventures

Tribes have increasingly diversified beyond gaming into mainstream hospitality through strategic joint ventures. (See Supplement H: Sample Joint Venture Agreement)

Multi-Tribal DreamCatcher Hotels Partnership

One of the most innovative tribal joint ventures brought together three major tribes, the Seminole Tribe of Florida, Mississippi Band of Choctaw Indians, and Eastern Band of Cherokee Indians, in partnership with

DreamCatcher Hotels to develop a high-end, AAA Four Diamond hotel in Pigeon Forge, Tennessee (The Neshoba Democrat 2025). This unprecedented collaboration leverages the development expertise of DreamCatcher while creating significant returns for each tribe's members through an investment in a prime tourism market.

The Doradus Fund Coalition
In an exceptional demonstration of tribal collaboration, six tribes joined together as limited partners to provide over $80 million in equity for an off-reservation hotel development fund called the Doradus Fund. Led by the Poarch Band of Creek Indians through Creek Indian Enterprises Development Authority (CIEDA), this fund is developing eight branded, select-service hotels in high-growth markets across the southeastern United States (Creek Indian Enterprises Development Authority 2025).

Energy Sector Innovations
Brown Venture Group and Big Navajo Energy
In the clean energy sector, Big Navajo Energy secured a significant investment from Brown Venture Group LLC, a Black-owned venture capital firm (Tribal Business News 2025). Founded in 2012, Big Navajo Energy specializes in sustainable hydrogen production on native lands, with the investment enabling "phase one" of their project.

Impact of Recent Federal Tax Policy Changes on Renewable Energy Ventures
The OBBBA has significantly modified the federal tax incentive landscape for tribal renewable energy development through accelerated phaseouts and shortened deadlines for many clean energy incentives. These changes particularly affect the Section 179D deduction for energy-efficient commercial buildings and various renewable energy tax credits that previously provided long-term investment incentives (U.S. Department of Treasury 2025).

For tribal energy enterprises, these modifications require strategic reassessment of project timing and financing structures. While the Inflation Reduction Act's direct payment provisions for renewable energy tax credits remain available to tribal governments, eliminating the need for complex tax equity partnerships, the accelerated phaseout of complementary incentives creates urgency for tribes pursuing comprehensive renewable energy development strategies (U.S. Department of Treasury 2024).

The enhanced rural development benefits introduced through the 2025 legislation may partially offset reduced energy incentives for tribal projects in rural areas, though tribes must carefully evaluate the net impact on project economics and financing feasibility. Strategic coordination between tribal energy development entities and enhanced rural opportunity programs may provide alternative pathways for sustainable renewable energy development while maintaining tribal control and long-term community benefits (Economic Innovation Group 2025).

Chapter 5: Sovereign Immunity Considerations in Business

Sovereign immunity is a recurring theme in all the above discussions, and it is crucial to structuring Native American businesses. To summarize key points and updates regarding immunity:

1. **Tribal Immunity is Inherent:** Tribal governments cannot be sued unless they consent or Congress clearly abrogates their immunity. This immunity extends to tribal business arms that are considered "arms of the tribe." The U.S. Supreme Court reaffirmed in *Michigan v. Bay Mills Indian Community* (2014) that tribes enjoy broad immunity even for off-reservation commercial activities, unless Congress says otherwise.

2. **Waivers:** Tribes can waive their immunity for business purposes, and this is often necessary to obtain financing or partners. A waiver must be unequivocal and is typically limited in scope (e.g., a waiver to be sued in a certain court regarding a particular contract). Best practice is to put waiver provisions in contracts rather than a blanket waiver.

3. **Entities and Immunity:** As detailed in each structure:

    - **Unincorporated tribal enterprises:** fully immune (cannot be sued directly; waiver must come from tribe).

    - **Section 17 corporations:** regarded as immune absent explicit waiver, though "sue and be sued" charters somewhat blur that, generally still immune to suits beyond the scope of consent.

- **Tribally chartered corporations/LLCs:** immune if functioning as arms of the tribe (wholly owned, serving tribal purposes). If partially owned by outsiders, likely not immune in a full sense. Clear charter language is important to claim immunity.

- **State-chartered entities:** generally not immune, as they are separate entities under state law (courts treat them like any corporate citizen). The tribe's immunity doesn't automatically shield them, though the tribe itself remains immune from any judgments against the company.

- **Individuals and partnerships:** individual Native business owners have no immunity; partnerships including a tribe could try to assert the tribe's immunity for partnership obligations, but practically it's messy, so tribes avoid being directly in general partnerships.

4. **Arm-of-the-Tribe Tests:** Courts have developed multi-factor tests to determine if a business entity is an "arm of the tribe" (hence immune). Factors often include: (1) how created (tribal law vs state law), (2) purpose (to further tribal governmental goals vs purely commercial for profit), (3) ownership and control (100% tribe-owned? tribe appoints board?), (4) how the entity's finances relate to tribe (do profits go to tribe, is liability covered by tribe, etc.), (5) intent of tribe/state in forming it. Recent decisions continue to apply these tests. For example, the California Supreme Court in *People v. Miami Nation Enterprises* (2016) set out such factors and ultimately recognized two tribal online lending companies as arms of the tribe (thus immune from state regulation), emphasizing the tribes' ownership and control, even though they were formed under tribal law primarily for profit.

5. **Congressional Abrogation:** Congress can subject tribes or their entities to suit through legislation. One new example is the 2018 amendment of the Bankruptcy Code. In *Lac du Flambeau Band v. Coughlin* (2023), the Supreme Court held that the U.S.

Bankruptcy Code's definition of "governmental unit" is broad enough to include tribes, thus Congress abrogated tribal immunity for bankruptcy proceedings.

6. **Waiver vs. Liability Shield:** It's important to distinguish that waiving immunity is not the same as accepting liability. A waiver just means the tribe or entity can be sued and the court can decide the case. The tribe or entity can still defend itself and is only liable if it loses on the merits.

7. **Insurance and Indemnity:** Many tribal entities mitigate risk by carrying insurance or requiring contractors to indemnify the tribe. This reduces the need to sue the tribe if something goes wrong (the insurance can pay).

Chapter 6: Federal Tax and Regulatory Considerations

Taxes and regulations often drive the choice of business structure. Here's an overview of how different structures interact with federal (and some state) tax rules, including developments since 2013:

1. **Tribal Tax Status Recap:** A tribe as a sovereign is not subject to federal income tax (Atkinson and Nilles 2008). Tribes also enjoy exemption from many federal excise taxes and state taxes when operating in their government capacity. However, tribal businesses can be taxed or not taxed depending on entity form, as summarized by GAO:

- federally chartered entities (Section 17/Section 3) are not taxed;
- state-chartered entities are generally taxed;
- tribally chartered may or may not be taxed (now moving toward not taxed, if wholly owned, per new guidance); and
- individually owned businesses are taxed (U.S. Government Accountability Office 2022, 45-48).

Enhanced Federal Tax Benefits from 2025 Legislation
Recent federal tax legislation has substantially enhanced the tax advantages available to tribal business entities through several permanent provisions that create significant opportunities for strategic business development and capital investment. These provisions became effective with the OBBBA's enactment in July 2025, with certain benefits available retroactively to 2022 for qual-

ifying small businesses. The permanent extension of 100% bonus depreciation enables tribal entities to immediately expense the full cost of qualifying equipment, machinery, and certain property improvements, providing substantial cash flow advantages for businesses investing in manufacturing equipment, technology infrastructure, telecommunications systems, or other qualifying business assets (Economic Innovation Group 2025).

This permanent bonus depreciation provision eliminates the uncertainty created by previous phaseout schedules and enables tribes to engage in long-term strategic planning for capital investments without concern about changing depreciation benefits. For tribal businesses considering significant equipment purchases or facility improvements, the ability to immediately expense these investments creates powerful incentives for business expansion and modernization while generating immediate tax benefits for entities subject to federal taxation.

The interaction between bonus depreciation and different tribal business structures creates varying strategic opportunities. Tax-exempt entities (including Section 17 corporations and qualifying tribally chartered entities) cannot directly benefit from depreciation deductions but may find that bonus depreciation enhances the attractiveness of partnerships with taxable entities or improves the economics of projects involving both exempt and taxable components.

2. **Employment Taxes:** One area to note is employment taxes. Tribes must pay and withhold federal employment taxes (income tax withholding, FICA) for their employees like any other employer. Tribes are exempt from FUTA (unemployment tax) if they participate in state unemployment systems or as per law since 2000.

3. **Excise and Other Taxes:** Tribes are exempt from certain federal excise taxes when the goods/services are for essential governmental functions. For instance, gasoline excise taxes refunded when fuel is used by tribal government vehicles.

4. **IRS Guidance and Developments:** The biggest recent development, as mentioned, is the IRS's proposed regulation in 2024 (REG-113628-21) confirming that tribally chartered entities (LLCs, corporations, etc.) wholly owned by tribes will generally not be recognized as separate taxable entities (Department of the Treasury 2024).

Treasury Consultations 2023: In June 2023, Treasury had consultations specifically on tax status of tribally chartered corporations. Tribes strongly supported treating them as governments for tax. Treasury's proposal in October 2024 reflects that input.

Research and Development Tax Considerations

The permanent reinstatement of research and development expense deductions represents a significant enhancement for tribal technology and innovation enterprises engaged in software development, business process improvement, product development, or other qualifying research activities. Under the 2025 federal tax legislation, domestic R&E expenses can again be deducted immediately rather than amortized over multiple years, providing substantial tax benefits for tribal businesses investing in innovation and technology development (U.S. Department of Treasury 2025).

Small tribal businesses with average annual gross receipts of $31 million or less over the prior three-year period qualify for particularly favorable treatment, including the ability to retroactively claim R&E deductions back to 2022. This retroactive provision can generate substantial tax refunds for qualifying tribal businesses that previously were required to amortize R&E expenses and provides significant cash flow benefits for ongoing innovation activities.

The strategic applications of these R&E deductions vary significantly across tribal business structures as discussed in Chapter 3's analysis of different entity types. Section 17 corporations and qualifying tribally chartered entities with tax-exempt status cannot directly benefit from R&E deductions but may find that these provisions enhance their ability to attract private sector partners or improve the economics of joint venture arrangements. State-chartered tribal corporations and taxable tribal entities can directly benefit from immediate R&E expense deductions, creating incentives for increased investment in innovation activities and technology development.

Tribal businesses should carefully document qualifying R&E activities to ensure compliance with federal requirements while maximizing available tax benefits. Qualifying activities include software development, product testing, process improvement, and certain technology adaptation activities that meet federal criteria for research and development.

Qualified Business Income Deduction Updates

Recent modifications to Qualified Business Income (QBI) deduction provisions have created additional tax planning considerations for tribal business entities organized as pass-through entities like LLCs, partnerships, and S-corporations. The 2025 federal tax legislation includes changes affecting specified service trade or business (SSTB) entities and businesses subject to wage and income limitations that may impact tribal enterprises operating in professional services, consulting, or other specified service industries (U.S. Department of Treasury 2025).

These QBI modifications particularly affect tribal businesses that generate substantial income from professional services, management consulting, legal services, accounting services, or other activities classified as specified service trades or businesses. Tribal entities must carefully evaluate whether their activities qualify for QBI deductions and how wage and income limitations may affect the availability and amount of deductions.

For tribal LLCs and partnerships with significant pass-through income, the modified QBI provisions create both opportunities and limitations that require careful tax planning. Tribal businesses may need to consider restructuring certain activities or adjusting compensation arrangements to optimize QBI benefits while maintaining compliance with tribal ownership requirements and operational objectives.

The interaction between QBI deductions and tribal tax-exempt status creates complex planning considerations for mixed-structure tribal enterprises. Wholly owned tribal entities that qualify for tax-exempt treatment under proposed IRS regulations would not directly benefit from QBI deductions, while partially taxable tribal entities or joint ventures with private partners may benefit from strategic QBI planning.

International Tax Provisions and Cross-Border Considerations

Recent federal tax legislation has modified several international tax provisions that may affect tribal businesses engaged in cross-border activities, including deductions for foreign-derived intangible income (FDII), global intangible low-tax income (GILTI) provisions, and the Base Erosion and Anti-Abuse Tax (BEAT). While most tribal businesses operate primarily within the United States, tribes engaging in international trade, cross-border partnerships, or ventures with foreign entities should understand these provisions' implications (U.S. Department of Treasury 2025).

The FDII deduction provides tax benefits for income derived from intangible property used to generate foreign sales, which may benefit tribal businesses engaged in technology licensing, software development, or intellectual property commercialization in international markets. GILTI provisions affect the taxation of foreign subsidiary income, which may impact tribal businesses with foreign operations or investments.

BEAT provisions impose minimum tax requirements on large corporations with substantial payments to foreign affiliates, which could affect tribal businesses engaged in significant international transactions or partnerships with foreign entities. While these provisions primarily target large multinational corporations, tribal businesses should evaluate their potential application to complex international business structures or joint ventures.

Tribal businesses considering international expansion or cross-border partnerships should coordinate international tax planning with tribal sovereignty considerations and ensure that international business structures preserve tribal governmental authority and cultural considerations while optimizing tax efficiency and compliance with both U.S. and foreign tax requirements. The complexity of coordinating enhanced federal tax benefits with tribal business structure selection and federal program participation requires specialized professional guidance familiar with both federal tax law and tribal sovereignty considerations.

Chapter 7: Best Practices for Choosing and Structuring Tribal Businesses

Selecting the optimal business structure requires balancing legal, financial, and cultural factors. There is no one-size-fits-all answer, each tribe's circumstances and goals differ. However, there are best practices and considerations that have emerged (Federal Reserve Bank of Minneapolis 2024):

1. **Define the Goals and Activities:** Clearly identify the purpose of the business. Is it a purely commercial profit-making venture, or does it have governmental or community service aspects?

2. **Maintain Sovereign Immunity Strategically:** Decide upfront how important retaining immunity is for the venture. If protecting the tribe's sovereignty is paramount (as it usually is), lean toward structures that preserve immunity.

3. **Limit Liability and Protect Tribal Assets:** A core principle is to never put the entire tribal treasury on the line for a business's debts. Use corporate veils (corporations/LLCs) to ensure creditors only have access to the assets of the business, not the tribe's general fund.

4. **Consider Tax Implications Thoroughly:** Work with tax advisers to evaluate how each structure affects federal, state, and tribal tax. Avoid unnecessary taxation.

5. **Access to Capital:** One of the biggest practical determinants is financing. If external capital (bank loans, bonds, investor equity) is needed, choose a structure palatable to financiers. (See Supplement I: Challenges and Solutions for Native American Tribes in Raising Capital.)

   Federal Contracting Opportunities: Federal contracting represents a significant revenue source for many tribal businesses, with specialized programs providing substantial advantages for Native American enterprises. Different business structures offer varying benefits for federal contracting, from 8(a) program eligibility to Buy Indian Act preferences. Structure selection should consider federal contracting objectives and compliance requirements. (See Supplement M: Federal Contracting and Procurement Programs.)

   Strategic Program Coordination: Successful tribal economic development often requires coordinating multiple federal programs, business structures, and funding sources to achieve comprehensive development objectives. Strategic program selection and coordination can maximize federal benefits while building sustainable institutional capacity and avoiding administrative conflicts. Effective coordination requires systematic assessment of program compatibility, sequencing considerations, and administrative capacity to ensure that multiple program participation enhances rather than overwhelms organizational capabilities. (See Supplement N: Strategic Selection and Coordination Framework.)

6. **Governance and Management:** Research by the Harvard Project on American Indian Economic Development demonstrates that separating politics from business operations, by creating a professional management structure, is essential for successful tribal economic development (Cornell and Kalt 2003).

7. **Adaptability:** As no single structure fits all, tribes sometimes mix and match structures. This is perfectly acceptable and often wise.

8. **Compliance and Legal Infrastructure:** Once a structure is chosen, maintain compliance with all legal formalities.

9. **Engage Tribal Members:** A sometimes overlooked factor is community buy-in. When structuring enterprises, consider how it affects tribal members.

10. **Legal Review of Agreements:** Whatever structure is used, every significant contract the business enters should be reviewed for consistency with tribal law and the tribe's interests.

Chapter 8: Indian Hiring Preference in Native American Business Structures

Legal Framework and Historical Context
Indian hiring preference is firmly established in U.S. law as a permissible practice due to the unique political relationship between tribal nations and the federal government (MacCourt, 2016, 18-21). This legal foundation rests on several key developments:

Morton v. Mancari (1974)
The Supreme Court unanimously upheld the constitutionality of Indian preference in Bureau of Indian Affairs hiring practices. The Court distinguished that this preference was based on political classification (membership in federally recognized tribes), not racial classification. Justice Blackmun wrote that the preference was "reasonably designed to further the cause of Indian self-government" and didn't constitute racial discrimination.

Indian Self-Determination and Education Assistance Act (1975)
This landmark legislation expanded the concept of preference beyond the BIA to tribally operated programs and services. Section 7(b) explicitly states that preference in training and employment opportunities should be given to Indians in connection with administration of federal contracts or grants to tribal organizations (Desiderio, 2016).

Additional Legal Support

- Title VII of the Civil Rights Act includes a specific exemption for Indian preference on or near reservations

- Tribal Employment Rights Ordinances (TEROs) have been consistently upheld by federal courts

- The 1987 case *Brendale v. Confederated Tribes and Bands of the Yakima Indian Nation.* 492 U.S. 408 (1989) Bureau of Indian Affairs confirmed tribal authority to regulate employment practices within reservation boundaries

Tribal Variation in Preference Systems

Tribes exercise sovereignty in designing preference policies that reflect their specific needs, values, and economic circumstances:

Common Tiered Preference Structures

1. **First Tier:** Enrolled members of the specific tribe

2. **Second Tier:** Often includes one or more of:

   - Enrolled members of other federally recognized tribes

   - Direct descendants of tribal members (sometimes with blood quantum requirements)

   - Spouses of enrolled tribal members

3. **Third Tier:** May include:

   - Other Native Americans

   - Parents of enrolled tribal members

   - Long-term reservation residents

Documentation and Verification Systems

Tribes have developed rigorous verification systems that typically require:

- Tribal enrollment cards or certificates with enrollment numbers

- Certificates of Indian Blood (CIB) documenting blood quantum if relevant

- Marriage certificates for spousal preference

- Birth certificates and lineage documentation for descendant status
- Residency documentation for geographic preferences

Geographic Considerations
Preference policies often vary based on:
- Whether employment is on or off reservation lands
- Proximity to reservation for urban enterprises
- Location within original treaty territories versus acquired lands

Tribal Economic Development Entities and Preference Structures
Different tribal economic development structures implement preference policies according to their specific organizational form and purpose:

Section 17 Corporations
These federally chartered tribal corporations often maintain strict preference policies consistent with tribal government policies, including:
- Explicit inclusion of preference in corporate charters
- Extension of tribal government preference tiers to corporate operations
- Board oversight to ensure preference implementation
- Example: Navajo Nation Oil and Gas Company maintains a multi-tiered preference system with specific goals for Navajo employment

Tribal Enterprise Boards/Authorities
Tribally chartered entities often have preference policies that:
- Include skill development components to increase qualified tribal candidates
- Establish enterprise-specific exemptions for specialized positions
- Create succession planning requirements for non-Native management positions

- Example: Chickasaw Nation Industries implements a "Chickasaw first" policy while maintaining specific exemptions for positions requiring specialized expertise

Tribal 8(a) Companies

These SBA-recognized disadvantaged businesses often structure preference to:

- Meet both SBA ownership/control requirements and tribal employment goals
- Include specific management transition plans for non-Native executives
- Balance federal contracting requirements with preference systems
- Example: Ho-Chunk Inc. maintains preference policies while operating businesses across multiple states and industries

Note: Each individual business that participates in the 8(a) program receives certification for a maximum of nine years (established by the Business Opportunity Development Reform Act of 1988) (U.S. Small Business Administration 2025). The nine-year term applies to each participating company individually - not to the program itself. The program continues to operate indefinitely, accepting new participants each year while others graduate or exit after their individual nine-year terms.

Participants can receive sole-source contracts up to $4.5 million for goods and services and $7 million for manufacturing (U.S. Small Business Administration 2025). Native American-owned businesses, including those owned by tribes, Alaska Native Corporations, Native Hawaiian Organizations, and Community Development Corporations, receive unique advantages, including exemption from sole-source contracting limits and the ability to own multiple 8(a) subsidiaries (U.S. Small Business Administration 2025).

However, justification requirements have been updated: the Department of Defense requires formal justification only for contracts exceeding $100 million, while other federal agencies require approval for contracts exceeding $25 million (Department of Defense 2020; Federal Acquisition Regulation 2025).

Gaming Enterprises

Tribal casinos typically have preference systems that:

- Follow IGRA requirements for tribal oversight and benefit

- Include regulatory compliance positions with strict preference requirements

- Offer training programs to prepare tribal members for management roles

- Address specialized positions like financial and surveillance roles

- Example: Mashantucket Pequot Tribal Nation's Foxwoods Resort Casino has a multi-tiered preference system with extensive training programs

Joint Ventures and Business Partnerships

The interface between tribal preference and non-Native business partnerships presents unique challenges and opportunities:

Legal Structure Considerations

The specific entity structure affects how preference is implemented:

- Limited Liability Companies (LLCs) often include preference requirements in operating agreements

- Limited Partnerships may address preference in partnership agreements

- Contractual joint ventures typically address preference in project labor agreements

- Example: The Native American Contractors Association provides model language for incorporating preference into various business structures

Geographic and Jurisdictional Factors

The location of business operations significantly impacts preference implementation:

- On-reservation operations generally fall under tribal TERO jurisdiction

- Off-reservation operations may be subject to state and federal employment laws
- Some tribes extend preference to aboriginal territories beyond current reservation boundaries
- Example: The Mississippi Band of Choctaw Indians implements preference across multiple industrial parks both on and adjacent to trust lands

Management and Operational Integration

Successful joint ventures develop systems to integrate preference with operational needs:

- Creation of training pipelines for technical positions
- Clear delineation of roles subject to preference and those with specific expertise requirements
- Mechanisms to resolve disputes about qualification assessments
- Example: The Southern Ute Growth Fund has established detailed protocols for implementing preference within its energy joint ventures

Financial Considerations and Investor Relations

Preference systems in joint ventures must address economic realities:

- Impact of training costs on profit distribution
- Disclosure requirements to non-Native investors or partners
- Performance metrics that account for workforce development goals
- Example: Energy partnerships between tribes and major oil companies often include provisions for training funds and employment targets as part of the financial structure

Tribal Employment Rights Offices (TEROs)

Many tribes have established formal TERO departments that oversee preference implementation:

TERO Functions

- Registration of tribal members seeking employment
- Certification of Native-owned businesses for contracting preference
- Enforcement of preference requirements through inspections and audits
- Collection of TERO fees from employers operating on reservations
- Resolution of disputes regarding preference implementation
- Example: The Navajo Nation TERO office maintains a comprehensive database of qualified Navajo workers and provides compliance training to employers

TERO Ordinances

These tribal laws often address:

- Specific percentage requirements for Native employment
- Training and apprenticeship requirements
- Reporting obligations for employers
- Penalties for non-compliance
- Example: The Confederated Salish and Kootenai Tribes' TERO ordinance requires employers to submit detailed workforce analysis and utilization plans

Best Practices and Implementation Strategies

Successful preference systems share certain characteristics:

Training and Capacity Building

- Pre-employment training programs targeted to business needs
- Apprenticeship programs for technical positions
- Management development initiatives

- Educational partnerships with tribal colleges
- Example: The Cherokee Nation Career Services department provides specific training aligned with tribal enterprise needs

Compliance and Reporting Systems
- Regular workforce analysis by position and department
- Documentation of good faith efforts when qualified Native candidates aren't available
- Transparent appeals processes for hiring decisions
- Example: The Gila River Indian Community requires quarterly compliance reports from all enterprises operating on tribal lands

Cultural Integration
- Incorporation of traditional values into workplace practices
- Recognition of cultural obligations like ceremonial leave
- Language preservation initiatives within business operations
- Example: The Seminole Tribe of Florida's Hard Rock enterprises incorporate cultural awareness training for all employees

Challenges and Future Directions
Skills Gaps and Educational Alignment
- Growing need for STEM-educated tribal members
- Competition with urban employers for skilled tribal members
- Need for specialized education in fields like healthcare and technology
- Example: The American Indian Science and Engineering Society partners with tribes to develop STEM pipelines

Geographic Dispersion of Tribal Members
- Many tribal members live away from reservations
- Remote work opportunities create new preference implementation challenges

- Urban tribal enterprises face different implementation considerations

- Example: The Citizen Potawatomi Nation has developed preference policies that accommodate their geographically dispersed membership

Evolving Legal Landscape
- Ongoing challenges to preference in specific contexts

- Intersection with state employment laws in Public Law 280 states

- Impact of federal contracting requirements on preference implementation

- Example: Recent cases involving the applicability of preference to tribally owned businesses operating in urban areas

The Role of Tribal Employment Rights Offices (TEROs) in Native American Business Development

Introduction

Tribal Employment Rights Offices (TEROs) are pivotal in advancing tribal sovereignty and economic self-determination. Established under the authority of federally recognized tribes, TEROs enforce tribal employment laws and preferences on tribal lands. Their primary purpose is to ensure that Native Americans gain their rightful share of employment, training, contracting, and business opportunities on or near reservations (Nilles, 2016, 22-25).

TERO Foundations and Legal Authority

TEROs derive their authority from the inherent sovereignty of tribal nations. This sovereignty allows tribes to enact and enforce employment preference laws without needing approval from federal or state governments. The legal foundation for TEROs is further reinforced by federal laws such as the Indian Self-Determination and Education Assistance Act and Title VII of the Civil Rights Act of 1964, which acknowledge the unique political status of tribes and their right to self-governance.

Impact on Internal Business Structures - Overview

Within tribal communities, TEROs influence internal business structures by promoting employment and contracting preferences for tribal members. This includes setting conditions for Indian preference in hiring, training, promotions, and subcontracting. TEROs often collaborate with tribal economic development departments and educational institutions to create pipelines of skilled Native workers and entrepreneurs, ensuring that tribal enterprises are both economically productive and culturally reinforcing.

TERO in External Business Engagements - Overview

TEROs play a strategic role in negotiations with external investors, contractors, and business partners. Tribal TERO ordinances may require non-tribal companies operating on reservation land to comply with tribal hiring preferences, pay TERO fees, or submit compliance plans. These requirements help ensure that economic benefits stay within the community and that outside entities respect tribal laws and sovereignty. When effectively integrated into business agreements, TERO policies reinforce tribal control and equitable benefit sharing.

TEROs are systematically structured programs. Key elements of the structure include:

- **Legal Framework:** TERO utilizes a sound and comprehensive framework that encompasses the use of Tribal, Federal, and/or State employment law.

- **Administrative Structure:** TEROs have a well developed administrative structure and enforcement process.

- **Synergistic Partnering:** TERO programs apply synergistic partnering principles in relationships with employers to the greatest extent possible.

Challenges and Strategic Opportunities - Overview

Despite their benefits, TEROs can face resistance from external partners unfamiliar with tribal sovereignty or concerned about additional compliance requirements. Tribal leaders and business developers must navigate the balance between asserting tribal preferences and maintaining a business-friendly environment. However, when TEROs are strategically framed as vehicles for local workforce development, long-term capacity building, and risk management, they can strengthen the tribe's negotiation position and contribute to more sustainable economic outcomes.

Conclusion

TEROs serve as critical tools in aligning tribal sovereignty with modern economic development strategies. Their influence extends beyond employment into the structural design of tribal businesses and their engagement with external markets. When properly implemented, TEROs not only protect and promote tribal employment but also help create business environments that are equitable, strategic, and rooted in self-determination.

Supplement A: Sovereign Immunity Decision Matrix For Tribal Business Entities

This matrix provides a framework for evaluating sovereign immunity considerations across different tribal business structures:

Entity Type	Immunity Status	Key Factors	Waiver Mechanisms	Risk Level
Unincorporated Tribal Enterprise	Full Immunity	• Direct tribal operation • No separate legal entity • Assets = tribal assets	• Tribal council resolution • Contract-specific waivers • Limited arbitration clauses	Low (for tribe) High (for creditors)
Section 17 Corporation	Presumed Immunity	• Federal charter • "Sue and be sued" clause interpretation • Wholly tribal-owned	• Board resolution • Charter amendments • Contract provisions	Medium
Tribally Chartered Corporation	Conditional Immunity	• Arm-of-tribe analysis • Tribal ownership % • Governmental purpose	• Charter language • Tribal code provisions • Operating agreements	Medium

Entity Type	Immunity Status	Key Factors	Waiver Mechanisms	Risk Level
State-Chartered Corporation	Limited/No Immunity	• State law creation • Separate legal entity • Commercial purpose	• Generally waived by formation • Contractual agreements • Insurance coverage	High
Tribal LLC (Single-Member)	Strong Immunity	• Tribal law formation • 100% tribal ownership • Disregarded entity status	• Operating agreement • Management decisions • Member resolutions	Low-Medium
State LLC (Tribal-Owned)	Uncertain Immunity	• State law creation • Factual analysis required • Jurisdictional considerations	• Operating agreement • Explicit waivers • Arbitration clauses	Medium-High

Decision Framework Questions:

1. Is preserving sovereign immunity essential for this venture?
2. What level of liability exposure is acceptable?
3. Do lenders/partners require immunity waivers?
4. Will the entity operate on or off reservation?
5. What dispute resolution mechanisms are preferred?

Supplement B: Sovereign Immunity Waiver

Sample Limited Sovereign Immunity Waiver Language for Commercial Contracts

LIMITED WAIVER OF SOVEREIGN IMMUNITY

[Tribal Entity Name], a [Section 17 corporation/tribally chartered corporation/LLC] of the [Tribe Name] ("Entity"), hereby provides this limited waiver of sovereign immunity solely for the purposes of this Agreement dated [Date] ("Agreement") with [Counterparty Name] ("Counterparty").

1. SCOPE OF WAIVER

The Entity hereby waives its sovereign immunity from suit solely:

a) For claims arising directly from this Agreement;

b) In the courts or arbitration forums specified in Section [X] below;

c) For the recovery of monetary damages not exceeding $[Amount];

d) For declaratory and injunctive relief directly related to performance under this Agreement.

2. LIMITATIONS

This waiver does NOT extend to:

a) Punitive, exemplary, or consequential damages;

b) Any claims against the [Tribe Name] or its other entities;

c) Any governmental or regulatory actions by the Entity;

d) Any assets other than those specifically pledged as collateral;

e) Any matters not directly arising from this Agreement.

3. FORUM SELECTION

Any disputes shall be resolved through:

[Option A: Binding arbitration under [AAA/JAMS] rules in [Location]]

[Option B: [Tribal Court Name] with appeal to [Federal District Court]]

[Option C: [State] court in [County], [State]]

4. GOVERNING LAW

This Agreement shall be governed by [Tribal/State/Federal] law, except as modified by applicable federal Indian law.

5. ENFORCEMENT

Any judgment or award may be enforced against the specific assets identified in Schedule [X] attached hereto, but not against any other assets of the Entity or the [Tribe Name].

By:_____ Date: _____

[Name], [Title]

[Tribal Entity Name]

Supplement C: Sample Section 17 Petition to the Secretary of the Interior

PETITION FOR FEDERAL CORPORATE CHARTER UNDER SECTION 17 OF THE INDIAN REORGANIZATION ACT

TO: The Honorable Secretary of the Interior U.S. Department of the Interior Washington, D.C. 20240

FROM: [Tribal Government Name] [Address] [City, State, ZIP]

DATE: [Date]

I. TRIBAL INFORMATION

- Tribal Name: [Full Legal Name]
- Federal Recognition: [Date of Recognition/Treaty Reference]
- Current Government: [IRA/Traditional/Other]
- Tribal Resolution: [Number and Date of Authorizing Resolution]

II. PROPOSED CORPORATION

- Corporate Name: [Proposed Name] Corporation
- Purpose: [Brief Description of Business Activities]
- Duration: Perpetual
- Principal Office: [Address on Tribal Lands]

III. PROPOSED CHARTER PROVISIONS

1. Corporate Powers: The corporation shall have the power to:

- Conduct business activities for the economic benefit of the Tribe
- Enter into contracts and agreements
- Acquire, hold, and dispose of property
- Borrow money and issue obligations
- Sue and be sued in its corporate name
- Exercise such other powers as may be necessary

2. Capital Structure:

- Authorized Shares: [Number] shares of common stock
- Par Value: $[Amount] per share
- Ownership: All shares to be owned by [Tribal Government Name]

3. Management:

- Board of Directors: [Number] members
- Appointment: Directors appointed by [Tribal Council/Chairman]
- Terms: [Length] years, staggered/concurrent

4. Financial Provisions:

- Fiscal Year: [January 1 - December 31/October 1 - September 30]
- Annual Reports: To be filed with Tribal Government and BIA
- Audit Requirements: Annual independent audit

IV. SUPPORTING DOCUMENTS

Attached hereto:

- Tribal Council Resolution [Number] dated [Date]
- Proposed Articles of Incorporation
- Proposed Bylaws
- Economic Development Plan
- Environmental Assessment (if required)

V. CERTIFICATION

The undersigned certifies that this petition is submitted pursuant to authority granted by the Tribal Council and that all information herein is true and correct.

_____   Date: _____

[Name], [Title] [Tribal Government Name]

Supplement D: Sample Tribal Corporate Charter

CHARTER OF [CORPORATION NAME] A SECTION 17 CORPORATION OF THE [TRIBE NAME]

ARTICLE I - NAME AND DURATION The name of this corporation shall be "[Corporation Name]" and it shall exist in perpetuity unless dissolved in accordance with federal law and this Charter.

ARTICLE II - PURPOSES AND POWERS Section 1. The corporation is organized for the purposes of: a) Promoting the economic development of the [Tribe Name]; b) Conducting business activities for the benefit of the Tribe and its members; c) Generating revenue for tribal governmental services; d) Creating employment opportunities for tribal members.

Section 2. The corporation shall have all powers necessary and proper to carry out its purposes, including but not limited to: a) Conducting any lawful business activity; b) Acquiring, holding, and disposing of real and personal property; c) Entering into contracts and joint ventures; d) Borrowing money and pledging assets as security; e) Sue and be sued in its corporate name, subject to any applicable sovereign immunity; f) Hiring employees and engaging contractors.

ARTICLE III - CAPITAL STOCK Section 1. The corporation is authorized to issue [Number] shares of common stock with a par value of $[Amount] per share.

Section 2. All issued shares shall be owned by the [Tribe Name] and may not be transferred without the express consent of the Tribal Council.

ARTICLE IV - BOARD OF DIRECTORS Section 1. The corporation shall be managed by a Board of Directors consisting of [Number] members appointed by the Tribal Council.

Section 2. Directors shall serve terms of [Number] years and may be reappointed.

Section 3. The Board shall meet at least quarterly and maintain minutes of all meetings.

ARTICLE V - OFFICERS The corporation shall have a President, Secretary, and Treasurer, who may be members of the Board or appointed by the Board.

ARTICLE VI - SOVEREIGN IMMUNITY Section 1. The corporation possesses the sovereign immunity of the [Tribe Name] except as specifically waived by the Board of Directors in accordance with tribal law.

Section 2. The inclusion of a "sue and be sued" clause in this Charter does not constitute a general waiver of sovereign immunity but merely grants the corporation the capacity to initiate and defend legal proceedings when authorized by the Board.

ARTICLE VII - DISSOLUTION This corporation may only be dissolved by mutual consent of the [Tribe Name] and the Secretary of the Interior, or by operation of federal law.

ARTICLE VIII - AMENDMENTS This Charter may be amended only with the approval of the Tribal Council and the Secretary of the Interior.

IN WITNESS WHEREOF, this Charter is executed on [Date].

APPROVED:

_____ Date: _____

Secretary of the Interior

ACCEPTED:

_____ Date: _____

[Name], Chairman [Tribe Name]

Supplement E: A Comparative Analysis of Section 17 IRA, OIWA, and Tax Implications

COMPARISON AND CONTRAST: SECTION 17 IRA, INTERNAL REVENUE CODE, AND OKLAHOMA INDIAN WELFARE ACT

SECTION 17 OF THE INDIAN REORGANIZATION ACT (IRA) - 1934

Purpose and Structure: Section 17 of the Indian Reorganization Act permits tribes to incorporate under federal law to "equip themselves with the devices of modern business organization, through forming themselves into business corporations." A Section 17 corporation is wholly owned by the tribe, but is separate and distinct from the tribal government.

Key Features:

- Federal charter issued by Secretary of Interior through Bureau of Indian Affairs[2]

- Powers include capacity to make contracts, adopt corporate seal, sue and be sued, purchase/dispose of property, and other corporate powers "not inconsistent with law"

- Cannot be dissolved or suspended except by act of Congress; cannot be amended without Secretary of Interior approval

- Many Section 17 corporations exist but most have been inactive since creation due to restrictive BIA-generated charters and extensive federal oversight

OKLAHOMA INDIAN WELFARE ACT (OIWA/THOMAS-ROGERS ACT) - 1936

Purpose and Structure: Also known as the Thomas-Rogers Act, it extends the 1934 Indian Reorganization Act to tribes within the boundaries of the state of Oklahoma. The Oklahoma Indian Welfare Act was an alternative to the Wheeler-Howard Act because Oklahoma's delegation believed the original IRA was for reservation Indians and did not relate to Oklahoma's unique situation.

Oklahoma's Unique Situation: Unlike most other states, Oklahoma had been formed largely from Indian Territory, where numerous tribes had been relocated during the 19th century removals. By the 1930s, most tribal lands in Oklahoma had been allotted to individual Indians under the Dawes Act, breaking up communal tribal ownership. Additionally, many Oklahoma tribes had lost their formal government structures during the allotment period and territorial transition to statehood in 1907. This created a fundamentally different legal and practical situation from reservation-based tribes elsewhere, where tribal governments and communal land ownership generally remained intact. Oklahoma tribes needed legislation that addressed their specific circumstances of landlessness, dissolved governments, and the complex aftermath of allotment and statehood.

Key Features:
- Any recognized tribe or band of Indians residing in Oklahoma has the right to organize and adopt a constitution and bylaws under rules prescribed by the Secretary of Interior
- Secretary may issue charter of incorporation, operative when ratified by majority vote of adult members (minimum 30% voter turnout required)
- Allows tribal organization when at least ten members of an existing tribe want to organize, with right to participate in revolving credit fund and other IRA privileges

THE FIVE CIVILIZED TRIBES: HISTORICAL CONTEXT

The Five Civilized Tribes—Cherokee, Chickasaw, Choctaw, Creek (Muscogee), and Seminole—earned this designation from European Americans because they adopted many aspects of European-American culture, including written constitutions, representative governments, and in some cases, plantation agriculture and slaveholding.[10] Originally from the Southeastern United States, these tribes were forcibly removed to Indian Territory (present-day Oklahoma) during the 1830s in what became known as the Trail of Tears.

Following the Civil War, these tribes faced unique challenges. Because some members had allied with the Confederacy, the federal government imposed new treaties in 1866 that required the tribes to abolish slavery and extend citizenship and rights to their formerly enslaved people, known as Freedmen. This historical context is crucial to understanding the later controversies surrounding the Oklahoma Indian Welfare Act.

THE FREEDMEN ISSUE: ORIGINS AND RESOLUTION

Historical Background: The Freedmen were formerly enslaved African Americans held by members of the Five Civilized Tribes. Under the post-Civil War treaties of 1866, each of the Five Tribes was required to extend full tribal citizenship to their former slaves and their descendants (Wikipedia 2025; Five Civilized Tribes 2025). This created a unique class of tribal citizens who were of African rather than Native American descent.

OIWA and Membership Disputes: When the Five Civilized Tribes began reorganizing under the Oklahoma Indian Welfare Act and establishing new governments, a critical question emerged: could they modify their membership rules to exclude Freedmen? In 1941, the Solicitor General noted that Congress had approved legislation enabling tribes to reconstitute their governments and create new constitutions with membership rules that limited membership to persons of Indian descent (Wikipedia 2025).

Modern Litigation and Resolution: While tribes initially resisted providing Freedmen with full tribal benefits, they did not generally take action to exclude them until the late 20th century, coinciding with increased assertions of tribal sovereignty. In 2007, Cherokee members voted overwhelmingly to strip 2,800 Freedmen of their membership, defining tribal citizenship as "by blood" (NPR 2017). This action triggered significant legal challenges that were resolved in 2017 when U.S. District Judge Thomas F. Hogan ruled that Freedmen descendants have full rights to Cherokee Nation citizenship. The judge determined that "The Cherokee Nation can continue to define itself as it sees fit, but must do so equally and evenhandedly with respect to native Cherokees and the descendants of Cherokee Freedmen" (NPR 2017). The Cherokee Nation did not appeal this federal court decision and began processing Freedmen citizenship applications. In 2021, the Cherokee Nation Supreme Court formally reaffirmed this ruling, ordering the removal of "by blood" language from the tribal constitution (CNN 2021).

Conclusion: The most significant controversy involving the Freedmen exclusion issue among the Five Civilized Tribes was largely resolved through federal court intervention in 2017. While this ruling specifically addressed the Cherokee Nation, it established important precedent regarding tribal citizenship and the federal government's treaty obligations with respect to Freedmen descendants. The Osage exclusion represents a deliberate political compromise that secured OIWA's passage but reflects the complex interplay of tribal sovereignty, mineral rights, and federal legislation.

INTERNAL REVENUE CODE TREATMENT

Tax Status Distinctions: The Internal Revenue Code creates different tax treatments:

- **IRA Section 17 corporations**: Not subject to federal income tax

- **OIWA Section 3 corporations**: Not subject to federal income tax

- **State chartered corporations**: Ordinarily subject to federal income tax on income earned after October 1, 1994

- **Tribal law entities**: Currently under IRS review with guidance forthcoming[15]

Recent Developments: In October 2024, Treasury and IRS issued proposed regulations addressing federal tax classification of entities wholly owned by Indian Tribal governments. The regulations would treat wholly owned Tribal entities as "disregarded entities" for federal tax purposes, similar to Section 17 and Section 3 corporations.

Enhanced Federal Tax Benefits from 2025 Legislation

The One Big Beautiful Bill Act (OBBBA) of 2025 has further enhanced the tax advantages available to tribal business entities through permanent extensions and modifications detailed throughout this guide's comprehensive analysis. These enhancements, including permanent bonus depreciation and reinstated R&E deductions, create additional strategic advantages for federally chartered tribal corporations compared to state-chartered entities (Economic Innovation Group 2025; U.S. Department of Treasury 2025). The enhanced rural development incentives introduced through the 2025 legislation provide particular benefits for tribal communities in rural areas, creating additional coordination opportunities between federal tax benefits and tribal sovereignty-based advantages that distinguish Native American business structures from conventional corporate entities.

CRITICAL DIFFERENCES BETWEEN IRA SECTION 17 AND OIWA

1. Geographic Application:

- **IRA Section 17**: Available to all federally recognized tribes

- **OIWA**: Oklahoma tribes are not eligible to incorporate under the Indian Reorganization Act of 1934 - they must use OIWA instead

2. Federal Oversight:

- **IRA Section 17**: Lengthy multi-step federal process with extensive federal oversight and approval, increased administrative costs, and requires act of Congress to dissolve

- **OIWA**: More streamlined process specifically designed for Oklahoma's unique situation

3. Land and Property Rights:

- **IRA Section 17**: Limited by specific prohibitions against sale, mortgage, or lease for more than ten years of any land within reservation boundaries

- **OIWA**: Broader land acquisition authority including trust lands and specific provisions for Oklahoma's gross-production tax on oil and gas

CONTROVERSIES AMONG OKLAHOMA TRIBES REGARDING OIWA COVERAGE

1. OSAGE NATION EXCLUSION

Explicit Exclusion: The Oklahoma Indian Welfare Act explicitly states that it "shall not relate to or affect Osage County, Oklahoma" and "does not affect the Osage Nation, which retained ownership of its own land." During legislative drafting, Osage County was eliminated from the language due to strong opposition.

Reason for Exclusion: The Osages were excluded by efforts of lobbyists with interest in Osage oil. There was much opposition to the original draft, particularly from Osage County representatives who were concerned about control of Native American financial interests, specifically regarding taxation of mineral rights.

2. TRIBAL ORGANIZATION PATTERNS

Successful Organizations: Many American Indian tribes of Oklahoma organized under this legislation, including the Caddo, Kansa, Peoria, and Cheyenne-Arapaho tribes.

Variations in Implementation: The Miami Tribe re-organized their government under the Oklahoma Indian Welfare Act on June 1, 1940, and adopted a corporate charter at that time. Some of the charters drafted and adopted in 1940 are now dated, and tribes like Miami have sought congressional approval to revoke outdated charters.

CONCLUSION

The three legal frameworks represent an evolution in federal Indian law:

    1. Section 17 IRA (1934) established the federal corporate structure but with extensive federal oversight

    2. OIWA (1936) provided Oklahoma tribes with a more tailored approach reflecting their unique post-allotment situation

    3. Internal Revenue Code created tax distinctions that favor federally chartered tribal corporations over state-chartered entities

The most significant ongoing controversy involves the **Freedmen exclusion issue** among the Five Civilized Tribes, which continues to generate litigation and political tension. The **Osage exclusion** was a deliberate political compromise to secure passage of OIWA but reflects the complex interplay of tribal sovereignty, mineral rights, and federal legislation.

Supplement F: Checklist: Determining If An Entity Qualifies As An "Arm of the Tribe"

ARM-OF-THE-TRIBE ANALYSIS CHECKLIST

Courts typically examine multiple factors to determine whether a business entity qualifies as an "arm of the tribe" entitled to sovereign immunity. Use this checklist to evaluate your entity's status:

FORMATION AND LEGAL STATUS
- Entity formed under tribal law (stronger) vs. state law (weaker)
- Express language in governing documents stating entity is an arm of the tribe
- Tribal council resolution declaring entity to be governmental instrumentality
- Entity charter/articles reference governmental purposes

OWNERSHIP AND CONTROL
- 100% owned by the tribe (strongest factor)
- Tribe owns majority interest (51%+)
- Tribal council appoints board members/managers
- Tribe retains power to dissolve entity

- Entity bylaws require tribal approval for major decisions

FUNCTION AND PURPOSE
- Entity serves essential governmental functions
- Activities benefit tribal members generally (not just investors)
- Entity provides governmental services (utilities, healthcare, etc.)
- Revenue supports tribal governmental operations
- Entity created to further tribal self-determination

FINANCIAL RELATIONSHIP
- Entity's liabilities backed by tribal treasury
- Profits flow to tribal government
- Tribe provides initial capitalization
- Entity shares tribal credit rating/financial standing
- Consolidated financial reporting with tribe

OPERATIONAL INTEGRATION
- Entity operates under tribal regulations
- Shared personnel/facilities with tribal government
- Entity subject to tribal audit requirements
- Coordination with other tribal enterprises
- Entity reports regularly to tribal council

TREATMENT BY EXTERNAL PARTIES
- IRS treats entity as disregarded/part of tribe
- Federal agencies recognize entity as tribal instrumentality
- Creditors look to tribal government for repayment
- Entity eligible for tribal government funding programs

SCORING GUIDE:

- **Strong Arm Status (20+ factors):** Very likely to be considered arm of tribe

- **Moderate Arm Status (15-19 factors):** Probably arm of tribe, but some risk

- **Weak Arm Status (10-14 factors):** Uncertain status, legal review recommended

- **Separate Entity (Under 10 factors):** Likely treated as separate from tribe

RECOMMENDATIONS BASED ON ANALYSIS:

- Structure clearly qualifies as arm of tribe - maintain current structure

- Structure has strong arm characteristics - minor modifications recommended

- Structure has moderate arm characteristics - significant changes advised Structure unlikely to qualify - consider restructuring or accept separate status

Supplement G: Sample Tribal Economic Development Ordinance

[TRIBE NAME] ECONOMIC DEVELOPMENT AUTHORITY ORDINANCE

Ordinance No. [Number]

SECTION 1. TITLE AND PURPOSE This Ordinance shall be known as the "[Tribe Name] Economic Development Authority Ordinance." The purpose is to establish a tribal authority to promote, facilitate, and coordinate economic development activities for the benefit of the [Tribe Name] and its members.

SECTION 2. DEFINITIONS a) "Authority" means the [Tribe Name] Economic Development Authority b) "Board" means the Board of Directors of the Authority c) "Council" means the [Tribe Name] Tribal Council d) "Economic Development" includes business enterprises, job creation, infrastructure development, and revenue generation activities

SECTION 3. ESTABLISHMENT There is hereby established the [Tribe Name] Economic Development Authority as an instrumentality and political subdivision of the [Tribe Name].

SECTION 4. BOARD COMPOSITION a) The Authority shall be governed by a Board of [Number] directors b) [Number] directors appointed by the Tribal Council c) [Number] directors appointed by the

Chairman (if applicable) d) [Number] ex-officio members from tribal government e) Directors serve [Number]-year staggered terms

SECTION 5. POWERS AND DUTIES The Authority is authorized to: a) Develop and implement economic development plans b) Create, acquire, and manage business enterprises c) Form corporations, LLCs, and other business entities d) Enter into contracts, leases, and joint ventures e) Acquire, hold, and dispose of real and personal property f) Issue bonds and other debt instruments (subject to tribal approval) g) Apply for and receive grants and loans h) Establish lending and investment programs i) Coordinate with federal, state, and local development agencies

SECTION 6. RELATIONSHIP TO TRIBAL GOVERNMENT a) The Authority operates as an arm of the tribal government b) Major policy decisions require Tribal Council approval c) Annual budget subject to Council review and approval d) Authority reports quarterly to Tribal Council e) Council may dissolve Authority by ordinance

SECTION 7. SOVEREIGN IMMUNITY a) The Authority possesses the sovereign immunity of the [Tribe Name] b) Immunity may be waived only by specific Board resolution c) Waivers limited to specific transactions and purposes d) No general waiver of immunity authorized

SECTION 8. CONFLICT OF INTEREST Board members must: a) Disclose any personal financial interest in Authority transactions b) Recuse themselves from decisions involving conflicts c) File annual financial disclosure statements d) Comply with tribal ethics codes

SECTION 9. EFFECTIVE DATE This Ordinance becomes effective upon adoption by the Tribal Council.

ADOPTED this _____ day of ____, *20.*

[Name], Chairman [Tribe Name]
ATTEST:

[Name], Secretary [Tribe Name]

Supplement H: Sample Joint Venture Agreement

JOINT VENTURE AGREEMENT Between [Tribe Name] and [Private Company Name]

PARTIES

- **Tribal Party:** [Tribe Name], a federally recognized Indian tribe
- **Private Party:** [Company Name], a [State] corporation

RECITALS WHEREAS, Tribal Party desires to develop [Project Description] on tribal lands; WHEREAS, Private Party has expertise and capital to contribute to the project; WHEREAS, the parties wish to form a joint venture to pursue mutual benefits;

ARTICLE 1 - FORMATION OF JOINT VENTURE 1.1 **Entity Formation:** The parties shall form [JV Entity Name], LLC under [State/Tribal] law. 1.2 **Ownership:** Tribal Party: [%], Private Party: [%] 1.3 **Management:** [Manager-managed/Member-managed structure]

ARTICLE 2 - CONTRIBUTIONS 2.1 Tribal Contributions:

- Land use rights: [Description]
- Regulatory advantages: [Tax benefits, etc.]
- Local workforce access
- [Other contributions]

2.2 Private Party Contributions:

- Capital: $[Amount]

- Technical expertise: [Description]

- Management services: [Description]

- [Other contributions]

ARTICLE 3 - GOVERNANCE 3.1 **Management Committee:** [Number] members from each party 3.2 **Major Decisions:** Require [unanimous/majority] consent 3.3 **Day-to-Day Operations:** Managed by [Party/Professional manager]

ARTICLE 4 - PROFIT AND LOSS ALLOCATION 4.1 **Distribution:** According to ownership percentages 4.2 **Tax Treatment:** Each party responsible for own tax obligations 4.3 **Reinvestment:** [Percentage] of profits retained for growth

ARTICLE 5 - EMPLOYMENT PREFERENCES 5.1 **Tribal Preference:** Priority hiring for qualified tribal members 5.2 **Training Programs:** Private Party to provide skills development 5.3 **Compliance:** All hiring subject to applicable TERO requirements

ARTICLE 6 - SOVEREIGN IMMUNITY 6.1 **Tribal Immunity:** Preserved except as specifically waived herein 6.2 **Limited Waiver:** Tribal Party waives immunity solely for:

- Contract disputes between parties

- Third-party claims arising from JV operations

- Limited to JV assets (not tribal assets)

ARTICLE 7 - DISPUTE RESOLUTION 7.1 **Negotiation:** Good faith discussions for [30] days 7.2 **Mediation:** [Neutral mediator/Tribal court mediation] 7.3 **Arbitration:** Binding arbitration under [AAA/JAMS] rules 7.4 **Venue:** [Location], subject to tribal court jurisdiction for tribal law issues

ARTICLE 8 - REGULATORY COMPLIANCE 8.1 **Environmental:** Comply with tribal and federal environmental laws 8.2 **Cultural Protection:** Respect tribal cultural sites and practices 8.3 **Tribal Law:** Operations subject to applicable tribal regulations

ARTICLE 9 - TERMINATION 9.1 **Term:** [Number] years, renewable by mutual consent 9.2 **Termination Events:** Material breach, insolvency, mutual agreement 9.3 **Asset Distribution:** According to ownership percentages

ARTICLE 10 - MISCELLANEOUS 10.1 **Governing Law:** [Tribal/State/Federal] law as applicable 10.2 **Amendment:** Requires written agreement of both parties 10.3 **Integration:** This agreement supersedes all prior negotiations

IN WITNESS WHEREOF, the parties execute this Agreement on [Date].

[TRIBE NAME] [COMPANY NAME]

By: _____ By:

_____ [Name], [Title] [Name], [Title] Date:

_____ Date: _____

Supplement I: Challenges and Solutions for Native American Tribes in Raising Capital

OVERVIEW OF CAPITAL ACCESS CHALLENGES

Native American tribes face unique obstacles in accessing capital markets due to their sovereign status, jurisdictional complexity, and historical factors. This supplement outlines common challenges and proven solutions.

PRIMARY CHALLENGES

1. Sovereign Immunity Concerns

- **Challenge:** Lenders fear inability to collect on defaulted loans
- **Solutions:**
  - Limited immunity waivers for specific transactions
  - Arbitration clauses in loan agreements
  - Third-party guarantees or insurance
  - Collateral structures using business assets (not tribal assets)

2. Jurisdictional Uncertainty

- **Challenge:** Unclear which courts have jurisdiction over disputes
- **Solutions:**
  - Clear forum selection clauses
  - Choice of law provisions

— Tribal court/state court cooperation agreements

— Federal court jurisdiction agreements

3. Collateral and Security Issues

- **Challenge:** Trust land cannot be mortgaged; tribal assets may be immune

- **Solutions:**

  — Personal property collateral (equipment, receivables)

  — Revenue pledges from specific projects

  — Third-party guarantees

  — Insurance and surety bonds

  — Off-reservation asset pledges

4. Limited Credit History

- **Challenge:** Tribes may lack extensive credit histories

- **Solutions:**

  — Start with smaller, secured transactions

  — Provide detailed financial statements and projections

  — Engage credit rating agencies

  — Use SBA guarantee programs

  — Partner with established entities

PROVEN FINANCING STRATEGIES

Traditional Bank Lending

- Relationship banking with institutions experienced in tribal finance

- Detailed business plans and financial projections

- Professional management teams

- Clear legal structure and governance

Government Programs

- SBA 8(a) lending programs

- USDA rural development loans

- HUD Section 184 loan guarantees
- BIA loan guarantee programs
- New Markets Tax Credits (See Supplement J: Treasury Department and IRS Programs)

Bond Financing
- Section 17 corporations can issue tax-exempt bonds
- Tribal government bonds for governmental purposes
- Taxable bonds for commercial projects
- Revenue bonds secured by specific income streams

Alternative Financing
- Equipment financing and leasing
- Factoring and receivables financing
- Crowdfunding for smaller projects
- Tribal investment partnerships
- Private placement offerings

BEST PRACTICES FOR TRIBES

Preparation Phase
- Develop comprehensive business plans
- Establish audited financial statements
- Create professional management structures
- Build relationships with potential lenders
- Obtain legal counsel experienced in tribal finance

Structure Selection
- Choose entity type based on financing needs
- Consider lender preferences and requirements
- Balance sovereignty protection with access needs
- Plan for growth and additional financing rounds

Due Diligence Support
- Prepare detailed information packages

- Address sovereignty and jurisdiction issues proactively
- Provide legal opinions on key issues
- Demonstrate strong governance and controls

Ongoing Relationship Management
- Maintain regular communication with lenders
- Provide timely financial reporting
- Honor all covenant requirements
- Build track record for future financing needs

EMERGING TRENDS

Impact Investing
- Growing interest in tribal economic development
- Focus on social and environmental returns
- Flexible terms and patient capital
- Alignment with tribal values

Opportunity Zones (See Supplement J: Treasury Department and IRS Programs)
- Many reservations designated as Opportunity Zones
- Tax incentives for long-term investments
- Potential for significant capital deployment
- Requires qualified opportunity funds

Green Financing
- Renewable energy project financing
- Environmental, social, and governance (ESG) criteria
- Federal and state incentive programs
- Carbon credit opportunities

Technology and Innovation
- Fintech solutions for tribal banking
- Blockchain and cryptocurrency applications
- Remote lending and underwriting
- Digital asset financing

CONCLUSION

While capital access challenges persist for tribal entities, numerous successful examples demonstrate that these obstacles can be overcome through careful planning, appropriate structuring, and professional execution. The key is balancing tribal sovereignty protection with lender comfort, while building long-term relationships that support ongoing economic development.

Supplement J: Treasury Department and IRS Programs

Introduction to Treasury's Role in Tribal Finance

Treasury's approach to tribal financing programs has evolved significantly since the establishment of the CDFI Fund in 1994, reflecting both growing recognition of tribal governments as sophisticated economic development entities and increasing understanding of the unique legal and cultural considerations that distinguish tribal communities from other low-income communities served by Treasury programs. This evolution parallels the broader federal policy development toward tribal self-determination discussed throughout our manuscript, emphasizing tribal control over development priorities and implementation approaches while providing federal resources and technical assistance to support tribal objectives (see cross-reference to main manuscript's discussion of federal policy evolution and business structure implications).

The integration of Treasury programs with tribal economic development strategies requires sophisticated understanding of both federal tax law and tribal sovereignty principles, as Treasury programs operate within the complex intersection of federal taxation, community development finance, and federal Indian law. This regulatory environment creates both opportunities and challenges that require careful analysis and professional guidance. (Treasury Department 2022).

Community Development Financial Institutions (CDFI) Fund Programs

CDFI Certification and Native American Applications

The CDFI Fund's certification process for Native American Community Development Financial Institutions (CDFIs) reflects specialized recognition of the unique legal, cultural, and economic circumstances of tribal communities, requiring modifications to standard CDFI certification criteria that accommodate tribal sovereignty, traditional governance structures, and cultural values that may differ from conventional community development approaches. The certification requirements under 12 C.F.R. Part 1805 establish fundamental criteria for CDFI designation, including community development focus, provision of development services, accountability to community, and non-government status, with specific provisions that recognize tribal governmental structures and traditional economic systems (12 C.F.R. § 1805.201).

Native American CDFI certification requires demonstration of service to Native American, Alaska Native, or Native Hawaiian communities, with geographic service areas that may encompass tribal lands, traditional territories, or urban areas with significant Native populations.

The Fund's guidance recognizes that tribal service areas may cross state boundaries and may include areas not traditionally considered "communities" under conventional CDFI definitions, reflecting the unique geographic and political circumstances of tribal nations (CDFI Fund 2023). This flexibility enables tribes to design CDFIs that serve their specific community configurations while meeting federal certification requirements.

The accountability requirements for Native American CDFIs acknowledge tribal governmental structures and traditional decision-making processes, enabling CDFIs to demonstrate community accountability through tribal governmental oversight, traditional council structures, or other governance mechanisms that reflect tribal cultural values and governmental authority. This approach recognizes that conventional nonprofit governance structures may not be appropriate for tribal CDFIs and that tribal governmental involvement may strengthen rather than compromise community accountability (12 C.F.R. § 1805.201(b)(3); CDFI Fund 2022).

CDFI Program Financial Assistance and Technical Assistance

The CDFI Fund provides both Financial Assistance (FA) awards and Technical Assistance (TA) grants to certified Native American CDFIs, with program design that recognizes the dual needs for capital and capacity building that characterize many tribal financial institutions. Financial Assistance awards provide grants, loans, deposits, and equity investments that capitalize CDFI lending activities and enable expansion of services to Native communities, while Technical Assistance grants support institutional development, staff training, and operational improvements that strengthen CDFI capacity and performance (12 U.S.C. § 4707; CDFI Fund 2023).

The Fund's evaluation criteria for Native American CDFI applications include specific recognition of tribal cultural considerations, traditional economic systems, and unique challenges facing Native communities, enabling tribal CDFIs to design programs that reflect cultural values while meeting federal performance requirements. Recent policy developments have emphasized the importance of culturally appropriate lending products, traditional knowledge integration, and community development approaches that honor tribal values while achieving measurable economic development outcomes (CDFI Fund 2022).

Financial Assistance awards for Native American CDFIs often support innovative lending products and services that address unique needs of tribal borrowers, including individual development accounts, microenterprise development programs, and business lending that accommodates traditional tribal business structures and collective ownership concepts. The Fund's performance measurement requirements have been adapted to recognize these innovative approaches while maintaining accountability for federal resources and community development outcomes (Native CDFI Network 2023).

Native American CDFI Assistance (NACA) Program

The Native American CDFI Assistance (NACA) program, authorized under 12 U.S.C. § 4707, provides specialized support for Native-controlled financial institutions through grants and technical assistance that recognize the unique developmental needs of tribal financial institutions. NACA grants support both emerging Native American CDFIs that are working toward certification and established CDFIs seeking to expand their capacity and service offerings (CDFI Fund 2023). The program's design reflects understanding that Native American CDFIs may require different developmental approaches and timelines compared to other community development financial institutions.

NACA program priorities emphasize institutional sustainability, community impact, and cultural appropriateness, enabling Native American CDFIs to build long-term capacity while serving immediate community needs. The program supports a range of activities including staff development, board training, product development, marketing, and operational improvements that strengthen institutional capacity and community development impact (12 C.F.R. § 1807.104; CDFI Fund 2022). Recent program enhancements have included specific support for technology development, regulatory compliance, and partnerships with mainstream financial institutions that expand access to capital and services.

The integration of NACA programming with broader tribal economic development strategies requires coordination with tribal governments, economic development authorities, and other tribal business structures discussed throughout our manuscript. Many successful Native American CDFIs serve as financing intermediaries that complement tribal governmental economic development activities while maintaining the independence and community focus required for CDFI certification (see cross-reference to main manuscript's discussion of tribal business coordination and the specialized financing intermediaries discussed in our categorical framework section).

Bank Enterprise Award (BEA) Program and Tribal Applications

The Bank Enterprise Award program provides financial incentives to FDIC-insured banks that increase their community development activities in distressed communities, including tribal communities that meet program eligibility criteria. While not exclusively targeted to tribal communities, the BEA program has proven valuable for encouraging mainstream financial institutions to expand services and lending activities in tribal communities, creating partnerships that complement tribal CDFIs and other specialized tribal financing mechanisms (12 U.S.C. § 4709; CDFI Fund 2023).

BEA program incentives include grants to participating banks that increase their lending, investment, or service activities in eligible distressed communities, with specific provisions that recognize tribal lands and Native American communities as eligible areas. The program's performance measurement system awards points for various community development activities, including loans to tribal businesses, investments in tribal CDFIs, and establishment of bank branches or services in tribal communities (12 C.F.R. § 1806.200; CDFI Fund 2022).

The coordination between BEA program activities and tribal economic development strategies creates opportunities for tribes to leverage mainstream banking relationships while maintaining specialized tribal financing mechanisms. Many tribes have worked with BEA-participating banks to develop lending programs, establish banking services, and create partnerships that combine conventional banking capacity with tribal economic development priorities (Independent Community Bankers of America 2023).

New Markets Tax Credit Program and Tribal Applications

Program Structure and Tribal Eligibility

The New Markets Tax Credit (NMTC) program, authorized under Section 45D of the Internal Revenue Code (26 U.S.C. § 45D), provides tax credits to investors who make qualified investments in designated Community Development Entities (CDEs) that serve low-income communities, with many tribal communities qualifying as eligible low-income areas based on census tract data and specialized tribal area designations. The program's structure, providing tax credits worth 39% of the investment amount over seven years, creates powerful incentives for private sector investment in tribal economic development projects while requiring that investments support genuine community development objectives rather than investor profit maximization (Internal Revenue Service 2023, 26 C.F.R. § 1.45D-1).

Tribal eligibility for NMTC investments depends upon census tract poverty rates, median family income comparisons, or designation as targeted populations that include tribal lands and Native American communities regardless of income levels. The targeted population provisions (26 U.S.C. § 45D(e)(2)) specifically include "an Indian reservation" and areas with significant Native American populations, enabling tribal communities to access NMTC investments even when census data may not accurately reflect community economic conditions (Treasury Department 2022).

The integration of NMTC investments with tribal sovereignty requires careful attention to program structure and governance arrangements that preserve tribal control while accessing private sector capital and complying with federal tax credit requirements. Many tribes have established tribally-controlled CDEs that can attract NMTC investment while maintaining tribal oversight of development activities, or have partnered with established CDEs that understand tribal governmental structures and cultural considerations (CDFI Fund 2023).

Enhanced Federal Tax Incentives

Recent federal tax legislation has substantially enhanced the capital access advantages available to tribal businesses through permanent extensions and modifications of key tax incentives. These enhanced benefits, detailed comprehensively in the main manuscript's Chapter 6, include permanent bonus depreciation, reinstated R&E deductions, and enhanced rural development opportunities that can significantly improve project economics and financing capacity (U.S. Department of Treasury 2025; Economic Innovation Group 2025). These enhanced tax benefits can significantly improve the economics of tribal business development projects while reducing the capital requirements for business expansion and modernization, creating additional pathways for accessing conventional financing sources and improving overall project feasibility for both debt and equity investors.

Enhanced Tax Incentive Coordination

The enhanced federal tax incentives introduced through 2025 legislation create new opportunities for coordinating impact investing with tribal economic development strategies. Impact investors can access enhanced tax benefits including permanent bonus depreciation and R&E deductions while supporting tribal community development objectives, creating improved investment returns that can attract additional patient capital to tribal communities. The enhanced rural development benefits available through Qualified Rural Opportunity Funds (QROFs) enable impact investors to access superior tax treatment for investments in rural tribal areas, while permanent Opportunity Zone benefits provide long-term investment incentives that align with impact investing timeframes and social return objectives (Economic Innovation Group 2025). This coordination between enhanced tax incentives and impact investing principles creates opportunities for tribal communities to access substantial private capital while maintaining community control and ensuring that investment activities serve tribal development priorities rather than purely financial objectives.

Tribal Community Development Entity Certification
The certification of tribal organizations as Community Development Entities requires demonstration of community development focus, accountability to low-income communities, and capacity to manage NMTC investments effectively while complying with complex federal tax credit requirements. Tribal CDE certification applications must address the unique characteristics of tribal communities and governmental structures while meeting federal certification criteria established in 26 C.F.R. § 1.45D-1(c) (Treasury Department 2023).

Tribal CDEs must demonstrate accountability to tribal communities through governance structures that include community representation and ensure that investment decisions reflect community priorities and needs. The accountability requirements can be satisfied through tribal governmental oversight, community advisory boards, or other mechanisms that ensure community input into CDE activities while maintaining the operational efficiency necessary for effective NMTC program participation (26 C.F.R. § 1.45D-1(c)(4); CDFI Fund 2022).

The management and operational capacity requirements for tribal CDEs include demonstration of experience in community development finance, understanding of NMTC program requirements, and capacity to structure and monitor qualified investments that meet program compliance requirements. Many tribal CDEs have developed this capacity through partnerships with experienced NMTC practitioners, technical assistance from national intermediaries, or staff development programs that build internal expertise in tax credit compliance and community development finance (Community Development Financial Institutions Fund 2023).

NMTC Investment Structures and Tribal Projects

NMTC investments in tribal communities utilize complex financing structures that combine tax credit equity with other financing sources to create comprehensive project financing while maintaining compliance with federal tax credit requirements and tribal sovereignty considerations. Typical NMTC transactions involve multiple layers of financing, including investor equity attracted by tax credits, CDE subordinated debt, senior debt from conventional lenders, and other public or private funding sources (Internal Revenue Service 2022).

The seven-year compliance period for NMTC investments requires ongoing monitoring and reporting to ensure that investments continue to serve community development purposes and maintain eligibility for tax credit benefits. Tribal NMTC projects must demonstrate ongoing community development impact through job creation, business development, community facility provision, or other measurable outcomes that satisfy federal tax credit requirements while serving tribal community development priorities (26 C.F.R. § 1.45D-1(d)(4); Treasury Department 2023).

Successful tribal NMTC projects have included healthcare facilities, educational institutions, manufacturing facilities, mixed-use developments, and infrastructure projects that combine community development impact with financial sustainability. The program's flexibility enables tribes to structure complex development projects that serve multiple community objectives while accessing substantial private sector investment through the tax credit incentive mechanism (New Markets Tax Credit Coalition 2023).

Opportunity Zone Incentives for Tribal Communities

Opportunity Zones - Enhanced and Permanent Program

The Opportunity Zones program has been significantly enhanced and made permanent through the One Big Beautiful Bill Act (OBBBA) of 2025, creating substantial new opportunities for long-term private investment in tribal economic development. The elimination of the original December 31, 2026 sunset for new investments establishes Opportunity Zones as a permanent feature of federal tax policy, enabling tribal communities to engage in long-term strategic planning without concern about program expiration (Economic Innovation Group 2025).

The creation of Qualified Rural Opportunity Funds (QROFs) provides enhanced benefits specifically designed to support rural and tribal community development. Investors in QROFs that maintain at least 90% of assets in qualifying rural areas receive a 30% basis step-up at five years (compared to 10% for standard Opportunity Zone investments). Additionally, QROFs benefit from 50% of standard substantial improvement requirements, significantly reducing capital requirements for qualifying tribal investments (Economic Innovation Group 2025).

The establishment of a rolling 10-year redesignation cycle beginning July 1, 2026, provides long-term predictability while ensuring continued targeting of communities with genuine economic development needs. Tribal governments should engage proactively in the redesignation process to ensure continued access to enhanced program benefits while advocating for recognition of unique tribal economic circumstances (U.S. Department of Treasury 2025).

Many tribal lands qualify for Opportunity Zone designation, and the enhanced permanent program creates powerful incentives for long-term private sector investment in tribal economic development projects. The program's emphasis on 10-year holding periods aligns well with tribal development priorities for sustainable, community-controlled economic development that serves long-term community interests rather than short-term profit maximization.

Qualified Opportunity Fund Structures and Tribal Control
Tribal approaches to Opportunity Zone investments include multiple strategies for accessing program benefits while maintaining tribal control over development activities, ranging from establishing tribal-controlled QOFs that can attract external investment to partnering with external QOFs that invest in tribal projects under tribal governmental oversight. The establishment of tribal-controlled QOFs requires compliance with federal tax regulations governing fund structure, investment requirements, and performance monitoring while accommodating tribal governmental authority and cultural considerations (26 C.F.R. § 1.1400Z2(a)-1; Treasury Department 2023).

Tribal QOFs must satisfy the same regulatory requirements as other qualified opportunity funds, including the requirement that at least 90% of fund assets consist of qualified opportunity zone property, compliance with substantial improvement requirements for existing property, and adherence to working capital safe harbor provisions for development projects. However, tribal QOFs can accommodate tribal governmental oversight, cultural considerations, and community development priorities while meeting federal tax compliance requirements (26 C.F.R. § 1.1400Z2(d)-1; Internal Revenue Service 2022).

The governance structures for tribal QOFs require careful attention to the intersection of federal tax requirements, tribal sovereignty, and investor protection concerns, often resulting in complex legal structures that preserve tribal authority while providing adequate investor protections and regulatory compliance. Many tribal QOFs utilize existing tribal business entities, such as Section 17 corporations or tribally chartered LLCs discussed throughout our manuscript, as management entities or investment vehicles while maintaining compliance with opportunity zone regulations.

Integration with Tribal Economic Development Strategies

The integration of Opportunity Zone investments with broader tribal economic development strategies requires systematic coordination with existing tribal business structures, economic development authorities, and community development priorities to ensure that tax credit-motivated investments serve tribal strategic objectives rather than merely providing investor tax benefits. This coordination parallels the strategic planning considerations discussed throughout our manuscript's Chapter 6, emphasizing the importance of aligning financing mechanisms with tribal governmental priorities and long-term community development objectives (Economic Innovation Group 2022).

Successful tribal Opportunity Zone projects have included mixed-use developments that combine housing with commercial and community facility components, manufacturing facilities that create employment opportunities for tribal members, infrastructure projects that support broader economic development activities, and tourism and cultural facilities that leverage tribal cultural assets while generating economic benefits. The program's flexibility enables tribes to pursue comprehensive development approaches that serve multiple community objectives while accessing substantial private sector investment (Opportunity Zones Database 2023).

The coordination between Opportunity Zone investments and other federal financing programs creates opportunities for layered financing structures that optimize federal benefits while accessing private sector capital. For example, tribes can combine Opportunity Zone equity investment with New Markets Tax Credits, federal grant funding, and tax-exempt bond financing to create comprehensive financing packages for large-scale development projects.

Treasury Tribal Consultation Processes and Program Development

Statutory and Policy Framework for Tribal Consultation

Treasury's tribal consultation obligations derive from multiple sources, including Executive Order 13175 (Consultation and Coordination with Indian Tribal Governments), the Presidential Memorandum on Tribal Consultation and Strengthening Nation-to-Nation Relationships (2021), and Treasury's own tribal consultation policy established to ensure meaningful government-to-government consultation on policies affecting tribal communities. These consultation requirements recognize tribal governments as sovereign entities with governmental authority over their communities and establish federal obligations to consult with tribal governments before implementing policies that may affect tribal interests (Treasury Department 2023).

The Treasury Department's tribal consultation policy establishes procedures for identifying policies requiring consultation, conducting meaningful consultation processes, and incorporating tribal input into policy development and implementation. The policy recognizes that effective consultation requires early engagement with tribal governments, provision of adequate information and time for tribal review, and genuine consideration of tribal concerns and recommendations in policy development (Executive Order 13175, 65 Fed. Reg. 67249; Treasury Department 2022).

Recent Treasury consultation activities have addressed CDFI program development, tax policy affecting tribal governments and businesses, opportunity zone implementation, and broader community development finance policy that affects tribal communities. These consultation processes have resulted in program modifications, regulatory clarifications, and policy developments that better serve tribal communities while maintaining program integrity and federal compliance requirements (Treasury Department 2023).

CDFI Fund Tribal Consultation and Program Development
The CDFI Fund conducts regular tribal consultation on program development, policy changes, and implementation issues affecting Native American CDFIs and tribal communities served by CDFI programs. Recent consultation topics have included NACA program enhancements, certification requirements for tribal CDFIs, performance measurement systems, and technical assistance priorities that address unique needs of Native communities (CDFI Fund 2023).

Tribal feedback from consultation processes has influenced significant CDFI program improvements, including modified certification requirements that accommodate tribal governmental structures, enhanced technical assistance for tribal CDFIs, and performance measurement systems that recognize cultural considerations and traditional economic systems. The Fund's responsiveness to tribal consultation input demonstrates the effectiveness of meaningful government-to-government consultation in improving federal program design and implementation (Native CDFI Network 2022).

The ongoing tribal consultation process for CDFI programs includes both formal consultation sessions and informal coordination with tribal governments, tribal organizations, and Native American CDFIs to ensure continuous program improvement and responsiveness to evolving tribal needs and priorities. This consultation framework enables the Fund to adapt programs to changing circumstances while maintaining accountability for federal resources and community development outcomes (CDFI Fund 2022).

Tax Policy Consultation and Tribal Economic Development
Treasury's Office of Tax Policy conducts tribal consultation on tax policy issues affecting tribal governments and tribal economic development, including implementation of tax credit programs, tax treatment of trib-

al business structures, and coordination between federal tax policy and tribal sovereignty. Recent consultation topics have included opportunity zone implementation, tribal tax-exempt bond issues (Treasury Department 2023).

The consultation process for tax policy development recognizes the complex intersection of federal tax law, tribal sovereignty, and economic development policy, requiring specialized expertise and careful attention to tribal governmental authority and cultural considerations. Treasury's tax policy consultation has resulted in regulatory clarifications, administrative guidance, and program modifications that better serve tribal governments while maintaining tax code integrity and compliance requirements (Internal Revenue Service 2022).

The integration of tribal consultation input into tax policy development requires coordination between Treasury's Office of Tax Policy, the Internal Revenue Service, and other Treasury components to ensure consistent policy implementation and effective program coordination. This coordination enables Treasury to provide comprehensive support for tribal economic development while maintaining appropriate oversight and compliance requirements (Treasury Department 2022).

IRS Guidance on Tribal Financing Structures and Tax Implications

Tax Treatment of Tribal Business Entities

The Internal Revenue Service's guidance on tax treatment of tribal business entities reflects the complex intersection of federal tax law, tribal sovereignty, and business entity classification that affects virtually all tribal financing structures and economic development activities. The fundamental principle underlying IRS guidance is that tribal governments, as sovereign entities, are not subject to federal income tax on income derived from essential governmental functions, while tribal business activities may be subject to taxation depending upon entity structure and operational characteristics (Revenue Ruling 67-284, 1967-2 C.B. 55; Internal Revenue Service 2023).

The proposed regulations issued in 2024 (REG-113628-21) provide significant clarification regarding tax treatment of entities wholly owned by tribal governments, establishing that such entities will generally be disregarded for federal tax purposes when they are formed under tribal law and wholly owned by federally recognized tribes. This guidance addresses longstanding uncertainty regarding tribal business entity taxation and provides tribes with greater clarity for structuring economic development activities while maintaining favorable tax treatment (Treasury Department 2024, Proposed Regulations on Tribal Entity Tax Treatment, 26 C.F.R. § 301.7701-2).

The application of these tax principles to specific tribal financing structures requires careful analysis of entity formation, ownership structure, operational characteristics, and relationship to tribal governmental functions. The IRS guidance emphasizes that tax treatment depends upon factual analysis rather than entity labels, requiring tribes to structure business activities carefully to achieve desired tax outcomes while maintaining compliance with federal tax law (Internal Revenue Service 2022).

Tax-Exempt Bond Coordination and Integration
The coordination between IRS guidance on tribal business entities and tribal tax-exempt bond authority creates opportunities for integrated financing strategies that optimize federal tax benefits while maintaining tribal control over economic development activities. The essential government function test that governs tribal tax-exempt bond eligibility (26 C.F.R. § 1.103-1(b)) intersects with tribal business entity tax treatment to create complex analytical frameworks that require sophisticated legal and tax analysis.

The integration of tax-exempt bond financing with tribal business entity structures enables tribes to create comprehensive financing strategies that utilize multiple federal tax benefits while maintaining appropriate legal structures and compliance requirements. For example, tribes can establish Section 17 corporations or tribally chartered entities that qualify for tax-exempt treatment while issuing tax-exempt bonds for qualifying governmental projects, creating layered tax benefits that substantially reduce financing costs.

The IRS guidance on post-issuance compliance for tribal tax-exempt bonds requires coordination with tribal business entity management to ensure continued compliance with essential government function requirements and other federal tax law obligations. This coordination requirement emphasizes the importance of integrated approach to tribal tax planning and business structure management that considers all federal tax implications rather than addressing individual programs in isolation (Internal Revenue Service 2023).

Tax Credit Program Compliance and Reporting
The IRS administration of tax credit programs affecting tribal communities, including the New Markets Tax Credit and renewable energy tax credits, requires comprehensive compliance monitoring and reporting that intersects with tribal business entity management and governmental operations. The complexity of tax credit compliance requirements necessitates sophisticated internal controls and professional support. (Internal Revenue Service 2022).

The Inflation Reduction Act's direct payment provisions for renewable energy tax credits (26 U.S.C. § 6417) represent a significant development in federal tax policy affecting tribal energy development, enabling tribal governments to receive direct payments in lieu of tax credits for qualifying renewable energy projects. This policy change eliminates the need for complex tax equity partnerships that could compromise tribal control while providing tribes with the same federal tax benefits available to private sector developers (Treasury Department 2022).

The coordination between different tax credit programs and tribal business entity structures requires systematic compliance management that addresses multiple federal tax obligations simultaneously while maintaining tribal governmental oversight and community development objectives. Many tribal governments have established specialized compliance systems or engaged professional service providers to manage these complex requirements effectively.

Coordination Between Treasury Programs and Tribal Business Structures
Strategic Integration Framework
The coordination between Treasury Department programs and tribal business structures discussed throughout our manuscript requires comprehensive strategic planning that considers the interaction between different financing mechanisms, tax implications, and tribal governmental

authority to optimize economic development outcomes while maintaining compliance with federal requirements. This strategic integration parallels the business structure selection methodology analyzed in our main manuscript, where tribal governments must balance multiple considerations including sovereignty preservation, operational efficiency, and regulatory compliance (see cross-reference to Chapter 6 and business structure selection analysis).

The integration of Treasury programs with tribal business structures typically involves establishing appropriate legal entities that can access Treasury programs while maintaining tribal governmental oversight and community development focus. For example, tribes may establish Section 17 corporations that can serve as Community Development Entities for NMTC programs while maintaining tax-exempt status and tribal governmental control, or create tribally chartered LLCs that can participate in Opportunity Zone investments while preserving tribal sovereignty and cultural considerations (Treasury Department 2023).

The professional service provider requirements for effective Treasury program integration include specialized expertise in federal tax law, community development finance, and tribal law that enables tribes to navigate complex regulatory requirements while achieving strategic objectives. (Government Finance Officers Association 2023).

Optimizing Enhanced Tax Benefits Through Strategic Structure Selection

Tribal businesses should evaluate their structure selection decisions in light of enhanced federal tax incentives that can substantially improve project economics and financing capacity. The permanent nature of 100% bonus depreciation enables long-term strategic planning for equipment and infrastructure investments without concern about changing tax benefits, while reinstated R&E deductions provide immediate tax advantages for tribal businesses engaged in innovation activities. Tribal entities should coordinate structure selection with tax planning to optimize the benefits of enhanced federal incentives while maintaining appropriate sovereignty protections and operational flexibility (U.S. Department of Treasury 2025). The interaction between different tribal business structures and enhanced tax benefits creates opportunities for sophisticated capital planning that coordinates tax-exempt tribal entities with taxable subsidiaries or partners to maximize overall tax efficiency while preserving tribal control and community development focus.

Compliance Coordination and Risk Management

The coordination of compliance requirements across multiple Treasury programs requires systematic management approaches that address overlapping federal obligations while maintaining tribal governmental oversight and community development accountability.

Risk management for integrated Treasury program participation includes both financial risks associated with program performance requirements and regulatory risks associated with compliance failures that could jeopardize program benefits or result in penalties. The development of comprehensive risk management systems requires understanding of each program's specific requirements and their interaction with tribal governmental operations and business entity management (Internal Revenue Service 2023).

The ongoing coordination between Treasury programs and tribal business operations requires systematic monitoring and reporting that demonstrates program compliance while providing tribal governments with information necessary for strategic decision-making and operational management. This monitoring requirement creates administrative burdens that must be balanced against program benefits through careful program selection and implementation planning (CDFI Fund 2023).

Business Structure Interface Analysis

The Treasury Department and IRS programs analyzed in this section demonstrate varying degrees of interface with tribal business structure selection, ranging from programs with minimal structural requirements to those where entity choice fundamentally affects program access and benefits. Understanding these interfaces enables tribes to make strategic decisions about both program participation and optimal business structure selection.

Community Development Financial Institutions (CDFI) Fund Programs

CDFI Certification and Native American Applications

Eligibility Considerations: CDFI certification has specific structural requirements that significantly affect tribal business structure selection. The certification requires "non-government status" under 12 C.F.R. § 1805.201, which creates important distinctions among tribal business structures. Unincorporated tribal enterprises typically cannot qualify for CDFI certification because they are indistinguishable from tribal government operations. Section 17 corporations and tribally chartered corporations can qualify more easily because they represent separate legal entities, even when wholly owned by tribes. State-chartered corporations face no structural barriers to CDFI certification. Individual/sole proprietorships and partnerships generally cannot meet CDFI certification requirements due to scale and institutional capacity requirements.

Compliance and Operational Impacts: Different business structures handle CDFI compliance requirements with varying effectiveness. Section 17 corporations benefit from established corporate governance frameworks that align well with CDFI accountability requirements, while their federal charter provides credibility with CDFI Fund reviewers. Tribally chartered corporations must demonstrate governance structures that meet federal accountability standards while respecting tribal law, sometimes requiring additional documentation and explanation. State-chartered corporations typically have the most straightforward compliance path due to familiar corporate structures and public filing requirements that demonstrate transparency.

Tax Implications: The interaction between CDFI status and tribal business structures creates complex tax considerations. Section 17 corporations maintain their tax-exempt status while operating as CDFIs, creating powerful combinations of federal tax benefits and CDFI program access. Tribally chartered corporations may maintain tax-exempt status under proposed 2024 IRS regulations while accessing CDFI benefits. State-chartered tribal corporations face standard corporate taxation but can access CDFI benefits, creating trade-offs between tax efficiency and program access.

Strategic Advantages/Disadvantages: Section 17 corporations represent the optimal structure for CDFI operations, combining tax exemption, sovereign immunity protections, and program eligibility. Tribally chartered corporations offer similar benefits with greater operational flexibility. State-chartered corporations provide maximum operational flexibility and program access but sacrifice tax benefits. The choice often depends on the tribe's broader economic development strategy and risk tolerance.

Sovereign Immunity Considerations: CDFI operations may require limited immunity waivers for commercial lending activities, with different structures offering varying flexibility. Section 17 and tribally chartered corporations can maintain broad immunity while waiving limited immunity for specific CDFI activities. State-chartered corporations typically operate without immunity protection, which may actually facilitate CDFI operations by reducing lender concerns about enforcement.

Bank Enterprise Award (BEA) Program
Eligibility Considerations: The BEA program has minimal direct interface with tribal business structures because it primarily incentivizes mainstream banks to serve tribal communities rather than requiring tribal entity participation. However, tribally owned banks or financial institutions seeking BEA recognition must be FDIC-insured, which typically requires state or federal banking charters rather than purely tribal charters.

Compliance and Operational Impacts: Tribal business structures have limited direct compliance obligations under BEA, though tribes may need to provide documentation of their status as eligible tribal communities to participating banks.

Tax Implications: BEA program participation has minimal direct tax implications for tribal business structures, as the tax benefits flow to participating banks rather than tribal entities.

Strategic Advantages/Disadvantages: All tribal business structures can potentially benefit from BEA program incentives through improved banking relationships, regardless of their specific structure.

Sovereign Immunity Considerations: Sovereign immunity generally does not affect BEA program access, as tribes are beneficiaries rather than direct program participants.

New Markets Tax Credit (NMTC) Program
NMTC Investment Structures and Community Development Entity Certification

Eligibility Considerations: NMTC program participation requires either Community Development Entity (CDE) certification or partnership with certified CDEs. Tribal business structure selection significantly affects these options. Unincorporated tribal enterprises cannot serve as CDEs due to the requirement for separate legal entity status. Section 17 corporations can serve as excellent CDEs, combining tax-exempt status with federal recognition and credibility. Tribally chartered corporations can qualify for CDE certification but may require additional documentation to demonstrate governance accountability. State-chartered corporations face the fewest barriers to CDE certification.

Compliance and Operational Impacts: NMTC compliance requirements vary significantly across business structures. Section 17 corporations benefit from federal charter credibility but may face compliance challenges due to minimal statutory guidance for corporate governance. Tribally chartered corporations must demonstrate corporate governance systems that meet federal standards while operating under tribal law. State-chartered corporations typically have established governance frameworks that align well with NMTC requirements.

Tax Implications: The intersection of NMTC benefits and tribal business structure taxation creates complex considerations. Section 17 corporations can serve as CDEs while maintaining tax-exempt status, though they cannot directly benefit from tax credits due to their tax-exempt nature. They can, however, attract NMTC investment from tax credit investors. Tribally chartered corporations with tax-exempt status face similar considerations. State-chartered tribal corporations can both serve as CDEs and potentially benefit from tax credits if structured appropriately.

Strategic Advantages/Disadvantages: Section 17 corporations offer optimal positioning for NMTC participation as CDEs, providing federal recognition, tax exemption, and sovereign immunity protections while enabling substantial community development investment. Tribally chartered corporations provide similar benefits with greater operational flexibility. State-chartered corporations sacrifice tax benefits but gain maximum operational and compliance flexibility.

Sovereign Immunity Considerations: NMTC participation may require limited immunity waivers for commercial investment activities. Section 17 and tribally chartered corporations can maintain broad immunity while providing limited waivers for specific NMTC transactions. The seven-year NMTC compliance period requires ongoing attention to immunity considerations in investment management.

Opportunity Zone Programs
Qualified Opportunity Fund Structures and Tribal Control

Eligibility Considerations: Opportunity Zone investment eligibility depends primarily on geographic designation rather than business structure, but Qualified Opportunity Fund (QOF) establishment and management involves significant structural considerations. Unincorporated tribal enterprises cannot serve as QOFs due to federal tax requirements for separate entity status. Section 17 corporations can establish or manage QOFs while maintaining their tax-exempt status, though they cannot directly benefit from capital gains deferrals. Tribally chartered corporations can serve similar functions under proposed IRS guidance. State-chartered corporations can both establish QOFs and benefit from program tax incentives. Individual/sole proprietorships can benefit from Opportunity Zone investments but cannot establish QOFs. Partnerships and joint ventures can serve as QOFs under appropriate structures.

Compliance and Operational Impacts: Opportunity Zone compliance requirements create different challenges across business structures. Section 17 corporations benefit from federal recognition but must navigate complex federal tax regulations while maintaining their tax-exempt status. Tribally chartered corporations must ensure compliance with both federal tax requirements and tribal law. State-chartered corporations face the most straightforward compliance path but must address potential conflicts between state corporate law and tribal sovereignty in tribal land investments.

Tax Implications: The interaction between Opportunity Zone benefits and tribal tax status creates complex planning opportunities. Section 17 and tribally chartered corporations with tax-exempt status cannot directly benefit from capital gains deferrals but can manage QOFs that provide benefits to investors. State-chartered tribal corporations can potentially benefit from both tax-exempt status (for qualifying activities) and Opportunity Zone benefits. Individual tribal members can benefit from Opportunity Zone investments regardless of their business structure choices.

Strategic Advantages/Disadvantages: The optimal structure for Opportunity Zone participation depends on whether the tribe seeks to attract outside investment (favoring Section 17 or tribally chartered structures that can manage QOFs while maintaining tribal control) or directly benefit from tax incentives (potentially favoring state-chartered structures or individual participation). The 10-year holding period requirements favor structures that provide long-term stability and clear governance frameworks.

Sovereign Immunity Considerations: Opportunity Zone investments on tribal lands require careful attention to sovereign immunity, particularly for QOFs managed by immune tribal entities. Limited immunity waivers may be necessary for commercial investment activities while preserving broader tribal immunity. The long-term nature of Opportunity Zone investments requires sustainable immunity waiver strategies.

IRS Guidance on Tribal Financing Structures
Tax Treatment of Tribal Business Entities

Eligibility Considerations: IRS guidance on tribal business entity taxation directly affects all tribal business structures, with different structures receiving different tax treatment based on their formation and ownership characteristics. The proposed 2024 regulations (REG-113628-21) create clear distinctions: wholly owned tribal entities formed under tribal law will generally be disregarded for tax purposes, while state-chartered entities face standard corporate taxation regardless of tribal ownership.

Compliance and Operational Impacts: Tax compliance requirements vary dramatically across structures. Section 17 corporations benefit from established tax-exempt treatment but must maintain compliance with federal corporate requirements. Tribally chartered corporations under proposed regulations would gain tax-exempt treatment but must ensure 100% tribal ownership and compliance with "disregarded entity" requirements. State-chartered corporations face standard corporate tax compliance regardless of tribal ownership.

Tax Implications: The proposed regulations create significant tax planning opportunities and challenges. Section 17 corporations maintain established tax-exempt status. Tribally chartered corporations would gain tax-exempt status if wholly owned by tribes, creating powerful incentives for tribal rather than state incorporation. State-chartered corporations face standard corporate taxation, creating potential double taxation issues. Individual/sole proprietorships remain fully taxable, while partnerships involving tax-exempt tribal entities create complex tax allocation issues.

Strategic Advantages/Disadvantages: The proposed regulations strongly favor tribal law entities for tax efficiency, particularly Section 17 corporations and wholly owned tribally chartered entities. State incorporation sacrifices significant tax benefits but may provide operational and financing advantages. Mixed ownership structures may lose tax benefits but enable outside investment and partnership opportunities.

Sovereign Immunity Considerations: Tax status generally does not affect sovereign immunity analysis, though tax-exempt entities may have stronger arguments for immunity in some contexts due to their governmental character.

Treasury Tribal Consultation and Program Development
Consultation Process Interface with Business Structures

Minimal Interface: Treasury's tribal consultation processes have minimal direct interface with specific business structure selection, as consultation focuses on policy development rather than entity-specific program participation. However, consultation outcomes may affect program design in ways that favor certain business structures over others.

Strategic Considerations: Tribes can use multiple business structures to participate in consultation processes, with different entities potentially providing different perspectives on program development needs. However, the consultation process itself does not require specific business structure choices.

Cross-Program Strategic Considerations

Several strategic considerations emerge from analyzing Treasury programs collectively:

Structural Flexibility: Tribes benefit from maintaining multiple business structures to optimize access to different Treasury programs. A combination of Section 17 corporations for CDFI operations and tax-exempt activities, tribally chartered LLCs for operational flexibility, and potential state-chartered entities for specific program access may provide optimal positioning.

Tax Optimization: The proposed IRS regulations significantly favor tribal law entities, creating strong incentives to establish tribally chartered corporations and LLCs while maintaining Section 17 corporations for activities requiring federal recognition and stability.

Compliance Coordination: Multiple Treasury program participation requires sophisticated compliance coordination that may favor larger, more institutionally developed business structures over simpler entities.

Sovereignty Preservation: Most Treasury programs can be accessed while preserving broad sovereign immunity through limited, program-specific immunity waivers, though this requires careful legal structuring and ongoing compliance management.

The Treasury Department programs demonstrate how business structure selection can significantly affect federal program access, compliance requirements, and strategic benefits, making structure selection a critical component of comprehensive tribal economic development planning.

Supplement K: Department of Commerce and EDA Programs

Introduction to Commerce Department Economic Development Authority

EDA's approach to tribal economic development recognizes both the unique challenges and opportunities present in Indian Country. The agency's programs address infrastructure deficits, business development needs, and planning capacity limitations that often constrain tribal economic growth. Unlike many federal programs that focus narrowly on specific sectors or activities, EDA programs provide flexible tools that can support diverse development strategies aligned with individual tribal priorities and circumstances (Economic Development Administration 2023; Government Accountability Office 2023).

The strategic importance of EDA programs extends beyond immediate project benefits to include long-term capacity building and institutional development. EDA investments often catalyze additional public and private investment, creating multiplier effects that enhance overall community development impact. The agency's emphasis on comprehensive economic development strategies aligns well with tribal approaches that consider economic development within broader community and cultural contexts (National Congress of American Indians 2024).

Understanding EDA programs requires recognition of their role within broader federal economic development frameworks. EDA programs work most effectively when coordinated with other federal resources, including Treasury Department financing, Agriculture Department rural development programs, and various agency-specific tribal programs. This coordination enables comprehensive approaches that address infrastructure, financing, business development, and planning needs simultaneously.

The integration of EDA resources with tribal development strategies should consider the business structure and governance principles outlined in Chapter 2, ensuring that EDA-funded activities align with appropriate organizational structures and sovereignty considerations. The planning and coordination approaches discussed in Chapter 7 provide valuable frameworks for optimizing EDA program utilization within broader tribal development strategies.

Public Works and Economic Adjustment Assistance

EDA's Public Works program represents the agency's largest source of infrastructure funding, providing grants for essential infrastructure projects that support economic development and community resilience. For tribal communities, Public Works grants can address critical infrastructure gaps that constrain economic growth while building the foundation for sustained development activities (Economic Development Administration 2024).

Infrastructure Development Grants

Public Works infrastructure grants support a wide range of projects including water and sewer systems, transportation improvements, telecommunications infrastructure, and facility construction or renovation. The program's flexibility allows tribal governments to address their most pressing infrastructure needs while aligning projects with broader economic development objectives. Successful tribal projects typically demonstrate clear connections between infrastructure improvements and economic development outcomes (Economic Development Administration 2024).

The application process for Public Works grants requires demonstration of economic distress, which most tribal areas easily meet based on unemployment rates, per capita income levels, or population decline criteria.

Projects must also show economic development impact, typically measured through job creation or retention projections, private investment leveraging, or enhanced economic competitiveness. The program's emphasis on measurable economic impact aligns well with tribal development projects that often serve multiple community needs simultaneously.

Grant amounts under the Public Works program typically range from $500,000 to $3 million, though larger grants are possible for major infrastructure projects. The program requires local matching funds, generally 50% of total project costs, though distressed communities may qualify for reduced match requirements. For tribal applicants, the match requirement can often be met through in-kind contributions, including tribal labor, materials, or previously completed related work.

Eligible applicants include tribal governments, tribal organizations, and other entities serving tribal areas. The program's broad applicant eligibility provides flexibility for tribal communities to structure applications through the most appropriate entities while ensuring projects serve tribal development objectives. Multi-tribal collaborations are also eligible, enabling regional approaches to infrastructure development that may achieve greater efficiency and impact.

The strategic value of Public Works grants extends beyond individual project benefits to include demonstration of tribal capacity for large-scale infrastructure development and relationship building with federal economic development agencies. Successful Public Works projects often position tribes for additional EDA assistance and enhance their competitiveness for other federal infrastructure programs.

Project planning for Public Works applications should consider integration with other tribal development initiatives and funding sources. Infrastructure projects can often be structured to leverage additional federal programs, private investment, or tribal resources to achieve greater scope and impact than would be possible with EDA funding alone. This comprehensive approach aligns with the strategic coordination principles discussed in Section IX.

Economic Adjustment Assistance for Tribal Communities

Economic Adjustment Assistance provides flexible support for communities experiencing sudden economic disruption or seeking to diversify their economic base. For tribal communities, this program can address economic challenges resulting from federal policy changes, natural disasters, industry closures, or other events that disrupt economic stability (Economic Development Administration 2024).

The program's flexibility makes it particularly valuable for tribal communities facing unique economic challenges that may not fit traditional program categories. Economic Adjustment projects can include infrastructure development, business development support, planning activities, and revolving loan fund capitalization. This flexibility enables tribal communities to design assistance packages that address their specific economic development needs and opportunities.

Recent tribal Economic Adjustment projects have addressed diverse challenges including tourism development following natural disasters, economic diversification from gaming revenues, transition planning for energy development projects, and recovery from pandemic- related economic impacts. The program's responsiveness to current economic conditions makes it valuable for addressing emerging challenges and opportunities.

Application requirements for Economic Adjustment assistance emphasize demonstration of economic disruption or adjustment needs, comprehensive response strategies, and community commitment to implementation. Tribal applicants typically excel in demonstrating economic challenges and community commitment, though they may need technical assistance in developing comprehensive response strategies that meet EDA requirements.

Grant amounts under Economic Adjustment assistance vary widely based on project scope and community needs, ranging from planning grants under $100,000 to major infrastructure or business development projects exceeding $2 million. The program's flexibility in grant sizing enables communities to access appropriate levels of assistance for their specific situations and organizational capacity.

The strategic importance of Economic Adjustment assistance includes its potential to serve as bridge funding while communities develop longer-term economic development strategies and access other federal programs. The program can provide immediate assistance for urgent needs while supporting development of capacity and partnerships necessary for sustained economic development efforts.

Coordination opportunities exist between Economic Adjustment assistance and other EDA programs, enabling comprehensive approaches that address immediate needs while building foundations for long-term development. This coordination can be particularly valuable for tribal communities that may need both immediate assistance and longer-term capacity building support.

Planning and Technical Assistance Programs

EDA planning and technical assistance programs provide essential support for organizational development, strategic planning, and project preparation activities that often determine the success of broader economic development efforts. For tribal communities, these programs can address capacity limitations while building the planning and implementation expertise necessary for sustained development activities (Economic Development Administration 2024).

Comprehensive Economic Development Strategy Support

The Comprehensive Economic Development Strategy (CEDS) program provides funding for regional economic development planning that creates frameworks for coordinated development activities. Tribal governments can participate in regional CEDS development or develop tribal- specific planning documents that guide their economic development priorities and strategies (Economic Development Administration 2024).

CEDS development involves comprehensive analysis of economic conditions, identification of development opportunities and challenges, and creation of strategic frameworks for coordinated development activities. For tribal communities, CEDS processes can provide valuable opportunities to engage community members, assess development options, and create consensus around development priorities and approaches.

The CEDS planning process typically involves stakeholder engagement, economic analysis, strategy development, and implementation planning phases. Tribal CEDS development often benefits from culturally appropriate engagement processes that ensure broad community participation and alignment with tribal values and priorities. The planning process can serve as community education and consensus-building activities that enhance support for subsequent development initiatives.

Funding for CEDS development typically supports planning activities over 12-24 month periods, including consultant support, community engagement activities, data collection and analysis, and strategy development. The investment in comprehensive planning often pays dividends through improved project quality, enhanced community support, and better coordination with other development activities.

The strategic value of CEDS development extends beyond the planning document itself to include the planning process benefits, relationship building with EDA and other federal agencies, and enhanced capacity for strategic planning and project development. Many tribes find that CEDS development significantly improves their competitiveness for subsequent federal funding opportunities.

Integration opportunities exist between CEDS development and broader tribal planning processes, including strategic planning, master planning, and sector-specific planning activities. Effective integration can create comprehensive planning frameworks that support both immediate development needs and longer-term community development objectives while avoiding duplication of planning efforts.

Technical Assistance and Capacity Building

EDA technical assistance programs provide specialized support for organizational development, project preparation, and implementation activities that enhance tribal capacity for economic development. These programs can address specific technical needs while building internal expertise that supports sustained development activities (Economic Development Administration 2024).

Technical assistance can support diverse activities including organizational development, financial planning, project feasibility analysis, market research, and implementation planning. For tribal organizations, technical assistance often addresses capacity gaps that may constrain their ability to access or effectively utilize other federal programs. The investment in technical assistance frequently enhances the effectiveness of other development investments.

The application process for technical assistance emphasizes demonstration of specific technical needs, clear project objectives, and commitment to utilizing assistance effectively. Tribal applicants typically qualify easily for technical assistance based on economic distress criteria, though they must demonstrate organizational readiness to benefit from assistance and implement recommendations.

Technical assistance projects typically range from $50,000 to $300,000, depending on scope and complexity. The program's flexibility enables communities to access appropriate levels of assistance for their specific needs and organizational capacity. Larger technical assistance projects can address comprehensive organizational development needs, while smaller projects can target specific technical challenges or opportunities.

Successful technical assistance projects often include combination of external expertise and internal capacity building, ensuring that tribal organizations not only address immediate technical needs but also develop enhanced internal capabilities for ongoing development activities. This approach maximizes the long-term value of technical assistance investments while building sustainable organizational capacity.

The strategic importance of technical assistance includes its role in preparing tribal organizations for larger development opportunities and enhancing their competitiveness for other federal programs. Technical assistance can help tribal organizations develop the sophisticated project development and management capabilities necessary for success with complex federal programs and large-scale development initiatives.

Coordination between technical assistance and other tribal development activities can create synergistic effects that enhance overall development effectiveness. Technical assistance can support project preparation for other federal programs, organizational development for new development initiatives, or strategic planning for comprehensive development approaches.

Business Development and Innovation Programs

EDA business development programs support entrepreneurship, innovation, and business growth activities that create employment opportunities and enhance economic competitiveness. For tribal communities, these programs can address business development challenges while building the entrepreneurial ecosystems necessary for sustained economic growth (Economic Development Administration 2024).

Revolving Loan Fund Programs

EDA Revolving Loan Fund (RLF) programs provide capital for business development lending that serves entrepreneurs and businesses in economically distressed communities. Tribal governments and tribal organizations can establish RLFs that provide ongoing access to business development capital while building local expertise in business lending and development support (Economic Development Administration 2024).

RLF capitalization grants typically range from $500,000 to $2 million, providing substantial capital bases for ongoing lending activities. The revolving nature of these funds enables continuous recycling of capital as loans are repaid, creating sustainable sources of business development financing that can serve tribal communities indefinitely. This sustainability makes RLFs particularly valuable for tribal communities that may have limited access to conventional business financing sources.

Eligible RLF lending activities include business start-up financing, expansion capital, equipment purchases, working capital, and other business development needs. The program's flexibility enables tribal RLFs to address diverse business development needs while maintaining focus on activities that create employment and enhance economic competitiveness. Many tribal RLFs also provide technical assistance and business development support to borrowers.

The administration of tribal RLFs requires development of lending policies, underwriting procedures, loan administration systems, and compliance monitoring capabilities. Successful tribal RLFs typically invest in staff development and systems that enable effective loan portfolio management while maintaining compliance with EDA requirements and sound lending practices.

RLF programs include ongoing compliance requirements including annual reporting, loan portfolio performance monitoring, and adherence to program guidelines for eligible lending activities. These requirements are designed to ensure effective use of federal resources while maintaining program sustainability, but they require ongoing organizational commitment and administrative capacity.

The strategic value of RLF programs extends beyond immediate business lending to include long-term institutional development and capacity building for comprehensive business development support. Tribal

RLFs often evolve into community development financial institutions or other specialized lending entities that provide ongoing business development infrastructure for their communities.

Integration opportunities exist between RLF programs and other business development resources, including SBA programs, CDFI resources, and private financing sources. Successful tribal RLFs often coordinate with multiple business development programs to create comprehensive support systems that address both financing and technical assistance needs of tribal entrepreneurs and businesses.

Innovation and Entrepreneurship Initiatives

EDA innovation programs support development of entrepreneurial ecosystems, technology commercialization, and business incubation activities that enhance regional innovation capacity. For tribal communities, these programs can support development of innovation infrastructure while building connections to broader innovation networks and resources (Economic Development Administration 2024).

The Build to Scale program supports development of entrepreneurial ecosystems through grants for business incubators, accelerators, and innovation support organizations. Tribal organizations can access Build to Scale funding to develop innovation infrastructure that serves tribal entrepreneurs while connecting them to broader innovation networks and resources. These programs can be particularly valuable for tribes pursuing technology-based economic development strategies.

University center programs support research and technical assistance activities that enhance regional innovation capacity and business development support. Tribal colleges and universities can participate in university center programs, providing business development support and applied research that serves tribal business development needs while building institutional capacity for ongoing innovation support.

Innovation challenge programs support development and commercialization of specific technologies or solutions to regional economic development challenges. Tribal organizations can participate in innovation challenges that address community development needs while building technical expertise and innovation capacity. These programs can support development of tribal enterprises that address both community needs and market opportunities.

The strategic importance of innovation programs includes their potential to position tribal communities for participation in knowledge-based economic sectors and technology commercialization opportunities. Innovation programs can also enhance tribal capacity for technology adoption and development that supports broader economic development objectives.

Planning for innovation and entrepreneurship initiatives should consider coordination with tribal educational institutions, existing business development resources, and broader tribal economic development strategies. Effective integration can create comprehensive innovation ecosystems that support both immediate business development needs and longer-term economic transformation objectives.

The business structure considerations discussed in Chapter 2 are particularly relevant for innovation and entrepreneurship initiatives, as these activities often involve complex organizational relationships and intellectual property considerations that require careful legal structuring and governance arrangements.

Infrastructure and Facilities Development

EDA infrastructure programs provide essential support for physical development projects that create foundations for economic growth and community development. For tribal communities, infrastructure development often represents a prerequisite for broader economic development activities, making EDA infrastructure programs particularly valuable for comprehensive development strategies (Economic Development Administration 2024).

Transportation and Utilities Infrastructure

Transportation infrastructure development through EDA programs can address critical connectivity challenges that often constrain tribal economic development opportunities. Projects can include road improvements, airport development, telecommunications infrastructure, and multimodal transportation facilities that enhance access to markets, workers, and resources (Economic Development Administration 2024).

EDA transportation projects often emphasize economic development impact rather than general transportation improvement, requiring demonstration of specific business development or employment benefits. Successful tribal transportation projects typically show clear connections to business development opportunities, tourism enhancement, or improved access to employment andmarkets.

Utilities infrastructure development can address fundamental barriers to business development and community growth in tribal areas. EDA-funded utilities projects can include water and sewer systems, electrical infrastructure, broadband development, and energy facilities that provide essential services for business development and community growth. The program's focus on economic development impact ensures that utilities projects serve business development objectives while addressing community needs.

The coordination between EDA infrastructure development and other federal infrastructure programs can create comprehensive approaches that address multiple infrastructure needs while maximizing federal investment efficiency. Programs such as USDA Rural Development, Indian Health Service, and Department of Transportation can provide complementary resources that enhance overall infrastructure development impact.

Project planning for transportation and utilities infrastructure should consider both immediate development needs and longer-term growth projections, ensuring that infrastructure investments support sustained economic development rather than simply addressing current deficits. This strategic approach aligns with the long-term planning principles discussed in Section IX and the strategic considerations outlined in Chapter 7.

The economic development focus of EDA infrastructure programs requires careful attention to project design and impact measurement, ensuring that infrastructure investments demonstrate clear economic development benefits that justify federal investment. This emphasis on economic impact measurement can enhance tribal capacity for performance-based project management and strategic planning.

Facility Development and Construction

EDA facility development programs support construction and renovation of buildings and facilities that serve economic development purposes, including business incubators, manufacturing facilities, technology centers, and tourism facilities. For tribal communities, facility development can provide essential infrastructure for business development while creating employment opportunities in construction and operations (Economic Development Administration 2024).

Business incubator and entrepreneurship facility development can create platforms for ongoing business development activities that serve tribal entrepreneurs while attracting outside businesses to tribal areas. These facilities often include office space, shared services, technical assistance resources, and networking opportunities that enhance business development success rates while building entrepreneurial ecosystems.

Manufacturing and industrial facility development can position tribal communities for participation in manufacturing sectors while creating substantial employment opportunities. EDA manufacturing facility projects often emphasize advanced manufacturing, value-added processing, or specialized manufacturing that builds on tribal resources or strategic advantages.

These projects can create anchor businesses that support broader economic development.

Tourism and hospitality facility development can support tribal tourism development strategies while showcasing tribal culture and creating employment opportunities. EDA tourism facility projects often include visitor centers, cultural facilities, conference facilities, and lodging developments that serve both tourism and community development objectives.

The strategic value of facility development extends beyond immediate project benefits to include demonstration of tribal capacity for large-scale development and attraction of additional investment. Successful facility development projects often catalyze additional private investment and business development activities that create multiplier effects throughout tribal communities.

Planning for facility development should consider operational sustainability, ongoing management requirements, and integration with broader tribal development strategies. Facilities that require ongoing operational support should include sustainable funding sources and management arrangements that ensure long-term viability and community benefit.

The sovereign immunity and business structure considerations discussed in Chapters 2 and 4 are particularly relevant for facility development projects, as these often involve commercial activities and third-party relationships that require careful legal structuring to protect tribal interests while enabling effective operations.

Regional Collaboration and Partnerships

EDA programs encourage regional collaboration and partnership development that can enhance the effectiveness of individual projects while building institutional capacity for ongoing development activities. For tribal communities, regional collaboration can provide access to resources and expertise while maintaining tribal sovereignty and self-determination (Economic Development Administration 2024).

Multi-Tribal Development Initiatives

Multi-tribal collaboration on EDA projects can achieve economies of scale while addressing shared development challenges and opportunities. Regional approaches can be particularly effective for infrastructure development, business development support, and planning activities that benefit from coordination across tribal boundaries (National Congress of American Indians 2024).

Regional infrastructure projects can address connectivity and utilities needs that cross tribal boundaries while achieving greater efficiency and impact than individual tribal projects. Multi- tribal transportation, telecommunications, and utilities projects can create regional infrastructure networks that enhance economic competitiveness while respecting individual tribal sovereignty and priorities.

Business development collaboration can create regional business networks, shared business development resources, and coordinated marketing and promotion activities that enhance the competitiveness of tribal businesses while building regional entrepreneurial ecosystems. Regional business incubators, loan funds, and technical assistance programs can serve multiple tribal communities while achieving operational efficiency.

Planning and technical assistance collaboration can build regional expertise and capacity while reducing costs for individual tribal communities. Regional planning initiatives can address shared challenges and opportunities while respecting individual tribal priorities and decision- making authority. Collaborative technical assistance can bring specialized expertise to tribal communities while building internal capacity across the region.

The governance and coordination challenges of multi-tribal collaboration require careful attention to sovereignty considerations, decision-making processes, and benefit distribution arrangements. Successful multi-tribal collaborations typically include formal agreements that clearly define roles, responsibilities, and benefit-sharing arrangements while respecting individual tribal sovereignty.

The strategic value of multi-tribal collaboration includes enhanced competitiveness for federal funding, access to specialized expertise and resources, and development of regional advocacy and policy influence. Multi-tribal collaborations can also create opportunities for knowledge sharing and capacity building that benefit all participating tribes.

State and Local Government Partnerships

Partnerships with state and local governments can enhance the effectiveness of EDA projects while building relationships that support broader tribal economic development objectives. These partnerships can provide access to additional resources, expertise, and markets while maintaining tribal sovereignty and self-determination (Council of State Governments 2024).

Infrastructure partnerships can coordinate tribal EDA projects with state and local infrastructure development to create regional networks that enhance connectivity and economic competitiveness. Transportation, utilities, and telecommunications partnerships can achieve greater efficiency and impact while addressing jurisdictional coordination challenges.

Economic development partnerships can create regional marketing and promotion activities, business development support systems, and workforce development programs that benefit both tribal and non-tribal communities. These partnerships can enhance the competitiveness of tribal businesses while building relationships that support broader economic development objectives.

Planning and policy partnerships can address regional development challenges and opportunities while building tribal influence in regional policy decisions. Tribal participation in regional planning processes can ensure that tribal interests are considered while contributing tribal expertise and perspectives to regional development strategies.

The legal and political complexities of tribal-state-local partnerships require careful attention to sovereignty considerations, jurisdictional issues, and intergovernmental relations. Successful partnerships typically include formal agreements that clearly define roles, responsibilities, and decision-making processes while respecting tribal sovereignty and government-to-government relationships.

The strategic importance of state and local partnerships includes enhanced access to resources and markets, improved coordination of regional development activities, and development of political relationships that support tribal interests. These partnerships can also provide opportunities for tribal governments to demonstrate their capabilities and build broader political support for tribal economic development.

Strategic Implementation and Coordination

Successful utilization of EDA programs requires strategic planning that aligns projects with broader tribal development objectives while maximizing the effectiveness of federal investments. The complexity and diversity of EDA programs create opportunities for comprehensive development approaches that address multiple community needs while building institutional capacity for sustained development activities (Harvard Project on American Indian Economic Development 2024).

Program Selection and Sequencing

Strategic program selection requires careful assessment of tribal development priorities, organizational capacity, and coordination opportunities with other federal programs. EDA's diverse program portfolio enables tribes to sequence projects that build capacity and demonstrate success while addressing priority development needs (Economic Development Administration 2024).

Planning and technical assistance programs often provide valuable starting points for tribes new to EDA programs, building organizational capacity and project development expertise while creating frameworks for subsequent project development. These early investments in planning and capacity building frequently enhance the success of subsequent infrastructure and business development projects.

Infrastructure development projects can create foundations for subsequent business development and economic growth activities, making them strategic early investments for comprehensive development strategies. However, infrastructure projects require substantial organizational capacity and often benefit from prior experience with smaller EDA projects or strong technical assistance support.

Business development programs can provide ongoing economic development benefits while building tribal expertise in financial management and business development support. RLF programs, in particular, create permanent community development infrastructure that can provide sustained benefits while demonstrating tribal capacity for complex program management.

The sequencing of EDA projects should consider both program readiness requirements and strategic development objectives, ensuring that early projects build capacity for subsequent activities while addressing priority community needs. This strategic approach can maximize both immediate project benefits and longer-term development impact.

Coordination opportunities between different EDA programs can create synergistic effects that enhance overall development effectiveness. For example, planning grants can support development of comprehensive strategies that guide subsequent infrastructure and business development investments, while technical assistance can enhance the effectiveness of other program investments.

Integration with Other Federal Programs
EDA programs achieve maximum effectiveness when coordinated with complementary federal programs that address related aspects of community and economic development. Strategic coordination can leverage federal investments while creating comprehensive approaches that address multiple community needs simultaneously (Government Accountability Office 2023; National Congress of American Indians 2024).

Treasury Department program coordination can combine EDA infrastructure development with CDFI lending, New Markets Tax Credit investments, or tax-exempt bond financing to create comprehensive development strategies that address both infrastructure and financing needs. This coordination can enhance project feasibility while maximizing community development impact.

Agriculture Department coordination can combine EDA business development support with USDA rural development programs to create comprehensive rural development strategies that address infrastructure, business development, and agricultural development needs simultaneously. This coordination is particularly valuable for rural tribal communities with significant agricultural resources or potential.

Small Business Administration coordination can combine EDA business development infrastructure with SBA business development support and financing programs to create comprehensive entrepreneurship support systems that address both infrastructure and business

development service needs. This coordination can enhance the effectiveness of tribal business development efforts while building sustainable support systems.

Housing and Urban Development coordination can address community development needs that complement EDA economic development investments, creating comprehensive approaches that consider both economic development and community development objectives. This coordination can be particularly valuable for tribal communities pursuing comprehensive community development strategies.

The strategic planning required for effective program coordination should consider the timing requirements, compliance obligations, and strategic objectives of different programs to ensure that coordination enhances rather than complicates project implementation. This planning often benefits from experienced technical assistance and legal support to navigate multiple regulatory frameworks simultaneously.

The business structure and governance considerations discussed in Chapter 2 are particularly relevant for coordinated program implementation, as different programs may have varying requirements for organizational structure, governance arrangements, and operational procedures that must be reconciled in comprehensive development strategies.

Business Structure Interface Analysis

The Economic Development Administration programs analyzed in this section demonstrate moderate to significant interface with tribal business structure selection, primarily through eligibility requirements, grant administration capabilities, and long-term asset management considerations. EDA programs generally focus on outcomes and capacity rather than specific entity types, but structural choices can significantly affect program access, implementation effectiveness, and sustainability.

Public Works and Economic Adjustment Assistance
Infrastructure Development Grants

Eligibility Considerations: EDA Public Works grants have broad eligibility that accommodates most tribal business structures, with specific advantages for different entity types. Tribal governments can apply directly through unincorporated tribal enterprises, which often provides the strongest application due to governmental status and demonstrated community benefit.

Section 17 corporations and tribally chartered corporations can serve as eligible applicants when designated by tribal governments, providing operational separation while maintaining tribal control. State-chartered corporations may face more complex eligibility analysis but can qualify when serving tribal development objectives. Individual/sole proprietorships and partnerships typically cannot meet the scale and public benefit requirements for Public Works funding.

Compliance and Operational Impacts: Different structures handle EDA compliance requirements with varying effectiveness. Unincorporated tribal enterprises benefit from direct tribal government backing but must integrate project management with governmental operations, potentially creating administrative complexity. Section 17 corporations provide operational separation that can enhance project management while maintaining tribal oversight, though their minimal statutory framework may create governance challenges. Tribally chartered corporations offer optimal flexibility for project management while maintaining clear accountability to tribal governments. State-chartered corporations provide established governance frameworks but may face additional oversight requirements due to their non-governmental status.

Tax Implications: EDA grant proceeds generally do not create taxable income for recipients, regardless of business structure. However, ongoing operations of EDA-funded facilities may create tax implications that vary by structure. Unincorporated tribal enterprises maintain full tax exemption for governmental activities. Section 17 and tribally chartered corporations with tax- exempt status can operate EDA-funded facilities without federal income tax obligations. State- chartered corporations may face taxation on revenues generated from EDA-funded facilities, potentially affecting long-term project economics.

Strategic Advantages/Disadvantages: Unincorporated tribal enterprises provide maximum credibility for EDA applications due to clear governmental status and community benefit, but may lack operational flexibility for complex project management. Section 17 corporations combine governmental association with operational separation, providing strong applications while enabling professional project management. Tribally chartered corporations offer optimal balance of tribal control, operational flexibility, and EDA eligibility. State-chartered corporations may provide superior project management capabilities but could face greater scrutiny regarding tribal benefit and governmental purpose.

Sovereign Immunity Considerations: EDA projects typically require limited immunity waivers for construction contracts and operational agreements. Unincorporated tribal enterprises require tribal-level immunity waivers, potentially exposing broader tribal assets. Section 17 and tribally chartered corporations can provide limited immunity waivers specific to EDA projects while preserving broader tribal immunity. State-chartered corporations operate without immunity protection, which may actually facilitate EDA project implementation by reducing contractor concerns about enforcement.

Economic Adjustment Assistance for Tribal Communities
Eligibility Considerations: Economic Adjustment Assistance provides even greater structural flexibility than Public Works programs, accommodating diverse tribal response strategies. The program's focus on economic disruption response enables creative structural approaches, including consortiums of multiple tribal entities or temporary special-purpose entities created to address specific economic challenges. All tribal business structures can potentially serve as eligible applicants or implementation vehicles.

Compliance and Operational Impacts: The flexible nature of Economic Adjustment assistance enables tribes to select business structures based on implementation needs rather than program requirements.

Complex multi-component responses may benefit from specialized entities like

Section 17 corporations or tribally chartered LLCs that can manage diverse activities while maintaining accountability to tribal governments.

Tax Implications: Similar to Public Works programs, Economic Adjustment grants generally do not create taxable income, but ongoing operations may have tax implications that vary by business structure selected for implementation.

Strategic Advantages/Disadvantages: The program's flexibility enables tribes to optimize business structure selection for specific adjustment strategies rather than program compliance, creating opportunities for innovative structural approaches that align with tribal strategic objectives.

Sovereign Immunity Considerations: Economic Adjustment projects may require various immunity waivers depending on implementation approach, with different structures providing different flexibility for limited waivers while preserving broader tribal immunity.

Planning and Technical Assistance Programs
Comprehensive Economic Development Strategy (CEDS) Support

Eligibility Considerations: CEDS planning programs have minimal business structure interface, as tribal governments typically participate directly regardless of their business entity structures. However, CEDS implementation may involve various tribal business structures, and the planning process should address how different structures will be utilized for economic development implementation.

Compliance and Operational Impacts: CEDS planning compliance focuses on planning processes and community engagement rather than specific business structure requirements. However, effective CEDS development should address how different tribal business structures will be deployed for plan implementation.

Tax Implications: CEDS planning grants have minimal direct tax implications, regardless of business structure. However, effective CEDS planning should address tax implications of different business structures for plan implementation.

Strategic Advantages/Disadvantages: CEDS planning provides opportunities to evaluate business structure options strategically, enabling tribes to plan optimal structural approaches for subsequent economic development activities. The planning process can inform business structure selection for future EDA program participation.

Sovereign Immunity Considerations: CEDS planning typically requires minimal immunity considerations, but the planning process should address how different business structures will handle immunity issues in implementation.

Technical Assistance and Capacity Building

Eligibility Considerations: EDA technical assistance programs accommodate all tribal business structures, with different structures potentially benefiting from different types of assistance.

Unincorporated tribal enterprises may benefit most from governmental capacity building, while corporate entities may need assistance with business operations and management.

Compliance and Operational Impacts: Technical assistance compliance requirements are minimal and generally do not vary by business structure. However, the effectiveness of technical assistance may depend on the recipient entity's institutional capacity and governance structure.

Tax Implications: Technical assistance grants generally do not create tax implications regardless of business structure, as they provide services rather than taxable income.

Strategic Advantages/Disadvantages: All business structures can benefit from EDA technical assistance, though the type and focus of assistance may vary based on structural needs and capacity requirements.

Sovereign Immunity Considerations: Technical assistance typically requires minimal immunity considerations, as it involves consultation and capacity building rather than commercial transactions.

Business Development and Innovation Programs

Revolving Loan Fund Programs

Eligibility Considerations: EDA Revolving Loan Fund capitalization requires careful business structure analysis, as the administering entity must have appropriate capacity for lending operations while maintaining tribal accountability. Unincorporated tribal enterprises can administer RLFs but may lack operational separation desirable for lending activities. Section 17 corporations provide excellent platforms for RLF administration, combining tribal accountability with operational separation and potential tax benefits. Tribally chartered corporations offer similar advantages with greater operational flexibility. State-chartered corporations can administer RLFs but may face tax implications on lending operations.

Compliance and Operational Impacts: RLF compliance requirements are substantial and ongoing, requiring sophisticated financial management and loan administration systems. Section 17 and tribally chartered corporations typically provide optimal compliance frameworks due to their corporate governance structures and operational separation from daily tribal government activities. Unincorporated tribal enterprises may struggle with the operational complexity of RLF administration while managing broader tribal governmental responsibilities.

Tax Implications: RLF operations may generate taxable income through interest and fees, creating different tax implications across business structures. Section 17 corporations maintain tax exemption on RLF operations, providing significant advantages. Tribally chartered corporations with tax-exempt status under proposed regulations could enjoy similar benefits. State-chartered corporations face standard corporate taxation on RLF income, potentially reducing funds available for community development lending.

Strategic Advantages/Disadvantages: Section 17 corporations provide optimal RLF platforms, combining tax exemption, operational flexibility, and tribal accountability. Tribally chartered corporations offer similar benefits with potentially greater governance flexibility. State-chartered corporations provide maximum operational flexibility but sacrifice tax benefits. Unincorporated tribal enterprises may lack the operational separation and management capacity necessary for effective RLF administration.

Sovereign Immunity Considerations: RLF operations require extensive immunity waivers for lending activities, including loan agreements, security interests, and collection activities. Section 17 and tribally chartered corporations can provide comprehensive immunity waivers for RLF operations while preserving broader tribal immunity (Economic Development Administration 2023; Bureau of Indian Affaires 2015).

Unincorporated tribal enterprises require tribal-level immunity waivers that may expose broader governmental assets.

Innovation and Entrepreneurship Initiatives
Eligibility Considerations: EDA innovation programs accommodate diverse business structures, with different structures providing different advantages for innovation and entrepreneurship development (Economic Development Administration 2023). Tribal colleges and universities can participate directly in university center programs. Various tribal business structures can develop business incubators and innovation centers, with corporate structures potentially providing better operational frameworks for complex innovation activities.

   Compliance and Operational Impacts: Innovation program compliance requirements vary by specific program but generally require sophisticated project management and performance measurement capabilities that may favor corporate structures over unincorporated enterprises.

   Tax Implications: Innovation program grants generally do not create direct tax implications, but ongoing operations of innovation facilities may generate taxable income that varies by business structure.

   Strategic Advantages/Disadvantages: Corporate structures may provide better frameworks for innovation activities due to operational flexibility and governance structures that can accommodate complex partnerships and intellectual property management.

   Sovereign Immunity Considerations: Innovation programs may require limited immunity waivers for partnerships and intellectual property agreements, with corporate structures potentially providing better flexibility for limited waivers.

Infrastructure and Facilities Development
Transportation and Utilities Infrastructure

Eligibility Considerations: EDA infrastructure programs have broad eligibility similar to Public Works programs, with tribal governments and designated tribal entities serving as eligible applicants. The choice of implementing entity may affect project management effectiveness and long-term operations.

Compliance and Operational Impacts: Infrastructure project compliance requirements favor entities with established project management capabilities and governance structures. Corporate entities may provide advantages for complex infrastructure projects requiring sophisticated procurement and construction management.

Tax Implications: EDA infrastructure grants do not create taxable income, but ongoing operations of infrastructure facilities may have tax implications that vary by operating entity structure.

Strategic Advantages/Disadvantages: The choice of business structure for infrastructure development should consider both project implementation capacity and long-term operational requirements, with corporate structures potentially providing advantages for complex projects.

Sovereign Immunity Considerations: Infrastructure projects typically require comprehensive immunity waivers for construction and operations, with corporate entities potentially providing better flexibility for project-specific immunity waivers.

Facility Development and Construction

Eligibility Considerations: EDA facility programs accommodate various tribal business structures, with the optimal choice depending on the facility's intended use and operational requirements. Business incubators and entrepreneurship facilities may benefit from corporate structures that can accommodate diverse tenant relationships and operational complexity.

Compliance and Operational Impacts: Facility development compliance requirements may favor corporate structures with established governance and operational frameworks, particularly for facilities requiring ongoing commercial operations.

Tax Implications: While EDA facility grants do not create taxable income, ongoing facility operations may generate taxable revenue that varies by business structure. Tax-exempt structures provide advantages for facilities serving governmental or charitable purposes.

Strategic Advantages/Disadvantages: Corporate structures may provide optimal platforms for facility development and operations, combining operational flexibility with accountability frameworks that satisfy EDA requirements while enabling effective facility management.

Sovereign Immunity Considerations: Facility operations may require ongoing immunity considerations for tenant relationships, operational agreements, and commercial activities, with corporate structures potentially providing better flexibility for managing complex immunity issues.

Regional Collaboration and Partnerships
Multi-Tribal Development Initiatives

Eligibility Considerations: Multi-tribal EDA projects create complex eligibility and structure considerations, often requiring specialized entities that can accommodate multiple tribal participants while satisfying EDA requirements. Joint powers authorities, multi-tribal corporations, or specialized partnership structures may be necessary to accommodate diverse tribal participation while meeting program requirements (White House 2024; Economic Development Administration 2023).

Compliance and Operational Impacts: Multi-tribal projects require sophisticated governance and coordination mechanisms that often favor formal corporate or partnership structures over informal collaboration. The complexity of multi-tribal coordination typically requires specialized entities with clear governance frameworks and accountability mechanisms.

Tax Implications: Multi-tribal entities may face complex tax implications depending on structure and ownership arrangements, with tax-exempt structures providing advantages when available and appropriate.

Strategic Advantages/Disadvantages: Multi-tribal projects often require innovative business structures that accommodate diverse tribal interests while meeting federal program requirements. Corporate structures may provide necessary governance frameworks while partnership structures may offer operational flexibility.

Sovereign Immunity Considerations: Multi-tribal projects create complex immunity considerations requiring coordination among multiple sovereign entities, often necessitating specialized legal structures and immunity waiver arrangements.

State and Local Government Partnerships

Eligibility Considerations: Tribal-state-local partnerships for EDA projects may require business structures that can accommodate diverse governmental participants while preserving tribal sovereignty. Specialized partnership entities or joint powers authorities may be necessary to manage complex intergovernmental relationships.

Compliance and Operational Impacts: Intergovernmental partnerships require sophisticated governance frameworks that respect different governmental authorities while meeting EDA program requirements. Corporate or partnership structures may provide necessary operational frameworks for complex intergovernmental collaboration.

Tax Implications: Intergovernmental partnerships may create complex tax implications that vary based on entity structure and operational arrangements, requiring careful analysis of tax treatment for different participants.

Strategic Advantages/Disadvantages: Intergovernmental partnerships often require innovative structural approaches that balance tribal sovereignty with collaborative effectiveness and EDA program compliance.

Sovereign Immunity Considerations: Tribal participation in intergovernmental partnerships requires careful attention to immunity preservation while enabling effective collaboration, often requiring specialized legal structures and limited immunity waivers.

Cross-Program Strategic Considerations

Structural Portfolio Approach: Tribes can optimize EDA program participation through strategic use of multiple business structures, with different entities serving different program purposes while maintaining coordinated tribal oversight. A Section 17 corporation might administer revolving loan funds, while a tribally chartered LLC manages infrastructure projects and an unincorporated enterprise handles planning activities.

Capacity Building Through Structure: EDA programs provide opportunities to build institutional capacity through appropriate business structure selection, with corporate entities potentially providing better frameworks for developing sophisticated project management and operational capabilities.

Long-Term Asset Management: EDA-funded infrastructure and facilities require long-term management consideration in business structure selection, with corporate entities potentially providing better frameworks for ongoing asset management and operational sustainability.

Immunity Strategy Coordination: Multiple EDA program participation requires coordinated immunity waiver strategies across different business structures, enabling programparticipation while preserving broader tribal sovereigntyprotection.

The EDA programs demonstrate significant interface with business structure selection, particularly for complex projects requiring sophisticated governance, ongoing operations, and multi-party coordination. Strategic business structure selection can enhance both EDA program access and implementation effectiveness while preserving tribal sovereignty and building institutional capacity.

Supplement L: Department of Agriculture Rural Development Programs

Introduction to USDA Rural Development Authority

USDA's approach to tribal economic development recognizes the unique status of tribal governments and the specific challenges facing Native American communities in rural areas. The agency's programs include both general rural development resources available to tribal areas and specialized programs designed specifically for tribal governments and Native American communities. This dual approach provides flexibility for tribal communities to access the most appropriate resources for their specific development needs and organizational structures (U.S. Department of Agriculture 2024; Government Accountability Office 2023).

The strategic importance of USDA Rural Development programs for tribal economic development extends beyond immediate project benefits to include long-term infrastructure development and capacity building that supports sustained economic growth. USDA programs often provide essential infrastructure that enables other economic development activities, making them foundational elements of comprehensive tribal development strategies (U.S. Department of Agriculture 2024). The agency's emphasis on rural community development aligns well with tribal values and approaches that consider economic development within broader community contexts (National Congress of American Indians 2024).

Understanding USDA Rural Development programs requires recognition of their role within federal rural policy and their coordination potential with other federal agencies serving tribal communities. USDA programs work most effectively when integrated with Treasury Department financing, Commerce Department business development resources, and agency-specific tribal programs to create comprehensive approaches that address infrastructure, business development, and community development needs simultaneously.

The integration of USDA resources with tribal development strategies should consider the organizational structure and governance principles outlined in Chapter 2, ensuring that USDA-funded activities align with appropriate tribal business structures and sovereignty considerations. The strategic planning and coordination approaches discussed in Chapter 7 provide valuable frameworks for optimizing USDA program utilization within broader tribal economic development strategies.

Infrastructure Development Programs

USDA Rural Development infrastructure programs address fundamental community needs that often constrain economic development in rural tribal areas. These programs provide grants and loans for water and sewer systems, telecommunications infrastructure, and community facilities that create essential foundations for business development and community growth (USDA Rural Development 2024).

Water and Sewer Systems Development

The Water and Environmental Programs provide grants and loans for water and sewer system development, improvement, and expansion in rural areas. For tribal communities, these programs can address critical infrastructure deficits that constrain both community health and economic development opportunities. Access to reliable water and sewer services represents a fundamental prerequisite for most business development activities and community growth initiatives (USDA Rural Development 2024).

Water and sewer grants are available to rural communities with populations under 10,000, with grant amounts available up to 75% of project costs for communities meeting income and population criteria that most tribal areas satisfy. The grant percentage can reach 100% for communities with extremely low incomes and small populations, making this program particularly accessible for economically distressed tribal communities.

Loan financing is available for the remaining project costs at favorable interest rates.

The application process requires demonstration of need, financial capacity, and environmental compliance. Tribal communities typically qualify easily for grants based on income criteria, though they must demonstrate technical and financial capacity for ongoing system operation and maintenance. The program emphasizes sustainability and requires comprehensive planning for long-term system viability.

Technical assistance is available to support project planning, application development, and system design. This assistance can be particularly valuable for tribal communities that may lack internal expertise in water and sewer system development. The technical assistance can help ensure that projects meet regulatory requirements while addressing specific tribal community needs and circumstances.

The strategic value of water and sewer system development extends beyond immediate health and safety benefits to include enabling business development and community growth that would otherwise be constrained by infrastructure limitations. Reliable water and sewer service often represents a prerequisite for manufacturing, food service, healthcare, and many other businesses that can provide employment and economic development opportunities.

Integration opportunities exist between water and sewer programs and other tribal development initiatives, including business development projects, housing development, and tourism development. Coordinated planning can ensure that infrastructure investments support broader development objectives while achieving maximum community benefit from federal investments.

Rural Utilities Service Programs
The Rural Utilities Service (RUS) provides financing for telecommunications, electric, and water infrastructure development in rural areas. For tribal communities, RUS programs can address connectivity and utilities challenges that often limit economic development opportunities while providing essential services for community development (Rural Utilities Service 2024).

Telecommunications programs provide loans and grants for broadband infrastructure development, telecommunications facility construction, and distance learning and telemedicine equipment. The broadband programs have become increasingly important for tribal economic development as internet connectivity becomes essential for business development, education, healthcare, and government services. RUS broadband programs can provide comprehensive solutions for tribal connectivity challenges.

Electric utility programs provide loans for electric system development, improvement, and expansion in rural areas. While most tribal areas have electric service, RUS programs can support system improvements, renewable energy development, and grid modernization that enhance reliability and support economic development activities. The programs can also support tribal utility development and ownership.

The Community Connect Grant Program provides grants for broadband infrastructure and community access points in rural areas lacking adequate broadband service. This program can provide comprehensive broadband solutions for tribal communities while creating community access points that serve educational, healthcare, and economic development needs. Grants can fund both infrastructure development and end-user equipment.

Distance Learning and Telemedicine (DLT) grants support telecommunications equipment and infrastructure that enables distance learning and telemedicine services in rural areas. For tribal communities, these programs can enhance access to education and healthcare services while building telecommunications infrastructure that supports broader economic development activities.

The strategic importance of telecommunications and utilities infrastructure includes enabling participation in knowledge-based economic activities, supporting business development that requires reliable communications and utilities, and enhancing access to markets, resources, and services that support community and economic development. Modern infrastructure often represents a prerequisite for economic diversification and growth.

Program coordination opportunities exist between RUS programs and other federal telecommunications and utilities programs, including Federal Communications Commission programs, Department of Energy programs, and tribal-specific infrastructure programs. Coordinated approaches can maximize infrastructure investment while addressing comprehensive community needs.

Community Facilities Development
The Community Facilities Direct Loan and Grant Program provides financing for essential community facilities including healthcare facilities, educational facilities, public safety facilities, and community centers. For tribal communities, community facilities development can address service delivery needs while creating employment opportunities and enhancing community capacity for economic development activities (USDA Rural Development 2024).

Healthcare facility development can address critical access needs in tribal communities while creating employment opportunities and supporting broader community development objectives. The program can finance construction, renovation, and equipment for hospitals, clinics, nursing homes, and other healthcare facilities that serve rural tribal communities. Healthcare facilities often represent significant employers and economic anchors in rural tribal areas.

Educational facility development can support tribal education priorities while creating community resources that enhance economic development capacity. The program can finance construction and renovation of schools, libraries, training facilities, and other educational infrastructure that serves both immediate educational needs and broader community development objectives. Educational facilities can also serve as community meeting spaces and resource centers.

Public safety facility development can address critical infrastructure needs while creating employment opportunities and enhancing community safety and security. The program can finance fire stations, police facilities, emergency services facilities, and other public safety infrastructure that serves essential governmental functions while contributing to economic development through employment and community security.

Community center development can create multipurpose facilities that serve diverse community needs while providing venues for economic development activities such as conferences, meetings, cultural events, and business development programs. Community centers often serve as focal points for community activities and can support both social and economic development objectives.

The application process emphasizes demonstration of community need, financial capacity, and project sustainability. Tribal applicants typically qualify for favorable terms based on rural location and community income levels. The program offers both grants and loans, with grant availability depending on community demographics and financial capacity.

Integration opportunities exist between community facilities development and other tribal development activities, including business development, tourism development, and cultural preservation initiatives. Community facilities can often be designed to serve multiple purposes and support diverse development objectives while meeting specific program requirements.

Business and Industry Development

USDA Rural Development business programs provide financing and technical assistance for business development activities in rural areas, including manufacturing, processing, retail, and service businesses that create employment and enhance economic competitiveness. For tribal communities, these programs can address business development challenges while building entrepreneurial capacity and creating sustainable employment opportunities (USDA Rural Development 2024).

Business and Industry Loan Guarantee Program

The Business and Industry (B&I) Loan Guarantee Program provides loan guarantees to lenders for business development activities in rural areas. The program guarantees up to 80% of loan amounts for eligible projects, reducing lender risk and improving access to conventional financing for rural businesses. For tribal businesses and businesses serving tribal areas, B&I guarantees can provide crucial access to capital for business development, expansion, and equipment purchases ((U.S. Department of Agriculture 2024).

Eligible business activities include manufacturing, processing, retail, service, and other businesses that create or preserve employment in rural areas. The program's broad eligibility enables diverse business development strategies while maintaining focus on employment creation and economic impact. Tribal businesses in various sectors can access B&I

guarantees for start-up, expansion, equipment, working capital, and other business development needs.

Loan amounts under the B&I program can reach $25 million, though most loans fall in the $500,000 to $5 million range. The substantial loan capacity enables significant business development projects while providing flexibility for smaller businesses and start-up enterprises. The program's loan guarantee structure makes it attractive to conventional lenders who might otherwise view rural business lending as too risky.

The application process involves both business applicants and participating lenders, requiring demonstration of business viability, management capacity, and economic impact. Tribal businesses must work with approved lenders to structure applications, though USDA provides technical assistance to support application development. The program emphasizes job creation and retention as primary evaluation criteria.

Eligible lenders include banks, credit unions, and other financial institutions that meet USDA requirements and have experience in business lending. Many lenders serving tribal areas participate in the B&I program, providing tribal businesses with access to guaranteed financing through established banking relationships. Some tribal financial institutions also participate as B&I lenders.

The strategic value of B&I loan guarantees includes enhanced access to conventional financing, improved borrowing terms and conditions, and demonstration of creditworthiness that can support future financing needs. Successful B&I borrowers often establish relationships with lenders that support ongoing business development and expansion activities beyond the initial guaranteed loan.

Coordination opportunities exist between B&I guarantees and other business development programs, including SBA lending programs, CDFI financing, and tribal business development resources. Layered financing approaches can address comprehensive business development needs while optimizing borrowing costs and terms for tribal businesses.

Rural Business Development Grant Program

The Rural Business Development Grant Program provides grants to support business development activities including business planning, training, technical assistance, and business incubation. For tribal communities, these grants can build business development infrastructure and capacity while providing ongoing support for entrepreneurship and business growth activities (USDA Rural Development 2024).

Grant recipients typically include nonprofit organizations, tribal governments, and economic development organizations that provide business development services to rural areas. Tribal governments and tribal organizations are eligible for grants to develop business incubation programs, provide technical assistance to tribal entrepreneurs, and support business development activities that create employment and economic opportunities.

Eligible activities include business planning assistance, technical assistance and training, business incubation services, economic development planning, and feasibility studies for business development projects. The program's flexibility enables comprehensive business development approaches that address both immediate business assistance needs and longer-term business development infrastructure requirements.

Grant amounts typically range from $50,000 to $500,000, depending on project scope and organizational capacity. The grants require matching funds, though in-kind contributions can often satisfy match requirements. For tribal organizations, the match requirement can often be met through tribal staff time, facilities, or other in-kind contributions that demonstrate organizational commitment to business development activities.

The application process emphasizes demonstration of business development experience, target area needs, and project sustainability. Tribal applicants often excel in demonstrating community needs and organizational commitment, though they may benefit from technical assistance in developing comprehensive project proposals that meet program requirements.

Successful grant projects often create ongoing business development infrastructure that continues to serve tribal entrepreneurs and businesses beyond the grant period. Business incubators, technical assistance programs, and training initiatives can provide sustained support for tribal business development while building organizational capacity for ongoing economic development activities.

Integration opportunities exist between business development grants and other tribal economic development resources, including revolving loan funds, business development corporations, and tribal business assistance programs. Coordinated approaches can create comprehensive business development ecosystems that address both financing and technical assistance needs of tribal entrepreneurs.

Value-Added Producer Grant Program
The Value-Added Producer Grant (VAPG) Program provides grants to agricultural producers to develop value-added enterprises that increase the value of agricultural commodities through processing, marketing, or other value-enhancement activities. For tribal agricultural producers and communities, VAPG can support development of food processing, agritourism, direct marketing, and other enterprises that enhance agricultural income while creating employment opportunities (U.S. Department of Agriculture 2024).

The program provides both planning grants and working capital grants to support value-added enterprise development. Planning grants fund feasibility studies, business planning, and market research activities that support enterprise development decisions. Working capital grants provide funding for marketing and operational expenses during enterprise start-up phases when revenues may not cover all operational costs.

Eligible applicants include individual agricultural producers, farmer cooperatives, agricultural producer groups, and tribal governments representing agricultural producers. The program's broad applicant eligibility provides flexibility for tribal communities to structure applications through the most appropriate entities while ensuring that projects serve tribal agricultural development objectives.

Value-added activities include agricultural processing, direct marketing, agritourism, renewable energy production from agricultural materials, and other activities that increase the value of agricultural commodities. For tribal communities, these activities can include traditional food processing, cultural tourism enterprises, farmers markets, and specialty agricultural products that reflect tribal cultural traditions and market opportunities.

Grant amounts range up to $250,000 for planning grants and $300,000 for working capital grants, with specific amounts depending on project scope and organizational capacity. The program requires matching funds, though in-kind contributions can satisfy match requirements. For tribal applicants, matching contributions can include tribal resources, facilities, or existing agricultural assets.

The strategic importance of value-added agricultural development includes diversification of tribal economies, enhancement of agricultural income, preservation of traditional agricultural practices and foods, and creation of employment opportunities in rural tribal areas. Value-added enterprises can also support tribal food sovereignty and cultural preservation objectives while generating economic benefits.

Coordination opportunities exist between VAPG and other agricultural development programs, including USDA agricultural marketing programs, Small Business Administration programs, and tribal agricultural development initiatives. Integrated approaches can address both agricultural production and marketing challenges while building comprehensive agricultural development capacity.

Housing and Community Development

USDA Rural Development housing programs address critical housing needs in rural areas while supporting broader community development objectives. For tribal communities, housing development often represents both a fundamental community need and an economic development opportunity that can create employment, support business development, and enhance overall community capacity for growth and development (USDA Rural Development 2024).

Rural Housing Service Programs

The Rural Housing Service provides grants and loans for housing development, rehabilitation, and homeownership assistance in rural areas. These programs can address housing shortages and quality issues that often constrain community development in rural tribal areas while creating construction employment and supporting local business development (Rural Housing Service 2024).

Single Family Housing Direct Loans provide homeownership financing for low- and moderate-income rural residents, including tribal members. The program offers below-market interest rates and flexible qualification criteria that make homeownership accessible for families who might not qualify for conventional financing. For tribal communities, these loans can increase homeownership rates while supporting local construction and real estate industries.

Multi-Family Housing Direct Loans finance rental housing development for low- and moderate-income residents in rural areas. These programs can address rental housing shortages in tribal communities while creating long-term assets and employment opportunities. Multi-family housing development can also support workforce development by providing affordable housing for workers in tribal economic development projects.

Housing Preservation Grants provide grants to nonprofit organizations and public agencies to rehabilitate housing for low- and moderate-income rural residents. These grants can address housing quality issues while creating employment opportunities in construction and rehabilitation activities. Housing preservation can also support community revitalization efforts that enhance economic development potential.

Rural Housing Site Loans provide financing for development of sites for housing construction, including infrastructure development such as water, sewer, and utilities. For tribal communities, site development loans can address infrastructure barriers to housing development while creating employment opportunities and supporting broader community development objectives.

The strategic value of housing development includes enhanced community capacity for workforce development, increased property values and community assets, creation of construction and related employment opportunities, and improved quality of life that can attract and retain residents and workers. Housing development often represents a fundamental prerequisite for other community and economic development activities.

Integration opportunities exist between housing programs and other tribal development initiatives, including business development, infrastructure development, and workforce development programs. Coordinated approaches can ensure that housing development supports broader development objectives while addressing immediate housing needs.

Community Development Programs

USDA community development programs support comprehensive approaches to rural community development that address infrastructure, housing, business development, and community facility needs simultaneously. For tribal communities, these programs can provide frameworks for integrated development approaches that address multiple community needs while building organizational capacity for sustained development activities (USDA Rural Development 2024).

The Rural Community Development Initiative provides grants to non-profit organizations to support rural community development activities including leadership development, strategic planning, and project development. Tribal organizations can access these grants to build community development capacity while addressing specific development challenges and opportunities.

Intermediary Relending Program provides loans to intermediary lenders who relend funds to rural businesses and community development projects. Tribal organizations can serve as intermediaries, providing ongoing access to development capital while building organizational capacity for business development and community lending activities. This program can create permanent community development infrastructure.

Rural Economic Area Partnership (REAP) Zones provide coordinated federal assistance to multi-county rural areas facing economic challenges. Tribal areas can participate in REAP Zones to access coordinated federal assistance while building partnerships with other rural communities and organizations. REAP participation can enhance access to federal resources while building regional development capacity.

The strategic importance of community development programs includes their potential to create comprehensive approaches to community development that address multiple needs simultaneously while building organizational capacity for sustained development activities. These programs often serve as frameworks for coordinating multiple federal programs and resources.

Planning for community development program participation should consider organizational capacity requirements, partnership opportunities, and coordination potential with other tribal development initiatives. Successful participation typically requires substantial organizational commitment and often benefits from technical assistance and partnership development support.

Agricultural Development and Rural Business

USDA agricultural development programs support both traditional agricultural activities and agricultural business development that can enhance rural economic opportunities. For tribal communities with agricultural resources or traditions, these programs can support agricultural enterprise development while preserving cultural practices and building economic opportunities based on traditional knowledge and resources (USDA Rural Development 2024).

Beginning Farmer and Rancher Development

The Beginning Farmer and Rancher Development Program provides grants to organizations that provide education, training, and technical assistance to beginning farmers and ranchers. For tribal communities, this program can support development of agricultural enterprises while preserving traditional agricultural knowledge and practices (USDA National Institute of Food and Agriculture 2024).

Grant recipients include nonprofit organizations, tribal governments, educational institutions, and other organizations that provide agricultural education and training. Tribal organizations can access grants to develop agricultural training programs that serve tribal members while preserving traditional agricultural practices and knowledge. These programs can combine traditional knowledge with modern agricultural techniques and business development support.

Eligible activities include agricultural education and training, business development assistance, mentoring programs, and technical assistance for beginning agricultural enterprises. The program's flexibility enables comprehensive approaches that address both agricultural production and business development needs of beginning tribal farmers and ranchers.

Grant amounts typically range from $50,000 to $750,000, depending on project scope and organizational capacity. The program requires matching funds, though in-kind contributions can satisfy match requirements. For tribal organizations, matching contributions can include tribal resources, traditional knowledge, existing agricultural assets, or community support.

The strategic value of beginning farmer and rancher development includes preservation of traditional agricultural knowledge, development of new agricultural enterprises, creation of agricultural employment opportunities, and enhancement of tribal food sovereignty. Agricultural development can also support cultural preservation and community development objectives while generating economic benefits.

Integration opportunities exist between beginning farmer programs and other agricultural development resources, including value-added producer grants, agricultural marketing programs, and tribal agricultural development initiatives. Coordinated approaches can create comprehensive agricultural development ecosystems that address production, processing, marketing, and business development needs.

Rural Cooperative Development

The Rural Cooperative Development Grant Program provides grants to support development of new cooperatives and improvement of existing cooperatives in rural areas. For tribal communities, cooperative development can provide organizational models for collective business development while preserving community ownership and control of economic development activities (USDA Rural Development 2024).

Eligible cooperatives include agricultural cooperatives, utility cooperatives, housing cooperatives, and other cooperative businesses that serve rural areas. Tribal communities can develop cooperatives to address shared business development needs while maintaining community ownership and democratic control of enterprises. Cooperatives can be particularly appropriate for tribal communities that emphasize collective decision-making and community benefit.

Grant activities include cooperative feasibility studies, business planning, training and education, and technical assistance for cooperative development. The program supports both new cooperative development and existing cooperative improvement, providing flexibility for tribal communities at different stages of cooperative development.

The application process emphasizes demonstration of cooperative development experience, community need, and project sustainability. Tribal applicants often excel in demonstrating community commitment and collective decision-making capacity, though they may benefit from technical assistance in cooperative business development and legal structuring.

Successful cooperative development often creates sustainable business models that provide ongoing economic benefits while maintaining community ownership and control. Cooperatives can provide vehicles for collective business development that align with tribal values and governance traditions while achieving commercial success.

The strategic importance of cooperative development includes creation of business models that maintain community ownership, provision of frameworks for collective business development, enhancement of community economic self-determination, and development of sustainable enterprises that serve community needs while generating economic benefits.

The business structure considerations discussed in Chapter 2 are particularly relevant for cooperative development, as cooperatives involve complex governance and ownership arrangements that must align with tribal sovereignty and governance traditions while meeting legal requirements for cooperative organization and operation.

Technical Assistance and Capacity Building

USDA Rural Development provides substantial technical assistance and capacity building support that can enhance tribal organizational capacity for economic development while building expertise in program management, project development, and business development activities. For tribal communities, technical assistance often represents a critical component of successful program utilization and long-term development capacity building (USDA Rural Development 2024).

Rural Development Technical Assistance Programs

USDA provides technical assistance through various mechanisms including direct agency support, contracted technical assistance providers, and grant-funded assistance programs. This assistance can support project development, application preparation, program management, and organizational development activities that enhance tribal capacity for rural development program utilization (U.S. Department of Agriculture 2024).

Direct technical assistance from USDA Rural Development staff includes project consultation, application support, program guidance, and ongoing project management assistance. Rural Development offices maintain staff with expertise in various program areas who can provide specialized assistance to tribal applicants and borrowers. This assistance is typically available at no cost to tribal communities.

Contracted technical assistance providers include engineering firms, financial consultants, organizational development specialists, and other professional service providers who work under contract with USDA to provide specialized assistance to rural communities. Tribal communities can access contracted technical assistance for complex projects that require specialized expertise beyond what is available from USDA staff.

Technical assistance grants provide funding for organizations to provide assistance to rural communities, including tribal communities. These grants can fund business development assistance, organizational development support, project preparation services, and other assistance activities that enhance rural community capacity for development activities.

The strategic value of technical assistance includes enhanced organizational capacity for program participation, improved project quality and success rates, development of internal expertise that supports ongoing development activities, and access to specialized knowledge and resources that may not be available locally.

Planning for technical assistance utilization should consider both immediate project needs and longer-term capacity building objectives, ensuring that assistance activities build rather than substitute for internal organizational capacity. Effective technical assistance typically combines external expertise with internal capacity development to achieve sustainable organizational enhancement.

Organizational Development and Training

USDA supports organizational development and training activities that enhance rural community capacity for economic development and program management. For tribal organizations, these resources can address capacity limitations while building the expertise necessary for sustained development activities and effective program utilization (USDA Rural Development 2024).

Leadership development programs provide training and support for rural community leaders, including tribal leaders, to enhance their capacity for economic development leadership and program management. These programs often include workshops, conferences, peer learning opportunities, and mentoring relationships that build leadership skills and knowledge.

Financial management training addresses the complex financial management requirements of rural development programs while building organizational capacity for financial planning, budgeting, and compliance monitoring. For tribal organizations, financial management training can enhance capacity for program management while building expertise that supports broader organizational development.

Project management training provides skills and knowledge necessary for successful management of complex development projects, including planning, implementation, monitoring, and evaluation activities. Tribal organizations can benefit from project management training that addresses both general project management principles and specific requirements of rural development programs.

Grant writing and application development training enhances organizational capacity for accessing federal programs and managing complex application processes. This training can be particularly valuable for tribal organizations that may have limited experience with federal grant programs or complex application requirements.

The strategic importance of organizational development and training includes enhanced organizational capacity for program participation, improved project management and implementation capabilities, development of sustainable internal expertise, and enhanced competitiveness for federal programs and other development opportunities.

Integration opportunities exist between USDA training and capacity building resources and other federal technical assistance programs, including EDA technical assistance, SBA training programs, and tribal-specific capacity building initiatives. Coordinated approaches can create comprehensive capacity building strategies that address multiple organizational development needs while avoiding duplication of effort.

Program Coordination and Integration

USDA Rural Development programs achieve maximum effectiveness when coordinated with other federal programs and integrated into comprehensive tribal development strategies. The diversity and scope of USDA programs create substantial opportunities for internal coordination while their focus on rural development makes them natural complements to other federal programs serving tribal communities (White House Office of Intergovernmental Affairs 2024).

Internal USDA Program Coordination

Coordination among different USDA Rural Development programs can create comprehensive development approaches that address infrastructure, business development, housing, and community development needs simultaneously. This internal coordination can achieve synergistic effects while reducing administrative complexity and enhancing overall development impact (USDA Rural Development 2024).

Infrastructure and business development coordination can ensure that infrastructure investments support business development opportunities while business development activities generate demand for infrastructure improvements. For example, water and sewer system development can support business development projects that require reliable utilities, while business development can provide rationale and financing support for infrastructure improvements.

Housing and community development coordination can create comprehensive approaches to community development that address both housing needs and broader community development objectives. Housing development can support workforce development for business and economic development projects, while community development activities can enhance the attractiveness and viability of housing development initiatives.

Agricultural and business development coordination can create integrated approaches that support both traditional agricultural activities and agricultural business development. Value-added agricultural enterprises can provide markets for agricultural production while creating business development opportunities that build on existing agricultural resources and expertise.

The strategic value of internal program coordination includes enhanced project feasibility through multiple funding sources, reduced administrative complexity through coordinated application and management processes, and creation of comprehensive development approaches that address multiple community needs simultaneously.

Planning for internal coordination should consider program timing requirements, compliance obligations, and administrative capacity to ensure that coordination enhances rather than complicates project implementation. Successful coordination typically requires careful project management and often benefits from technical assistance to navigate multiple program requirements simultaneously.

Integration with Other Federal Agencies

USDA Rural Development programs complement programs from other federal agencies serving tribal communities, creating opportunities for comprehensive approaches that leverage multiple federal resources while addressing diverse community development needs. Strategic integration can maximize federal investment effectiveness while building tribal capacity for complex development initiatives (Government Accountability Office 2024).

Treasury Department integration can combine USDA infrastructure and business development resources with Treasury financing programs to create comprehensive development strategies that address both infrastructure and capital needs. For example, USDA infrastructure grants can complement CDFI lending or New Markets Tax Credit investments to create feasible development projects that address comprehensive community needs.

Commerce Department integration can coordinate USDA business development support with EDA infrastructure and business development programs to create regional development approaches that address both local and regional development needs. This coordination can be particularly valuable for tribal communities pursuing development strategies that require both local capacity building and regional market access.

Small Business Administration integration can combine USDA business development infrastructure with SBA business development support and financing to create comprehensive entrepreneurship support systems. This coordination can enhance the effectiveness of tribal business development efforts while providing access to specialized business development resources and financing.

Housing and Urban Development integration can address community development needs that complement USDA rural development investments, creating comprehensive approaches that consider both rural development and community development objectives. This coordination can be particularly valuable for tribal communities pursuing comprehensive community development strategies.

The strategic importance of inter-agency coordination includes enhanced access to federal resources, creation of comprehensive development approaches that address multiple community needs, demonstration of tribal capacity for complex development initiatives, and development of relationships with multiple federal agencies that support ongoing development activities.

The coordination frameworks and strategic planning approaches discussed in Chapter 7 provide valuable guidance for managing complex inter-agency coordination while ensuring that coordinated approaches support rather than complicate tribal development objectives and governance arrangements.

Strategic Implementation Considerations

Successful utilization of USDA Rural Development programs requires strategic planning that aligns projects with broader tribal development objectives while building organizational capacity for sustained development activities. The diversity and complexity of USDA programs create opportunities for comprehensive development approaches that can transform rural tribal communities while preserving tribal values and sovereignty (Harvard Project on American Indian Economic Development 2024).

Comprehensive Development Strategy Development

USDA programs work most effectively when integrated into comprehensive development strategies that address multiple community needs while building organizational capacity for sustained development activities.

Infrastructure development strategy should prioritize investments that enable broader economic development while addressing immediate community needs. Water, sewer, telecommunications, and utilities infrastructure often represent prerequisites for business development and community growth, making infrastructure development strategic early investments for comprehensive development initiatives.

Business development strategy should consider both immediate business development opportunities and longer-term capacity building for sustainable entrepreneurship and enterprise development. Business development infrastructure such as incubators, loan funds, and technical assistance programs can provide ongoing support for tribal entrepreneurs while building organizational capacity for sustained business development activities.

Housing and community development strategy should address both immediate housing needs and broader community development objectives that support economic development and community growth. Housing development can support workforce development while community facilities can provide venues and infrastructure for business development and community activities.

The strategic value of comprehensive development strategy includes enhanced project feasibility through coordinated planning and implementation, creation of synergistic effects that enhance overall development impact, and development of organizational capacity for complex development initiatives that positions tribal communities for ongoing development opportunities.

Sustainability and Long-Term Planning
USDA programs require attention to long-term sustainability and ongoing operational requirements that continue beyond initial project implementation. Planning for sustainability ensures that USDA investments create lasting benefits while building tribal capacity for ongoing development activities (Government Accountability Office 2024).

Financial sustainability planning addresses ongoing operational costs, maintenance requirements, and revenue generation necessary for long-term project viability. Infrastructure projects require ongoing maintenance and operational support, while business development programs require sustained funding for ongoing activities. Financial sustainability planning should consider both tribal financial capacity and revenue generation potential from USDA-funded activities.

Organizational sustainability planning addresses staffing, training, and systems necessary for ongoing program management and operational excellence. USDA programs often require sophisticated organizational capacity for compliance monitoring, performance measurement, and ongoing program management. Organizational sustainability planning should consider both immediate capacity needs and longer-term capacity development requirements.

Community sustainability planning addresses community support, leadership development, and institutional arrangements necessary for sustained development impact. Successful USDA projects typically require ongoing community engagement and support, making community sustainability planning essential for long-term success. This planning should consider both immediate community needs and longer-term community development objectives.

Environmental sustainability planning addresses environmental stewardship and natural resource management considerations that affect long-term project viability and community development sustainability. USDA programs often involve natural resource utilization or environmental impact, making environmental sustainability planning important for both compliance and community values alignment.

The strategic importance of sustainability planning includes creation of lasting development benefits, enhancement of tribal capacity for ongoing development activities, demonstration of tribal capacity for complex project management, and positioning for additional development opportunities that build on successful USDA program implementation.

Integration of sustainability planning with broader tribal planning processes can create comprehensive approaches that align USDA investments with long-term tribal development objectives while ensuring that projects contribute to rather than detract from broader community sustainability and self-determination goals. This approach aligns with the strategic planning principles outlined in Chapter 7 and the long-term planning considerations discussed in Section IX.

Business Structure Interface Analysis

The USDA Rural Development programs analyzed in this section demonstrate significant interface with tribal business structure selection, particularly for programs involving ongoing operations, business development, and multi-year commitments. USDA programs generally emphasize rural community benefit and operational sustainability, creating important considerations for entity selection that can affect program access, compliance effectiveness, and long-term project success.

Infrastructure Development Programs
Water and Sewer Systems Development

Eligibility Considerations: USDA water and sewer programs strongly favor governmental entities, making unincorporated tribal enterprises the most straightforward applicants due to their direct governmental status and clear public benefit mission. Section 17 corporations can serve as eligible applicants when designated by tribal governments, providing operational benefits while maintaining governmental character. Tribally chartered corporations may qualify as instrumentalities of tribal governments but require clear documentation of their governmental purpose and tribal control. State-chartered corporations face more complex eligibility analysis and may need to demonstrate clear public benefit and governmental relationship. Individual/sole proprietorships and partnerships typically cannot meet the public benefit and scale requirements for water and sewer infrastructure funding.

Compliance and Operational Impacts: Water and sewer system compliance requires long-term operational capacity and regulatory compliance that varies significantly across business structures. Unincorporated tribal enterprises benefit from direct governmental backing but must integrate complex utility operations with broader tribal governmental responsibilities, potentially creating administrative challenges. Section 17 corporations provide operational separation that can enhance utility management while maintaining clear governmental accountability, though their minimal statutory framework may create governance complexities for ongoing utility operations. Tribally chartered corporations offer optimal flexibility for utility operations, enabling professional utility management while maintaining tribal oversight and accountability. State-chartered corporations provide established operational frameworks but may face additional oversight requirements and potential conflicts between corporate duties and tribal governmental objectives.

Tax Implications: USDA water and sewer grants generally do not create taxable income for recipients. However, ongoing utility operations may generate revenue that creates different tax implications across structures. Unincorporated tribal enterprises maintain full tax exemption for governmental utility operations. Section 17 and tribally chartered corporations with tax-exempt status can operate utilities without federal income tax obligations on revenues. State-chartered corporations may face taxation on utility revenues, potentially affecting long-term system sustainability and rate structures.

Strategic Advantages/Disadvantages: Unincorporated tribal enterprises provide maximum credibility for USDA applications but may lack operational expertise for complex utility management. Section 17 corporations combine governmental credibility with operational separation, enabling professional utility management while maintaining tribal control. Tribally chartered corporations offer optimal balance of tribal oversight, operational flexibility, and regulatory compliance capability. State-chartered corporations may provide superior utility management expertise but could face tax burdens that affect system economics.

Sovereign Immunity Considerations: Water and sewer operations require ongoing commercial relationships with contractors, suppliers, and potentially customers that may necessitate immunity waivers. Unincorporated tribal enterprises require tribal-level immunity waivers that could expose broader governmental assets. Section 17 and tribally chartered corporations can provide limited immunity waivers specific to utility operations while preserving broader tribal immunity. State-chartered corporations operate without immunity protection, which may facilitate utility operations by reducing contractor and vendor concerns about enforcement.

Rural Utilities Service (RUS) Programs

Eligibility Considerations: RUS telecommunications and electric programs accommodate various tribal business structures, with specific advantages for different entity types depending on the utility service. Tribal governments through unincorporated enterprises can access RUS programs directly, providing strong eligibility for governmental telecommunications and electric infrastructure. Section 17 corporations can serve as eligible utility entities, combining governmental character with operational separation beneficial for complex utility operations. Tribally chartered corporations may qualify as tribal instrumentalities for RUS programs. State-chartered corporations can access RUS programs but may face more complex eligibility analysis regarding tribal benefit and control.

Rural electric cooperatives represent a specialized structure that many tribes have utilized effectively for electric utility development.

Compliance and Operational Impacts: RUS programs involve substantial ongoing compliance requirements including financial reporting, operational standards, and federal oversight that vary significantly across business structures. Cooperative structures have proven particularly effective for RUS electric programs, providing operational expertise while maintaining community accountability. Section 17 corporations provide operational separation beneficial for utility management while maintaining clear tribal accountability. Tribally chartered corporations offer flexibility for customized governance arrangements that can accommodate both RUS requirements and tribal oversight needs.

Tax Implications: RUS loan and grant programs generally do not create taxable income for recipients. However, utility operations funded through RUS programs may generate taxable revenue. Tax-exempt entities maintain advantages for utility operations, while state-chartered corporations may face taxation that affects utility economics and rate structures.

Strategic Advantages/Disadvantages: Cooperative structures have proven particularly successful for tribal electric utility development, providing operational expertise and access to cooperative networks while maintaining community control. Section 17 corporations provide operational separation and tax advantages. State-chartered corporations may provide access to utility expertise and financing but sacrifice tax benefits.

Sovereign Immunity Considerations: Utility operations require extensive commercial relationships that may necessitate immunity waivers. Corporate and cooperative structures typically provide better frameworks for managing utility-specific immunity waivers while preserving broader tribal immunity.

Community Facilities Development

Eligibility Considerations: USDA Community Facilities programs strongly favor governmental entities and nonprofit organizations, making unincorporated tribal enterprises and tribal governments the preferred applicants. Section 17 corporations qualify easily due to their governmental character and tax-exempt status. Tribally chartered nonprofit corporations can qualify for Community Facilities funding. State-chartered corporations may qualify but face more complex eligibility analysis regarding governmental purpose and community benefit.

Compliance and Operational Impacts: Community facilities require ongoing operational management that may benefit from corporate structures with established governance frameworks. Healthcare, educational, and community center operations may require professional management capabilities that corporate structures can provide more effectively than unincorporated enterprises integrated with broader tribal governmental operations.

Tax Implications: Community Facilities grants do not create taxable income, and ongoing operations of community facilities typically qualify for tax exemption under governmental or charitable purposes. Tax-exempt structures provide clear advantages for community facility operations.

Strategic Advantages/Disadvantages: The optimal structure depends on the type and complexity of community facilities. Simple facilities may be effectively operated through unincorporated tribal enterprises, while complex facilities like hospitals or multi-purpose centers may benefit from corporate structures that provide operational separation and professional management frameworks.

Sovereign Immunity Considerations: Community facilities may require limited immunity waivers for operational contracts, professional services, and potentially user agreements. Corporate structures may provide better flexibility for facility-specific immunity waivers.

Business and Industry Development
Business and Industry (B&I) Loan Guarantee Program

Eligibility Considerations: USDA B&I loan guarantees accommodate all tribal business structures, with different structures providing different advantages for business development and lender relationships. Tribal businesses organized as corporations (Section 17, tribally chartered, or state-chartered) typically provide stronger applications due to established business governance and operational separation from tribal government functions. Individual/sole proprietorships can access B&I guarantees for smaller business development. Partnerships and joint ventures can qualify when properly structured and documented.

Compliance and Operational Impacts: B&I loan compliance requires sophisticated business operations and financial management that generally favor corporate structures over unincorporated enterprises. Lenders typically prefer corporate borrowers due to established governance, operational separation, and familiar legal frameworks. Section 17 corporations provide federal recognition that can enhance lender confidence. State-chartered corporations offer familiar legal structures that lenders understand, potentially facilitating loan approval and management.

Tax Implications: B&I loan proceeds are not taxable income, but business operations funded through B&I loans may generate taxable income. Corporate structures with tax-exempt status provide significant advantages for business operations, while state-chartered corporations face standard corporate taxation that affects business economics and debt service capacity.

Strategic Advantages/Disadvantages: Section 17 corporations provide optimal B&I platforms, combining federal recognition, potential tax exemption, and operational separation that lenders value. Tribally chartered corporations offer similar benefits with greater governance flexibility. State-chartered corporations provide maximum lender comfort but sacrifice tax benefits. Individual businesses can access smaller B&I loans but may lack capacity for larger business development projects.

Sovereign Immunity Considerations: B&I loans require comprehensive immunity waivers for loan agreements, security interests, and enforcement mechanisms. Corporate structures can provide loan-specific immunity waivers while preserving broader tribal immunity. Unincorporated tribal enterprises require tribal-level immunity waivers that may expose broader governmental assets. Individual tribal member businesses operate without immunity protection.

Rural Business Development Grant Program

Eligibility Considerations: Rural Business Development grants accommodate various tribal business structures as both recipients and beneficiaries. Tribal governments and tribal organizations can receive grants to provide business development services. Section 17 corporations and tribally chartered corporations can serve as grant recipients for business development programming. State-chartered corporations may qualify as grant recipients when serving tribal business development objectives.

Compliance and Operational Impacts: Business development grant compliance requires program management and service delivery capabilities that may favor organizations with established operational frameworks. Corporate structures may provide better platforms for complex business development programming requiring diverse services, partnerships, and performance measurement.

Tax Implications: Business development grants generally do not create taxable income for recipients. However, ongoing business development operations may generate revenue that creates different tax implications across structures. Tax-exempt structures provide advantages for business development organizations.

Strategic Advantages/Disadvantages: Corporate structures may provide optimal platforms for business development programming, offering operational flexibility and governance frameworks that can accommodate complex program requirements while maintaining tribal accountability and community focus.

Sovereign Immunity Considerations: Business development programs typically require limited immunity waivers for service agreements, partnerships, and client relationships. Corporate structures may provide better flexibility for program-specific immunity waivers.

Value-Added Producer Grant (VAPG) Program
Eligibility Considerations: VAPG accommodates various business structures including individual agricultural producers, agricultural cooperatives, producer groups, and tribal governments representing agricultural producers. Individual tribal member farmers and ranchers can access VAPG directly. Tribal agricultural enterprises can be structured as cooperatives, corporations, or other business entities depending on the agricultural activity and producer relationships.

Compliance and Operational Impacts: VAPG compliance requirements vary by grant type (planning vs. working capital) and generally accommodate diverse business structures. However, value-added agricultural operations may benefit from corporate structures that can accommodate complex processing, marketing, and distribution activities.

Tax Implications: VAPG grants are generally not taxable income, but value-added agricultural operations may generate taxable revenue. Tax-exempt structures provide advantages for tribal agricultural enterprises, while individual producers face standard taxation on agricultural income.

Strategic Advantages/Disadvantages: The optimal structure depends on the scale and complexity of value-added agricultural activities. Individual producers can access VAPG for smaller value-added enterprises. Cooperative structures may provide advantages for larger-scale processing and marketing operations involving multiple producers. Corporate structures may be optimal for complex agribusiness operations requiring substantial capital and operational sophistication.

Sovereign Immunity Considerations: Value-added agricultural operations may require immunity waivers for processing contracts, marketing agreements, and commercial relationships. Individual producers operate without immunity protection. Tribal agricultural corporations can provide limited immunity waivers for agricultural operations while preserving broader tribal immunity.

Housing and Community Development
Rural Housing Service Programs

Eligibility Considerations: USDA housing programs accommodate various tribal structures with different programs serving different entity types. Tribal governments can access multi-family housing programs through unincorporated enterprises. Tribal housing authorities or Section 17 corporations can serve as housing developers and operators. Individual tribal members can access single-family housing programs regardless of tribal business structure choices.

Compliance and Operational Impacts: Housing development and management requires long-term operational capacity that may favor corporate structures with established governance and management frameworks. Multi-family housing operations require sophisticated property management that corporate structures may provide more effectively than unincorporated tribal enterprises.

Tax Implications: USDA housing grants and loans generally do not create taxable income for recipients. However, ongoing housing operations may generate revenue that creates different tax implications. Tax-exempt structures provide advantages for affordable housing operations, while individual homeowners face standard homeownership tax treatment.

Strategic Advantages/Disadvantages: Corporate structures may provide optimal platforms for complex housing development and management, offering operational separation and governance frameworks that enhance housing program effectiveness. Individual programs accommodate homeownership regardless of business structure choices.

Sovereign Immunity Considerations: Housing operations may require immunity waivers for tenant relationships, property management contracts, and maintenance agreements. Corporate structures may provide better flexibility for housing-specific immunity waivers while preserving broader tribal immunity.

Community Development Programs

Eligibility Considerations: USDA community development programs accommodate various tribal structures, with different programs favoring different entity types. Tribal governments can participate directly through unincorporated enterprises. Nonprofit organizations including tribally chartered nonprofits can access various community development programs. Economic development corporations can serve as intermediaries for community development activities.

Compliance and Operational Impacts: Community development program compliance varies by specific program but generally requires sustained organizational capacity and performance measurement that may favor corporate structures with established governance and operational frameworks.

Tax Implications: Community development grants generally do not create taxable income, and community development operations typically qualify for tax-exempt treatment under governmental or charitable purposes.

Strategic Advantages/Disadvantages: Corporate structures may provide better platforms for complex community development programming requiring diverse partnerships, services, and long-term sustainability planning.

Sovereign Immunity Considerations: Community development programs may require limited immunity waivers for partnerships, service agreements, and community relationships. Corporate structures may provide better flexibility for program-specific immunity waivers.

Agricultural Development and Rural Business
Beginning Farmer and Rancher Development

Eligibility Considerations: Beginning farmer programs accommodate various structures as both grant recipients (organizations providing services) and beneficiaries (beginning farmers and ranchers). Tribal organizations can receive grants to provide agricultural education and support. Individual tribal members can benefit from beginning farmer programs regardless of business structure. Agricultural training organizations can be structured as nonprofits, corporations, or other entities.

Compliance and Operational Impacts: Agricultural education and training programs require educational capacity and program management that may favor organizations with established operational frameworks. Corporate structures may provide better platforms for complex agricultural training and support programming.

Tax Implications: Beginning farmer grants to organizations are generally not taxable income. Educational and training operations typically qualify for tax-exempt treatment. Individual beginning farmers face standard agricultural taxation regardless of program participation.

Strategic Advantages/Disadvantages: Corporate structures may provide optimal platforms for agricultural education and training programs, offering operational flexibility and governance frameworks that can accommodate diverse training needs while maintaining tribal cultural integration and community focus.

Sovereign Immunity Considerations: Agricultural training programs typically require limited immunity waivers for educational contracts, partnerships, and participant relationships. Corporate structures may provide better flexibility for program-specific immunity waivers.

Rural Cooperative Development

Eligibility Considerations: Cooperative development programs specifically support cooperative business structures, creating unique considerations for tribal business development. Tribal members can form agricultural, utility, housing, or other cooperatives. Tribal governments can support cooperative development without directly forming cooperatives. Existing tribal cooperatives can access improvement grants.

Compliance and Operational Impacts: Cooperative development requires understanding of cooperative law, governance, and operations that differs significantly from corporate structures. Cooperatives provide democratic member control and profit-sharing that may align well with tribal values and community development objectives. However, cooperative governance can be complex and may require significant member education and engagement.

Tax Implications: Cooperatives have specialized tax treatment under federal law, including potential for patronage refunds and exemptions that can provide tax advantages for agricultural and utility operations. Tribal member participation in cooperatives generally does not affect tribal tax status, though cooperative profits distributed to tribal members may be taxable.

Strategic Advantages/Disadvantages: Cooperatives provide democratic governance and community control that may align well with tribal values. They can be particularly effective for agricultural marketing, utility operations, and shared services. However, cooperative governance requires member engagement and education that may be challenging to sustain. Cooperatives may provide better community ownership and control than corporate structures for certain types of businesses.

Sovereign Immunity Considerations: Cooperatives formed by tribal members generally operate without sovereign immunity protection. Tribal government support for cooperative development typically does not extend tribal immunity to cooperative operations. However, this lack of immunity may actually facilitate cooperative operations by reducing legal complexity in member and commercial relationships.

Technical Assistance and Capacity Building
Rural Development Technical Assistance Programs

Eligibility Considerations: USDA technical assistance programs accommodate all tribal business structures as beneficiaries, with different structures potentially benefiting from different types of assistance. The type of technical assistance needed may vary based on business structure complexity and operational requirements.

Compliance and Operational Impacts: Technical assistance compliance is minimal and generally does not vary by business structure. However, the effectiveness of technical assistance may depend on the recipient entity's capacity to implement recommendations and sustain improvements.

Tax Implications: Technical assistance grants generally do not create tax implications regardless of business structure, as they provide services rather than taxable income.

Strategic Advantages/Disadvantages: All business structures can benefit from USDA technical assistance, though the focus and type of assistance may vary based on structural complexity and operational needs. Corporate structures may benefit from business management assistance, while unincorporated enterprises may need governmental capacity building support.

Sovereign Immunity Considerations: Technical assistance typically requires minimal immunity considerations, as it involves consultation and capacity building rather than ongoing commercial relationships.

Organizational Development and Training

Eligibility Considerations: Organizational development programs accommodate various tribal structures both as service recipients and providers. Training organizations can be structured as nonprofits, corporations, or tribal governmental departments depending on focus and operational requirements.

Compliance and Operational Impacts: Organizational development compliance focuses on training effectiveness and capacity building outcomes rather than specific business structure requirements. However, training organizations may benefit from corporate structures that provide operational frameworks for educational programming.

Tax Implications: Training and organizational development grants generally do not create taxable income. Educational operations typically qualify for tax-exempt treatment under governmental or charitable purposes.

Strategic Advantages/Disadvantages: Corporate structures may provide better platforms for educational and training organizations, offering governance frameworks that can accommodate diverse educational partnerships while maintaining accountability and effectiveness.

Sovereign Immunity Considerations: Educational and training programs typically require limited immunity considerations, though educational partnerships and contracts may benefit from limited immunity waivers that corporate structures can provide more flexibly.

Cross-Program Strategic Considerations

Agricultural Enterprise Development: Tribes pursuing comprehensive agricultural development may benefit from diverse business structures serving different functions: cooperatives for producer services and marketing, corporations for processing and value-added activities, and individual enterprises for direct farming and ranching operations.

Infrastructure and Business Integration: USDA programs often enable integrated approaches combining infrastructure development with business development. Corporate structures may provide optimal platforms for managing complex integrated projects that combine infrastructure operations with business development activities.

Community Development Coordination: USDA community development programs work most effectively when coordinated with broader tribal development strategies. Corporate structures may provide better frameworks for comprehensive community development that integrates housing, business development, and infrastructure improvements.

Long-Term Sustainability: Many USDA programs create long-term operational obligations that may favor corporate structures with established governance frameworks and operational separation from tribal governmental functions. However, unincorporated tribal enterprises maintain advantages for clearly governmental activities.

Cooperative Development Strategy: Cooperatives represent underutilized business structures for tribal communities that may provide advantages for agricultural marketing, utility operations, and community services while maintaining democratic control and community ownership.

The USDA Rural Development programs demonstrate significant interface with business structure selection, particularly for programs involving ongoing operations, business development, and community services. Strategic business structure selection can enhance both USDA program access and operational effectiveness while preserving tribal sovereignty and building sustainable community development capacity.

Supplement M: Federal Contracting and Procurement Programs

Introduction to Federal Contracting Authority for Tribal Enterprises

Federal contracting and procurement represent substantial market opportunities for tribal enterprises, with billions of dollars in annual federal procurement that can provide stable revenue sources, capacity building opportunities, and pathways to broader market development. The federal government's commitment to supporting disadvantaged businesses through various procurement programs creates significant opportunities for tribal businesses to access government markets while building competitive capabilities for commercial market success (Federal Acquisition Regulation 2024).

Federal contracting authority for tribal enterprises stems from multiple legislative sources, including the Small Business Act, the Indian Self-Determination and Education Assistance Act, the Buy Indian Act, and various executive orders that establish procurement preferences and set-aside programs designed to support Native American business development. These legal foundations create a comprehensive framework of opportunities that can transform tribal enterprises while contributing to broader tribal economic development objectives (Government Accountability Office 2023).

The strategic importance of federal contracting extends beyond immediate revenue generation to include capability development, market positioning, demonstration of business competitiveness, and creation of business relationships that can open additional market opportunities. Successful federal contractors often develop expertise, capacity, and credibility that enables them to pursue larger federal contracts while also accessing commercial markets with enhanced competitive positioning (Bureau of Indian Affairs 2024).

Understanding federal contracting opportunities requires recognition of the complex regulatory environment that governs federal procurement, including acquisition regulations, socioeconomic programs, compliance requirements, and performance standards that shape contracting opportunities and requirements. Successful participation in federal contracting typically requires sophisticated understanding of procurement processes, customer requirements, and competitive positioning strategies that maximize opportunities while ensuring compliance with federal requirements.

The integration of federal contracting strategies with broader tribal business development should consider the organizational structure and governance principles outlined in Chapter 2, ensuring that contracting activities align with appropriate tribal business structures and sovereignty considerations. The strategic planning and business development approaches discussed in Chapter 7 provide valuable frameworks for optimizing federal contracting participation within broader tribal economic development strategies.

Indian Small Business and Economic Enterprise Development Program

The Indian Small Business and Economic Enterprise Development (ISEED) Program represents a comprehensive approach to supporting Native American business development through federal contracting opportunities, technical assistance, and business development support. ISEED addresses the unique challenges facing Native American businesses while providing tools and resources specifically designed to enhance their competitiveness in federal markets (Bureau of Indian Affairs 2024).

Program Structure and Business Development Support

The ISEED Program provides a comprehensive framework for Native American business development that combines procurement opportunities with business development assistance, recognizing that successful federal contracting requires both market access and business capability development. The program's structure addresses common barriers to Native American business success while building long-term competitive capabilities (Bureau of Indian Affairs 2024).

Business development assistance includes comprehensive support for business planning, financial management, marketing, operations development, and strategic planning that addresses both general business development needs and specific requirements of federal contracting. This assistance is designed to build business capabilities that support both immediate contracting success and long-term business growth and diversification.

Technical assistance addresses specific aspects of federal contracting including proposal preparation, compliance requirements, performance management, and customer relationship development. Technical assistance helps Native American businesses navigate the complex requirements of federal contracting while building internal expertise that supports ongoing contracting success.

Training programs address diverse topics including federal procurement processes, proposal writing, project management, financial management, and business development strategies that enhance competitiveness in federal markets. Training programs build business capabilities while creating peer networks that support ongoing business development and problem-solving.

Networking and relationship development opportunities connect Native American businesses with federal customers, prime contractors, and other business partners while building professional relationships that support market access and business development. Networking is particularly important for businesses entering federal markets where relationships and reputation often significantly influence contracting opportunities.

Market intelligence and business development support provide Native American businesses with information about contracting opportunities, customer requirements, and market trends that support strategic planning and business development activities. Market intelligence helps businesses identify opportunities while developing competitive positioning strategies that maximize their prospects for contract awards.

The strategic value of ISEED business development support includes enhancement of business capabilities, improvement of competitive positioning, development of federal market expertise, and creation of business relationships that support both immediate contracting success and longer-term business development objectives.

Procurement Opportunities and Set-Aside Programs

ISEED facilitates access to various federal procurement opportunities specifically designed to support Native American business development, including set-aside programs, sole-source opportunities, and competitive preferences that enhance Native American businesses' prospects for federal contract awards (Bureau of Indian Affairs 2024).

Indian Small Business set-asides limit competition to qualified Native American businesses, providing enhanced opportunities for contract awards while maintaining competitive dynamics among qualified businesses. Set-aside opportunities can provide Native American businesses with access to substantial federal contracts that might otherwise go to larger established contractors.

Sole-source contracting authority enables federal agencies to award contracts directly to qualified Native American businesses under certain circumstances, providing opportunities to establish federal customer relationships while demonstrating capabilities for future competitive opportunities. Sole-source authority can be particularly valuable for businesses developing specialized capabilities or serving unique market needs.

Subcontracting opportunities arise through prime contractors' efforts to meet Native American subcontracting goals, creating additional market access for tribal businesses. Subcontracting can provide entry points to federal markets while building capabilities and relationships for future prime contracting opportunities.

Economic development contracts provide opportunities for Native American businesses to provide goods and services specifically related to Indian economic development activities. These contracts often align with tribal development priorities while providing business development opportunities that serve both commercial and community development objectives.

Self-determination contracts enable tribal governments and tribal organizations to assume responsibility for federal programs and services, creating business opportunities while enhancing tribal self-determination and governance capacity. Self-determination contracting can provide substantial revenue sources while building tribal institutional capacity.

The federal procurement preference structure creates substantial market opportunities for Native American businesses while contributing to tribal economic development through increased business activity, employment creation, and capability development. Successful ISEED participants often become significant federal contractors while also developing commercial market capabilities.

Strategic utilization of ISEED procurement opportunities requires understanding federal procurement processes, customer requirements, and competitive positioning strategies that maximize the value of program benefits while building long-term business competitiveness and market positioning.

Business Certification and Compliance Requirements
ISEED participation requires business certification that demonstrates Native American ownership and control while ensuring compliance with program requirements designed to maintain program integrity and effectiveness. Certification processes verify business eligibility while providing frameworks for ongoing compliance monitoring and support (Bureau of Indian Affairs 2024).

Native American ownership requirements specify that qualifying businesses must be at least 51% owned by enrolled tribal members who control the management and daily operations of the enterprise. Ownership requirements accommodate various business structures while ensuring that program benefits flow to Native American entrepreneurs and tribal communities.

Management and control requirements ensure that Native American owners have actual authority over business operations, strategic decisions, and day-to-day management activities. Control requirements address situations where Native American ownership might exist without meaningful business control, ensuring that program benefits serve their intended purposes.

Business registration and documentation requirements include federal, state, and tribal business registrations, tax identification numbers, and other administrative requirements that demonstrate legitimate business operations. Registration requirements ensure that participating businesses meet basic legal and administrative standards while maintaining appropriate regulatory compliance.

Financial capability demonstration requires businesses to show adequate financial resources, management systems, and operational capacity to perform federal contracts successfully. Financial capability requirements protect both businesses and government customers while ensuring that contract awards go to businesses capable of successful performance.

Past performance evaluation considers businesses' track records in contract performance, customer satisfaction, and compliance with contract requirements. Performance evaluation helps ensure that contract awards consider businesses' demonstrated capabilities while providing incentives for excellence in contract performance.

Ongoing compliance requirements include annual certification renewals, performance monitoring, and adherence to program guidelines that maintain business eligibility and program integrity. Compliance requirements ensure that businesses continue to meet program criteria while maintaining accountability for program benefits and opportunities.

The strategic importance of certification and compliance includes demonstration of business legitimacy and capability, access to program benefits and opportunities, maintenance of good standing with federal agencies, and positioning for ongoing contracting opportunities and business development support.

Buy Indian Act Implementation and Tribal Preferences

The Buy Indian Act provides federal agencies with authority to establish procurement preferences for Native American businesses when purchasing goods and services for Indian programs and activities (Buy Indian Act, 25 U.S.C. § 47; Bureau of Indian Affairs 2024). This authority creates substantial market opportunities for tribal businesses while ensuring that federal spending on Indian programs contributes to Native American economic development and tribal self-determination (25 U.S.C. § 47).

Legal Authority and Implementation Framework
The Buy Indian Act establishes clear legal authority for federal agencies to provide procurement preferences to Native American businesses when purchasing goods and services for the benefit of Indians. This authority recognizes the federal trust responsibility while creating market opportunities that support tribal economic development and business development objectives (Bureau of Indian Affairs 2024).

Statutory authority requires federal agencies to give preference to Native American businesses when purchasing goods and services for Indian programs, provided that such businesses can provide goods and services that meet agency requirements at fair and reasonable prices. The statutory framework balances procurement preferences with requirements for responsible government spending and program effectiveness.

Implementation guidelines provide federal agencies with procedures for identifying contracting opportunities appropriate for Buy Indian Act preferences, soliciting proposals from Native American businesses, and evaluating proposals to ensure that preferences are applied consistently and effectively. Implementation guidelines ensure that agencies understand their obligations while providing clear procedures for program administration.

Eligible contracting activities include goods and services purchased for Indian programs, services provided on or near Indian reservations, and activities that directly benefit Indian communities or tribal governments. Eligibility criteria ensure that Buy Indian Act preferences apply to appropriate contracting opportunities while maintaining focus on Indian program support and community benefit.

Business eligibility requirements specify that qualifying businesses must be at least 51% owned by Indians and controlled by Indians who manage daily business operations. Eligibility requirements ensure that program benefits flow to Indian entrepreneurs while accommodating various business structures and ownership arrangements.

Agency implementation responsibilities include identifying appropriate contracting opportunities, establishing procurement procedures that incorporate Buy Indian Act preferences, training contracting officers on program requirements, and monitoring program effectiveness and compliance. Agency responsibilities ensure consistent program implementation while building institutional capacity for ongoing program administration.

The strategic importance of Buy Indian Act implementation includes creation of substantial market opportunities for Native American businesses, demonstration of federal commitment to tribal economic development, and development of institutional frameworks that support ongoing procurement preferences and business development opportunities.

Procurement Preferences and Market Opportunities

Buy Indian Act implementation creates significant procurement preferences that can provide Native American businesses with enhanced access to federal contracts while building competitive capabilities and market relationships that support long-term business development. These preferences are designed to increase Native American business participation in federal procurement while supporting broader tribal economic development objectives (Bureau of Indian Affairs 2024).

Procurement preferences enable federal agencies to limit competition to Native American businesses or provide evaluation advantages that enhance Native American businesses' competitiveness in federal contracting. Preferences create market access opportunities that might not otherwise be available while maintaining competitive dynamics that encourage business excellence and capability development.

Market opportunity identification includes systematic review of federal procurement activities to identify contracting opportunities appropriate for Buy Indian Act preferences. Market identification helps agencies maximize program utilization while providing Native American businesses with information about contracting opportunities and requirements.

Competitive advantages provided through Buy Indian Act preferences can include price preferences, evaluation credits, or set-aside opportunities that enhance Native American businesses' prospects for contract awards. Competitive advantages are designed to level the playing field for

Native American businesses while maintaining incentives for competitive pricing and performance excellence.

Contract bundling restrictions limit agencies' ability to combine multiple contracting requirements into large contracts that may exceed Native American businesses' capabilities. Bundling restrictions ensure that contracting opportunities remain accessible to smaller Native American businesses while maintaining agency flexibility for efficient procurement.

Subcontracting opportunities arise when large contracts include requirements for Native American subcontractor participation, creating additional market access for tribal businesses. Subcontracting can provide entry points to federal markets while building capabilities and relationships for future prime contracting opportunities.

Performance measurement and evaluation track Buy Indian Act utilization, Native American business participation rates, and program effectiveness in supporting tribal economic development. Performance measurement provides accountability while supporting continuous improvement efforts and program advocacy.

The strategic value of procurement preferences includes enhanced market access for Native American businesses, creation of competitive advantages that support business development, demonstration of business capabilities that attract additional contracting opportunities, and contribution to broader tribal economic development through increased business activity and employment creation.

Agency Coordination and Program Development
Effective Buy Indian Act implementation requires coordination among federal agencies, tribal governments, and Native American businesses to ensure that program opportunities are maximized while meeting federal procurement requirements and tribal economic development objectives. Coordination creates synergistic effects that enhance program effectiveness while building institutional capacity for ongoing program improvement and expansion (Bureau of Indian Affairs 2024).

Inter-agency coordination ensures that Buy Indian Act implementation is consistent across federal agencies while sharing best practices and lessons learned that improve program effectiveness. Coordination helps agencies understand program requirements while building institutional knowledge and expertise that supports ongoing program development.

Tribal government consultation provides tribal leaders with opportunities to influence Buy Indian Act implementation while ensuring that program activities align with tribal economic development priorities and objectives. Consultation respects tribal sovereignty while building partnerships that enhance program effectiveness and tribal economic development impact.

Business development coordination aligns Buy Indian Act procurement opportunities with business development assistance, technical assistance, and capacity building support that enhances Native American businesses' ability to compete successfully for federal contracts. Coordination creates comprehensive support systems that address both market access and business capability development needs.

Training and outreach programs educate federal contracting officers, tribal governments, and Native American businesses about Buy Indian Act requirements, opportunities, and procedures. Training builds institutional capacity while ensuring that program participants understand their roles and responsibilities in effective program implementation.

Performance monitoring and evaluation assess program effectiveness, identify improvement opportunities, and demonstrate program impact on tribal economic development. Monitoring provides accountability while supporting continuous improvement efforts and advocacy for program expansion and enhancement.

Policy development activities address regulatory improvements, implementation guidance, and program expansion opportunities that enhance Buy Indian Act effectiveness and impact. Policy development ensures that programs evolve to meet changing needs while maintaining focus on tribal economic development support and federal trust responsibility fulfillment.

The strategic importance of agency coordination includes enhanced program effectiveness, creation of institutional capacity for ongoing program improvement, development of partnerships that support tribal economic development, and demonstration of federal commitment to tribal economic development and self-determination.

Section 8(a) Sole Source and Competitive Contracting

Section 8(a) sole source and competitive contracting represents one of the most powerful tools available for tribal business development, providing substantial federal contracting opportunities through both direct awards and set-aside competitions. The 8(a) program's contracting mechanisms create pathways for tribal businesses to establish themselves in federal markets while building capabilities for long-term competitive success (Small Business Administration 2024).

Sole Source Contracting Authority and Procedures

Section 8(a) sole source contracting authority enables federal agencies to award contracts directly to qualified 8(a) businesses without competitive bidding, subject to specific dollar thresholds and justification requirements. This authority provides tribal businesses with opportunities to establish federal customer relationships while demonstrating capabilities for future competitive opportunities (Small Business Administration 2024).

Dollar thresholds for sole source contracting vary by procurement type, with current limits of $4.5 million for manufacturing contracts and $7 million for all other contracts. These substantial thresholds enable tribal businesses to receive significant contract awards while building organizational capacity and customer relationships that support future business development.

Justification requirements ensure that sole source awards serve legitimate business development purposes while meeting federal procurement standards for responsibility and effectiveness. Justifications must demonstrate that sole source awards contribute to 8(a) business development while providing government customers with satisfactory goods and services at fair and reasonable prices.

Market research requirements ensure that agencies understand market conditions and business capabilities before making sole source awards. Market research helps agencies identify qualified businesses while ensuring that sole source awards are appropriate for specific procurement requirements and business development objectives.

Price reasonableness determination requires agencies to ensure that sole source contract prices are fair and reasonable compared to market rates and historical pricing. Price analysis protects government interests while ensuring that sole source awards provide value for taxpayer funds.

Performance requirements ensure that 8(a) businesses receiving sole source awards meet contract specifications, delivery schedules, and quality standards. Performance requirements maintain accountability while providing businesses with opportunities to demonstrate their capabilities and build positive customer relationships.

Contract modification and option exercise authority provides flexibility for agencies and businesses to adjust contract terms, extend performance periods, or exercise contract options based on performance and changing requirements. Modification authority enables ongoing business relationships while accommodating evolving needs and circumstances.

The strategic value of sole source contracting includes rapid market entry for tribal businesses, establishment of customer relationships and performance track records, demonstration of business capabilities and reliability, and creation of platforms for future competitive opportunities and business growth.

Set-Aside Competition and Business Development

Section 8(a) set-aside competitions limit contract competition to 8(a) businesses, providing enhanced competitive opportunities while maintaining competitive market dynamics that encourage business excellence and capability development. Set-aside competitions enable tribal businesses to compete against similarly situated businesses rather than large established contractors, improving their prospects for contract awards while building competitive capabilities (Small Business Administration 2024).

Competition structure limits participation to qualified 8(a) businesses that meet specific eligibility and capability requirements for particular procurement opportunities. Limited competition improves tribal businesses' prospects for success while maintaining competitive pressure for performance excellence and competitive pricing.

Evaluation criteria for 8(a) set-aside competitions typically emphasize technical capability, past performance, and price competitiveness while accommodating the business development focus of the 8(a) program. Evaluation criteria balance government procurement objectives with business development goals to ensure that awards support both effective procurement and business development.

Proposal preparation support helps 8(a) businesses develop competitive proposals that meet government requirements while effectively presenting their capabilities and competitive advantages. Proposal support addresses common challenges facing small businesses in federal procurement while building internal capabilities for ongoing competitive success.

Teaming and partnership opportunities enable 8(a) businesses to collaborate with other businesses, including larger contractors, to compete for opportunities that might exceed their individual capabilities. Teaming provides access to larger opportunities while building business relationships and capabilities that support long-term business development.

Protest and dispute resolution procedures provide mechanisms for addressing procurement protests and contract disputes that may arise during competition or contract performance. Dispute resolution procedures protect business interests while maintaining the integrity of the procurement process and business development objectives.

Performance evaluation and feedback provide 8(a) businesses with information about their competitive performance, areas for improvement, and strategies for enhanced competitiveness in future opportunities. Performance feedback supports continuous improvement while building business capabilities for ongoing competitive success.

The strategic value of set-aside competition includes enhanced competitive opportunities for tribal businesses, development of competitive capabilities and market positioning, establishment of performance track records and customer relationships, and creation of pathways to larger opportunities and full and open competition.

Transitioning to Full and Open Competition
The 8(a) program's ultimate objective involves preparing participating businesses for successful competition in full and open federal markets, where they compete against businesses of all sizes and capabilities. Transition planning and preparation represent critical components of 8(a) program participation that ensure businesses develop sustainable competitive capabilities (Small Business Administration 2024).

Transition planning begins early in 8(a) program participation and involves systematic development of capabilities, market relationships, and competitive strategies that enable businesses to compete successfully after graduating from the program. Transition planning ensures that businesses maximize program benefits while building sustainable competitive advantages.

Capability development addresses technical capabilities, organizational capacity, financial strength, and market positioning that enable businesses to compete effectively against larger and more established competitors. Capability development often requires substantial investment in systems, personnel, and infrastructure that support competitive excellence.

Market diversification involves developing business relationships and opportunities beyond 8(a) program benefits, including commercial markets, state and local government markets, and full and open federal competitions. Market diversification reduces dependence on 8(a) benefits while building sustainable revenue sources and competitive positioning.

Customer relationship development focuses on building long-term relationships with federal customers that continue beyond 8(a) program participation. Strong customer relationships often provide ongoing contracting opportunities while supporting business development through referrals and recommendations.

Financial strengthening involves building financial resources, credit relationships, and capital access that enable businesses to compete for larger opportunities while managing the working capital requirements of major federal contracts. Financial strength represents a critical factor in competitive success and sustainable business development.

Alumni network participation provides graduated businesses with ongoing peer support, business development opportunities, and advocacy resources that support continued success in competitive markets. Alumni networks often provide valuable business relationships and market intelligence that support ongoing competitive success.

The strategic importance of transition planning includes development of sustainable competitive advantages, creation of long-term business viability, demonstration of program effectiveness in building competitive businesses, and contribution to broader tribal economic development through successful business development and growth.

HUBZone Contracting Advantages and Tribal Designations

HUBZone contracting advantages provide tribal businesses located in qualified areas with significant competitive benefits in federal procurement, including set-aside opportunities and price evaluation preferences that can substantially enhance their prospects for contract awards (SBA 2025; Federal Acquisition Regulation 2025). The automatic qualification of tribal lands as HUBZone areas makes this program broadly accessible to tribal businesses while providing meaningful competitive advantages (Small Business Administration 2024).

HUBZone Set-Aside Opportunities and Preferences

HUBZone set-aside contracting limits competition to qualified HUBZone businesses, providing enhanced opportunities for contract awards while maintaining competitive dynamics among qualified businesses. Set-aside opportunities can provide tribal businesses with access to substantial federal contracts while building competitive capabilities and customer relationships (Small Business Administration 2024).

Set-aside eligibility requires businesses to maintain HUBZone certification while meeting specific location and employment requirements that ensure program benefits flow to designated economically distressed areas. Eligibility requirements ensure program focus while accommodating business development and growth that may affect location and employment patterns.

Competitive advantages in set-aside competitions include enhanced prospects for contract awards while competing against similarly situated businesses rather than large established contractors. Set-aside competitions can provide tribal businesses with meaningful opportunities to establish federal market presence while building competitive capabilities.

Price evaluation preferences provide HUBZone businesses with competitive advantages in full and open competition by allowing contracting officers to add up to 10% to competing offers when evaluating HUBZone proposals. Price preferences can be decisive in competitive situations while encouraging federal agencies to consider the economic development benefits of contracting with HUBZone businesses.

Sole-source contracting authority enables federal agencies to award contracts directly to HUBZone businesses under certain circumstances, providing opportunities for tribal businesses to establish federal customer relationships while demonstrating capabilities for future competitive opportunities.

Subcontracting opportunities arise through prime contractors' efforts to meet HUBZone subcontracting goals, creating additional market access for tribal businesses. Subcontracting can provide entry points to federal markets while building capabilities and relationships for future prime contracting opportunities.

Contract bundling restrictions limit agencies' ability to combine multiple contracting requirements into large contracts that may exceed HUBZone businesses' capabilities. Bundling restrictions ensure that contracting opportunities remain accessible to smaller HUBZone businesses while maintaining agency flexibility for efficient procurement.

The strategic value of HUBZone contracting advantages includes enhanced market access and competitive positioning, establishment of federal customer relationships and performance track records, demonstration of business capabilities and reliability, and contribution to tribal economic development through increased business activity and employment creation.

Tribal Land Designations and Geographic Advantages

Tribal lands' automatic qualification as HUBZone areas provides tribal businesses with broad access to program benefits while recognizing the economic development challenges facing many tribal communities. Geographic advantages create opportunities for tribal businesses to leverage their locations for competitive advantage while contributing to local economic development (Small Business Administration 2024).

Automatic HUBZone qualification eliminates the need for tribal areas to meet specific economic distress criteria, recognizing the unique circumstances and challenges facing tribal communities while ensuring broad program accessibility across Indian Country. Automatic qualification simplifies certification processes while ensuring that tribal businesses can access program benefits regardless of specific economic conditions.

Principal office requirements specify that HUBZone businesses must maintain their primary business locations within HUBZone areas, ensuring that program benefits contribute to economic development in designated areas. Location requirements align with tribal business development while ensuring that program benefits serve intended geographic areas.

Employee residency requirements ensure that HUBZone businesses employ workers who reside in HUBZone areas, creating employment opportunities for local residents while ensuring that business development contributes to community economic development. Residency requirements often align with tribal employment preferences while supporting community development objectives.

Geographic service area advantages can provide tribal businesses with competitive positioning for contracts requiring services in or near tribal areas. Geographic proximity often represents a competitive advantage in service contracting while supporting tribal businesses' understanding of local conditions and requirements.

Cultural and linguistic advantages can provide tribal businesses with competitive positioning for contracts requiring cultural knowledge, language skills, or community relationships that may be particularly important for services provided to tribal communities or Native American populations.

Traditional knowledge and expertise can provide tribal businesses with competitive advantages for contracts requiring understanding of traditional practices, cultural protocols, or specialized knowledge that may be unique to tribal communities and Native American populations.

The strategic importance of tribal land designations includes broad program accessibility for tribal businesses, recognition of unique tribal circumstances and challenges, alignment of program benefits with tribal development priorities, and creation of competitive advantages based on geographic location and cultural expertise.

Performance and Compliance Monitoring

HUBZone program participation requires ongoing compliance with location, employment, and performance requirements that maintain program integrity while accommodating business development and growth. Performance and compliance monitoring ensure that program benefits serve intended purposes while supporting business development objectives (Small Business Administration 2024).

Location compliance monitoring ensures that businesses maintain principal offices in HUBZone areas while accommodating business expansion and development that may involve multiple locations. Monitoring procedures balance program requirements with business development flexibility while maintaining program focus on designated geographic areas.

Employment compliance tracking ensures that businesses maintain required percentages of employees residing in HUBZone areas while accommodating workforce development and expansion activities. Employment tracking supports program objectives while recognizing business needs for qualified personnel and operational flexibility.

Performance measurement addresses contract performance, customer satisfaction, and business development outcomes that demonstrate program effectiveness and business success. Performance measurement provides accountability while supporting continuous improvement efforts and program advocacy.

Financial performance monitoring tracks business revenue, employment, and growth indicators that demonstrate program impact on business development and community economic development. Financial monitoring provides information for program evaluation while supporting business development planning and strategic decision-making.

Certification maintenance requires periodic recertification that verifies ongoing compliance with program requirements while accommodating changes in business circumstances or area designations. Recertification maintains program integrity while providing flexibility for business development within program parameters.

Violation resolution procedures provide mechanisms for addressing compliance issues while supporting businesses' efforts to maintain program eligibility and benefits. Resolution procedures balance program integrity with business development support while ensuring that violations are addressed appropriately.

The strategic importance of performance and compliance monitoring includes maintenance of program integrity and effectiveness, demonstration of business capability and reliability, protection of program benefits and competitive advantages, and support for ongoing business development within program parameters.

Service-Disabled Veteran-Owned Small Business and Tribal Coordination

Service-Disabled Veteran-Owned Small Business (SDVOSB) programs provide federal contracting opportunities for businesses owned by service-disabled veterans, including Native American veterans who may face unique challenges in business development and market access. Coordination between SDVOSB programs and tribal economic development initiatives can create comprehensive approaches that support veteran entrepreneurship while contributing to tribal economic development (Department of Veterans Affairs 2024).

SDVOSB Certification and Program Benefits

SDVOSB certification provides businesses owned and controlled by service-disabled veterans with access to federal contracting set-asides and sole-source opportunities that can significantly enhance their market access and competitive positioning. For Native American veterans, SDVOSB certification can provide valuable business development opportunities while supporting broader tribal economic development objectives (Department of Veterans Affairs 2024).

Certification requirements specify that qualifying businesses must be at least 51% owned by one or more service-disabled veterans who control management and daily operations. Certification requirements accommodate various business structures while ensuring that program benefits flow to service-disabled veterans and support their business development objectives.

Ownership and control requirements ensure that service-disabled veterans have actual authority over business operations, strategic decisions, and day-to-day management activities. Control requirements address situations where veteran ownership might exist without meaningful business control, ensuring that program benefits serve their intended purposes.

Service-disabled veteran definition includes veterans with service-connected disabilities as determined by the Department of Veterans Affairs, ensuring that program benefits serve veterans whose military service resulted in disabilities that may affect their business development and employment opportunities.

Set-aside contracting opportunities limit competition to qualified SDVOSB businesses, providing enhanced prospects for contract awards while maintaining competitive dynamics among qualified businesses. Set-aside opportunities can provide Native American veteran-owned businesses with access to substantial federal contracts.

Sole-source contracting authority enables federal agencies to award contracts directly to qualified SDVOSB businesses under specific circumstances, providing opportunities to establish federal customer relationships while demonstrating capabilities for future competitive opportunities.

Subcontracting opportunities arise through prime contractors' efforts to meet SDVOSB subcontracting goals, creating additional market access for Native American veteran-owned businesses. Subcontracting can provide entry points to federal markets while building capabilities and relationships for future prime contracting opportunities.

The strategic value of SDVOSB certification includes enhanced market access and competitive positioning for Native American veteran entrepreneurs, recognition of veterans' service and sacrifice through business development support, and contribution to tribal economic development through veteran entrepreneurship and business development.

Native American Veteran Entrepreneurship Support
Native American veterans face unique challenges in business development that stem from both their veteran status and their cultural backgrounds, creating opportunities for specialized support programs that address these intersecting considerations while building on cultural strengths and community resources (National Center for American Indian Enterprise Development 2024).

Cultural integration opportunities enable Native American veteran entrepreneurs to develop businesses that reflect both their military experience and cultural heritage while serving both veteran and tribal community needs. Cultural integration can create unique market positioning while supporting cultural preservation and community development.

Community-based support systems can leverage tribal organizations, veteran service organizations, and economic development entities to create comprehensive support networks for Native American veteran entrepreneurs. Community support can address isolation and resource access challenges while building peer networks and mentoring relationships.

Traditional knowledge and skills integration can enable Native American veterans to develop businesses based on traditional knowledge, cultural practices, or specialized skills while combining these with military experience and training. Skills integration can create unique business opportunities while supporting cultural preservation and economic development.

Military skills transfer programs can help Native American veterans identify business opportunities that leverage their military training, experience, and networks while addressing tribal community needs and market opportunities. Skills transfer can create pathways for veteran entrepreneurship while contributing to tribal economic development.

Access to capital assistance can address financing challenges facing Native American veteran entrepreneurs while coordinating veteran-specific financing programs with tribal economic development resources and CDFI programs. Capital access coordination can create comprehensive financing solutions while building veteran business development capacity.

Market development support can help Native American veteran entrepreneurs identify market opportunities, develop customer relationships, and build competitive positioning strategies that leverage both their veteran status and cultural knowledge. Market development can enhance business competitiveness while supporting sustainable business growth.

The strategic importance of Native American veteran entrepreneurship support includes recognition of veterans' service through business development opportunities, leverage of veteran skills and experience for tribal economic development, creation of role models and leadership examples within tribal communities, and demonstration of successful coordination between veteran and tribal support systems.

Coordination with Tribal Economic Development

SDVOSB programs can be effectively coordinated with tribal economic development initiatives to create comprehensive approaches that support veteran entrepreneurship while contributing to broader tribal economic development objectives. Coordination can enhance both veteran business development and tribal economic development outcomes while building sustainable support systems (White House Office of Intergovernmental Affairs 2024).

Program coordination can align SDVOSB business development support with tribal economic development programs, business incubators, and workforce development initiatives to create comprehensive approaches that address both veteran entrepreneurship and broader tribal economic development needs.

Resource coordination can combine veteran-specific resources with tribal economic development resources to create comprehensive support systems that address financing, technical assistance, market development, and business development needs of Native American veteran entrepreneurs.

Mentoring and networking coordination can connect Native American veteran entrepreneurs with both veteran business leaders and tribal business leaders to create comprehensive mentoring and support networks that address both veteran and cultural considerations in business development.

Market development coordination can align veteran business development with tribal economic development marketing, tourism development, and cultural preservation initiatives to create business opportunities that serve both veteran entrepreneurship and tribal community development objectives.

Training and education coordination can integrate veteran business development training with tribal business development programs, educational institutions, and workforce development initiatives to create comprehensive learning opportunities that address both veteran and tribal considerations.

Policy coordination can align veteran business development policies with tribal economic development policies to ensure that programs complement rather than conflict with each other while maximizing opportunities for coordinated support and resource leveraging.

The strategic importance of coordination includes enhanced resource efficiency and effectiveness, creation of comprehensive support systems for Native American veteran entrepreneurs, demonstration of successful intergovernmental cooperation, and development of models for coordination that can be replicated in other contexts and communities.

Integration opportunities exist between SDVOSB programs and other federal programs serving tribal communities, creating potential for comprehensive approaches that address veteran entrepreneurship within broader tribal economic development strategies while leveraging multiple federal resources and support systems.

Women-Owned Small Business and Native American Participation

Women-Owned Small Business (WOSB) federal contracting programs provide market access opportunities for businesses owned and controlled by women, including Native American women who may face unique challenges in accessing business development resources and market opportunities. The intersection of gender and cultural considerations creates both challenges and opportunities for Native American women entrepreneurs in federal contracting (Small Business Administration 2024).

WOSB Certification and Federal Contracting Opportunities

WOSB certification provides businesses owned and controlled by women with access to federal contracting set-asides in specific industries where women-owned businesses are underrepresented. For Native American women entrepreneurs, WOSB certification can provide valuable market access opportunities while addressing persistent barriers to women's participation in federal contracting (Small Business Administration 2024).

Certification requirements specify that qualifying businesses must be at least 51% owned by one or more women who control management and daily operations. Certification requirements accommodate various business structures while ensuring that program benefits flow to women entrepreneurs and support their business development objectives.

Economically disadvantaged women-owned small business (EDWOSB) certification provides additional opportunities for women entrepreneurs who meet specific economic disadvantage criteria. EDWOSB certification can provide Native American women with enhanced access to federal contracting opportunities while addressing economic barriers that may limit business development.

Industry eligibility for WOSB set-asides includes specific NAICS codes where women-owned businesses are underrepresented in federal contracting. Industry eligibility ensures that set-aside opportunities target sectors where women face particular challenges while providing meaningful market access opportunities.

Set-aside contracting opportunities limit competition to qualified WOSB or EDWOSB businesses in eligible industries, providing enhanced prospects for contract awards while maintaining competitive dynamics among qualified businesses. Set-aside opportunities can provide Native American women-owned businesses with access to substantial federal contracts.

Sole-source contracting authority enables federal agencies to award contracts directly to qualified WOSB businesses under specific circumstances, providing opportunities to establish federal customer relationships while demonstrating capabilities for future competitive opportunities.

Market research and opportunity identification help women entrepreneurs understand federal contracting opportunities while developing strategies for competitive positioning and market access. Market research can be particularly important for Native American women who may lack access to established business networks and market intelligence.

The strategic value of WOSB certification includes enhanced market access for Native American women entrepreneurs, recognition of gender-based barriers in federal contracting, creation of pathways for women's economic empowerment, and contribution to tribal economic development through women's entrepreneurship and business development.

Addressing Barriers to Native American Women's Business Development

Native American women entrepreneurs face intersecting barriers related to both gender and cultural considerations that can limit their access to business development resources, market opportunities, and capital sources. Addressing these barriers requires comprehensive approaches that recognize unique circumstances while building on cultural strengths and community resources (National Women's Business Council 2024).

Access to capital challenges often affect Native American women disproportionately due to limited credit histories, collateral availability, and access to mainstream financial institutions. Capital access barriers require coordinated approaches that combine women-specific financing programs with tribal economic development resources and CDFI programs.

Geographic isolation and limited infrastructure can constrain Native American women's access to business development resources, markets, and customers. Geographic barriers require innovative approaches to service delivery, market access, and business development support that accommodate remote locations and limited transportation options.

Cultural considerations may affect Native American women's approaches to business development, including preferences for collective decision-making, community benefit orientation, and integration of traditional knowledge and practices. Cultural considerations require business development approaches that respect traditional values while building competitive business capabilities.

Family and community responsibilities often create unique challenges for Native American women entrepreneurs who may balance business development with family care, community service, and cultural responsibilities. Balancing responsibilities requires flexible business development approaches that accommodate diverse priorities and obligations.

Limited access to business networks and mentoring relationships can constrain Native American women's business development opportunities and market access. Network limitations require targeted efforts to build professional relationships, mentoring opportunities, and peer support systems that address both gender and cultural considerations.

Educational and training barriers may limit Native American women's access to business development knowledge, specialized expertise, and professional development opportunities. Educational barriers require comprehensive approaches that combine formal education, practical training, and culturally appropriate learning opportunities.

The strategic importance of addressing barriers includes enhanced participation of Native American women in economic development, creation of inclusive business development environments, recognition of intersecting challenges and opportunities, and development of models for comprehensive support that can benefit other underrepresented groups.

Building Support Systems for Native American Women Entrepreneurs
Effective support systems for Native American women entrepreneurs require coordination among multiple organizations and resources to create comprehensive approaches that address both gender-specific and culturally specific needs while building sustainable business development capacity (National Women's Business Council 2024).

Mentoring and networking programs can connect Native American women entrepreneurs with experienced business leaders, successful women entrepreneurs, and tribal business leaders to create comprehensive support networks that address both business development and cultural considerations. Mentoring relationships can provide ongoing guidance while building professional networks and business relationships.

Business incubation and support services can provide Native American women entrepreneurs with access to shared facilities, business development services, and peer support networks that address common challenges while building business capabilities. Incubation services can be particularly valuable for women entrepreneurs who may lack access to traditional business support infrastructure.

Financial literacy and business education programs can address knowledge gaps while building business development capabilities that enhance Native American women's competitiveness in federal contracting and commercial markets. Education programs should accommodate diverse learning styles and cultural preferences while providing practical business development skills.

Access to capital coordination can combine women-specific financing programs with tribal economic development resources, CDFI programs, and other financing sources to create comprehensive capital access solutions. Financing coordination can address both immediate capital needs and longer-term business development financing requirements.

Child care and family support services can address practical barriers that may limit Native American women's participation in business development activities while accommodating family responsibilities and community obligations. Support services can enable greater participation while respecting cultural values and family priorities.

Technology and infrastructure support can help Native American women entrepreneurs overcome geographic barriers while accessing markets, resources, and business development opportunities through telecommunications, e-commerce, and digital marketing technologies.

The strategic value of comprehensive support systems includes enhanced business development success rates for Native American women entrepreneurs, creation of sustainable support infrastructure, demonstration of effective coordination among multiple organizations and resources, and development of models that can support other underrepresented entrepreneurs.

Subcontracting and Joint Venture Opportunities

Subcontracting and joint venture opportunities provide tribal business-es with pathways to participate in larger federal contracts while building capabilities, relationships, and experience that support long-term busi-ness development. These arrangements can provide access to substantial business opportunities while enabling capability development and market positioning that supports future prime contracting success (Federal Ac-quisition Regulation 2024).

Subcontracting Programs and Requirements

Federal subcontracting programs create opportunities for tribal busi-nesses to participate in major federal contracts as subcontractors to large prime contractors. Subcontracting requirements and incentives encour-age prime contractors to include small and disadvantaged businesses in contract performance while providing tribal businesses with access to substantial business opportunities (Small Business Administration 2024).

Small business subcontracting plans require large prime contractors to establish goals for subcontracting with small businesses, including var-ious socioeconomic categories such as small disadvantaged businesses, women-owned small businesses, veteran-owned small businesses, and HUBZone businesses. Subcontracting plans create opportunities for trib-al businesses while establishing accountability for prime contractor inclu-sion efforts.

Subcontracting goal achievement provides prime contractors with in-centives to meet or exceed subcontracting goals while creating business opportunities for tribal businesses. Goal achievement is evaluated as part of contractor performance assessment and can influence future contract-ing opportunities for prime contractors.

Good faith effort requirements ensure that prime contractors make meaningful attempts to identify and engage qualified small businesses for subcontracting opportunities. Good faith effort standards provide protec-tion for small businesses while maintaining flexibility for prime contrac-tors in subcontractor selection and management.

Subcontractor payment protection ensures that prime contractors pay subcontractors promptly and in accordance with contract terms. Payment protection addresses cash flow challenges that can significantly affect small business performance while maintaining accountability for prime contractor payment obligations.

Mentor-protégé relationships can provide tribal businesses with access to subcontracting opportunities while receiving guidance, technical assistance, and capability development support from experienced contractors. Mentor-protégé arrangements can create pathways for business development while building long-term business relationships.

Subcontractor performance evaluation provides tribal businesses with feedback about their performance while building track records that support future subcontracting and prime contracting opportunities. Performance evaluation creates accountability while supporting continuous improvement and business development.

The strategic value of subcontracting opportunities includes access to substantial business opportunities that might otherwise be unavailable, development of capabilities and experience that support future prime contracting, establishment of relationships with large contractors and federal customers, and demonstration of performance that enhances business credibility and market positioning.

Joint Venture Development and Management

Joint ventures enable tribal businesses to partner with other businesses to compete for federal contracts that might exceed their individual capabilities while sharing risks, resources, and expertise. Joint venture arrangements can provide access to larger opportunities while enabling capability development and market expansion (Small Business Administration 2024).

Joint venture structures can include various partnership arrangements that accommodate different business objectives, capability contributions, and risk-sharing preferences. Structure selection should consider business development objectives, regulatory requirements, and long-term strategic planning while ensuring that arrangements serve all partners' interests effectively.

Capability complementarity enables joint venture partners to combine different strengths and expertise to create comprehensive solutions for federal contracting opportunities. Complementarity can include technical capabilities, geographic presence, past performance, financial resources, and specialized expertise that enhance competitive positioning.

Risk and responsibility sharing arrangements define how joint venture partners allocate contract performance responsibilities, financial obligations, and business risks. Sharing arrangements should ensure that responsibilities align with capabilities while providing appropriate incentives for performance excellence and partnership success.

Revenue and profit sharing agreements specify how joint venture partners distribute contract revenues and profits based on their contributions, responsibilities, and risk assumptions. Sharing agreements should provide fair compensation while maintaining incentives for partnership cooperation and performance excellence.

Performance management systems ensure that joint venture partners coordinate effectively while maintaining accountability for contract performance and customer satisfaction. Management systems should address communication, decision-making, quality control, and conflict resolution while supporting partnership effectiveness.

Small business status maintenance requires careful attention to joint venture structure and operations to ensure that arrangements do not compromise partners' small business status or eligibility for socioeconomic programs. Status maintenance is essential for accessing small business contracting opportunities while participating in joint ventures.

The strategic importance of joint venture development includes access to larger contracting opportunities, development of capabilities and expertise through partnership collaboration, establishment of business relationships that support future opportunities, and demonstration of ability to manage complex business arrangements successfully.

Building Long-Term Business Relationships
Successful subcontracting and joint venture participation requires attention to relationship building and management that extends beyond individual contract performance to create ongoing business partnerships and market access opportunities. Long-term relationship development can provide sustained business opportunities while building market positioning and competitive capabilities (Harvard Project on American Indian Economic Development 2024).

Trust and reliability development through consistent performance, communication, and partnership cooperation creates foundations for ongoing business relationships that can provide sustained contracting opportunities. Trust building requires attention to both contract performance and partnership management while demonstrating commitment to long-term business success.

Mutual benefit creation ensures that subcontracting and joint venture arrangements provide value for all participants while supporting continued partnership cooperation and development. Mutual benefit requires attention to both immediate contract objectives and longer-term business development goals for all partners.

Performance excellence demonstration through superior contract performance, customer satisfaction, and partnership cooperation enhances tribal businesses' reputations while building market positioning that supports future business opportunities. Excellence demonstration creates competitive advantages while building customer and partner confidence.

Capability development through subcontracting and joint venture participation builds tribal businesses' expertise, resources, and market positioning while preparing them for future prime contracting and partnership opportunities. Capability development creates sustainable competitive advantages while supporting business growth and diversification.

Market expansion through partnership relationships can provide tribal businesses with access to new customers, geographic markets, and business sectors while building market knowledge and competitive positioning. Market expansion creates growth opportunities while reducing dependence on limited market segments.

Networking and relationship management maintain ongoing connections with partners, customers, and industry professionals while building professional networks that support future business development and market access. Networking creates social capital that supports ongoing business success while providing access to market intelligence and opportunities.

The strategic importance of long-term relationship building includes creation of sustainable business partnerships, development of market positioning and competitive advantages, establishment of ongoing business opportunities and revenue sources, and creation of foundations for continued business growth and development within federal and commercial markets.

Agency-Specific Tribal Contracting Programs

Various federal agencies have developed specialized contracting programs specifically designed to support tribal business development and address unique procurement needs related to Indian programs and services. These agency-specific programs create additional market opportunities while recognizing the specialized expertise and cultural knowledge that tribal businesses can provide (Government Accountability Office 2024).

Bureau of Indian Affairs Contracting Opportunities

The Bureau of Indian Affairs (BIA) provides substantial contracting opportunities for tribal businesses through both direct procurement activities and self-determination contracting that enables tribal governments and tribal organizations to assume responsibility for federal programs and services. BIA contracting creates significant market opportunities while supporting tribal self-determination and governance capacity development (Bureau of Indian Affairs 2024).

Self-determination contracting under the Indian Self-Determination and Education Assistance Act enables tribal governments and tribal organizations to assume responsibility for federal programs and services traditionally provided by federal agencies. Self-determination contracting can provide substantial revenue sources while building tribal institutional capacity and governance capabilities.

Direct service contracting includes procurement of goods and services needed for BIA operations, program implementation, and service delivery to tribal communities. Direct service contracting creates business opportunities while enabling tribal businesses to contribute directly to federal program effectiveness and community service delivery.

Construction and infrastructure contracting includes substantial opportunities for tribal businesses to participate in federal construction projects, infrastructure development, and facility maintenance activities on tribal lands and in tribal communities. Construction contracting can provide significant business opportunities while contributing to tribal community development.

Professional services contracting includes opportunities for tribal businesses to provide specialized services such as consulting, technical assistance, planning, and program evaluation services that support BIA program implementation and tribal capacity development. Professional services contracting can leverage tribal expertise while building business capabilities.

Natural resource management contracting includes opportunities for tribal businesses to provide services related to natural resource conservation, environmental protection, and resource development activities on tribal lands. Natural resource contracting can align with tribal environmental stewardship priorities while creating business opportunities.

Cultural and educational services contracting includes opportunities for tribal businesses to provide services related to cultural preservation, language revitalization, and educational program delivery that serve tribal communities. Cultural services contracting can support tribal cultural priorities while creating business opportunities that align with community values.

The strategic value of BIA contracting opportunities includes substantial market access for tribal businesses, alignment of business opportunities with tribal community development needs, support for tribal self-determination through contract assumption, and creation of business opportunities that leverage tribal expertise and cultural knowledge.

Indian Health Service Business Opportunities
The Indian Health Service (IHS) provides significant contracting opportunities for tribal businesses through healthcare service delivery, medical equipment and supplies procurement, and health facility construction and maintenance activities. IHS contracting creates business opportunities while supporting tribal health and community development objectives (Indian Health Service 2024).

Healthcare service delivery contracting includes opportunities for tribal businesses to provide direct healthcare services, support services, and specialized medical services that serve tribal communities. Healthcare contracting can address critical service needs while creating business opportunities that directly benefit tribal communities.

Medical equipment and supplies procurement includes substantial opportunities for tribal businesses to provide medical equipment, pharmaceuticals, medical supplies, and healthcare technology needed for IHS operations and tribal health programs. Medical procurement can create significant business opportunities while supporting tribal health system development.

Health facility construction and maintenance includes opportunities for tribal businesses to participate in hospital construction, clinic development, and facility maintenance activities that serve tribal communities. Construction contracting can provide substantial business opportunities while contributing to tribal healthcare infrastructure development.

Health information technology contracting includes opportunities for tribal businesses to provide technology services, system development, and technical support that enhance IHS operations and tribal health programs. Technology contracting can leverage specialized expertise while building business capabilities in growing markets.

Public health and prevention services contracting includes opportunities for tribal businesses to provide public health services, health education, disease prevention, and community health programs that serve tribal populations. Public health contracting can align with tribal community health priorities while creating service-oriented business opportunities.

Traditional and complementary medicine integration creates opportunities for tribal businesses to provide traditional healing services, cultural health programs, and complementary medicine approaches that serve tribal communities while preserving traditional knowledge and practices.

The strategic importance of IHS contracting opportunities includes creation of business opportunities that directly serve tribal health needs, development of tribal expertise in healthcare services and technology, support for tribal health system development and capacity building, and integration of traditional knowledge with contemporary healthcare delivery.

Environmental Protection Agency Tribal Programs
The Environmental Protection Agency (EPA) provides contracting opportunities for tribal businesses through environmental assessment, remediation, monitoring, and protection activities that serve tribal communities and support tribal environmental sovereignty. EPA contracting creates business opportunities while supporting tribal environmental stewardship and protection priorities (Environmental Protection Agency 2024).

Environmental assessment and monitoring contracting includes opportunities for tribal businesses to provide environmental sampling, monitoring, analysis, and assessment services that support EPA programs and tribal environmental protection activities. Assessment contracting can leverage tribal knowledge while building technical capabilities.

Environmental remediation contracting includes opportunities for tribal businesses to participate in contaminated site cleanup, restoration, and remediation activities on tribal lands. Remediation contracting can provide substantial business opportunities while addressing environmental protection needs in tribal communities.

Air and water quality monitoring includes opportunities for tribal businesses to provide specialized monitoring services, equipment installation and maintenance, and data collection activities that support environmental protection programs. Monitoring contracting can create ongoing business opportunities while supporting environmental stewardship.

Environmental compliance and regulation support includes opportunities for tribal businesses to provide consulting, technical assistance, and compliance monitoring services that help tribal governments and businesses meet environmental regulatory requirements. Compliance contracting can leverage tribal expertise while building specialized business capabilities.

Climate change and sustainability program support includes opportunities for tribal businesses to provide services related to climate adaptation, renewable energy development, and sustainability planning that support tribal environmental and economic development objectives. Sustainability contracting can align with tribal values while creating business opportunities in emerging markets.

Traditional ecological knowledge integration creates opportunities for tribal businesses to provide services that combine traditional environmental knowledge with contemporary environmental science and management approaches. Knowledge integration can preserve traditional practices while creating unique business positioning.

The strategic importance of EPA contracting opportunities includes creation of business opportunities that support tribal environmental protection priorities, development of tribal expertise in environmental services and technology, support for tribal environmental sovereignty and stewardship, and integration of traditional knowledge with contemporary environmental protection approaches.

Bonding and Financial Support for Tribal Contractors

Bonding and financial support represent critical components of successful federal contracting participation, particularly for tribal businesses that may face unique challenges in accessing conventional bonding and financing sources. Understanding bonding requirements and accessing appropriate financial support can significantly enhance tribal businesses' competitiveness and success in federal contracting (Small Business Administration 2024).

Surety Bond Requirements and SBA Support

Federal contracts typically require various types of surety bonds that guarantee contractor performance, payment obligations, and compliance with contract terms. SBA provides surety bond guarantee programs that help small businesses, including tribal businesses, access bonding that might otherwise be unavailable or unaffordable (Small Business Administration 2024).

Performance bonds guarantee that contractors will complete contract work in accordance with specifications, schedules, and quality requirements. Performance bonds protect government customers while providing assurance that contracts will be completed successfully. For tribal businesses, performance bonding can represent both a requirement and an opportunity to demonstrate reliability and capability.

Payment bonds guarantee that contractors will pay subcontractors, suppliers, and workers in accordance with contract terms and applicable laws. Payment bonds protect subcontractors and suppliers while ensuring that contract performance does not create financial liability for government customers. Payment bonding can be particularly important for tribal businesses that rely on subcontractor relationships.

Bid bonds guarantee that winning bidders will accept contract awards and provide required performance and payment bonds. Bid bonds protect government customers from bidder default while ensuring that competitive processes result in viable contract awards. Bid bonding enables tribal businesses to participate in competitive bidding while demonstrating financial capability.

SBA bond guarantee programs provide guarantees to surety companies that issue bonds to qualified small businesses, reducing surety risk and improving access to bonding for businesses that might not otherwise qualify. SBA guarantees can make bonding available to tribal businesses while providing competitive bonding rates and terms.

Quick-pay program enables SBA to reimburse sureties quickly when bond claims occur, improving surety willingness to bond small businesses while reducing processing delays that can affect business operations. Quick-pay provisions can enhance tribal businesses' access to bonding while providing efficient claim resolution.

Bond amount limits under SBA programs currently reach $6.5 million per contract, with higher limits available for qualified businesses and specific circumstances. Substantial bond limits enable tribal businesses to compete for major federal contracts while providing flexibility for business growth and diversification.

The strategic value of SBA bonding support includes enhanced access to federal contracting opportunities, improved competitive positioning through bonding capability, demonstration of financial reliability and business capability, and development of relationships with surety companies that support ongoing business development.

Working Capital and Cash Flow Management

Federal contracting often involves significant working capital requirements due to contract performance timing, payment cycles, and cash flow patterns that can strain business finances. Effective working capital and cash flow management represent critical capabilities for successful federal contracting participation (Small Business Administration 2024).

Contract financing needs typically include costs for labor, materials, equipment, and overhead expenses that must be incurred before contract payments are received. Working capital requirements can be substantial for large contracts while representing ongoing challenges for business financial management and cash flow planning.

Progress payment structures enable contractors to receive partial payments as work progresses, reducing working capital requirements while providing cash flow support during contract performance. Progress payments can be particularly important for tribal businesses with limited working capital resources or credit access.

Invoice and payment processing can involve significant delays between work completion and payment receipt, requiring businesses to manage cash flow gaps while maintaining operations and meeting obligations. Payment timing affects working capital requirements while influencing business financial planning and management strategies.

Line of credit and working capital loans provide businesses with access to financing that can bridge cash flow gaps while supporting contract performance and business operations. Working capital financing can be essential for businesses pursuing large contracts or managing multiple contract performance requirements simultaneously.

Invoice factoring and receivables financing enable businesses to convert contract receivables into immediate cash flow, reducing working capital requirements while providing financing based on contract performance rather than traditional credit criteria. Receivables financing can be particularly valuable for businesses with limited credit access or collateral availability.

Cash flow forecasting and management systems help businesses plan for working capital requirements while managing payment timing and operational cash needs. Effective cash flow management can prevent financial difficulties while supporting successful contract performance and business operations.

The strategic importance of working capital management includes successful contract performance and completion, maintenance of business operations and financial stability, demonstration of financial management capability and business reliability, and creation of capacity for pursuing larger and more complex contracting opportunities.

Building Financial Relationships and Credit History

Successful federal contracting participation often requires development of strong financial relationships and credit history that support bonding access, working capital financing, and business growth opportunities. Building financial relationships represents a strategic investment in long-term business competitiveness and market access (Small Business Administration 2024).

Banking relationship development involves establishing relationships with financial institutions that understand federal contracting requirements and can provide appropriate financing products and services.

Banking relationships provide access to working capital, equipment financing, and other financial services while building credit history and financial credibility.

Credit history establishment requires careful management of business finances, debt obligations, and payment patterns that demonstrate financial reliability and creditworthiness. Strong credit history enhances access to financing while improving borrowing terms and conditions for business development activities.

Financial reporting and record-keeping systems provide documentation of business financial performance, cash flow patterns, and management capabilities that support financing applications and credit evaluations. Strong financial reporting demonstrates business professionalism while providing information necessary for financing and bonding decisions.

Surety company relationships involve building ongoing relationships with bonding companies that understand tribal business circumstances and can provide competitive bonding rates and terms. Surety relationships require demonstration of business capability and financial strength while providing access to bonding for contract opportunities.

Professional advisory relationships include relationships with accountants, attorneys, and financial advisors who can provide guidance on financial management, tax planning, and business development strategies. Professional relationships provide expertise while supporting business development and financial management decisions.

Industry network development creates relationships with other contractors, suppliers, and customers that can provide business opportunities, references, and market intelligence. Industry networks provide social capital while supporting business development and market access activities.

The strategic importance of financial relationship building includes enhanced access to financing and bonding resources, improved competitive positioning through financial capability demonstration, development of business support networks and advisory resources, and creation of foundations for sustained business growth and market expansion.

Protest and Dispute Resolution Procedures

Federal contracting includes comprehensive procedures for addressing procurement protests, contract disputes, and performance disagreements that may arise during the contracting process or contract performance. Understanding protest and dispute resolution procedures enables tribal businesses to protect their interests while maintaining positive relationships with customers and partners (Federal Acquisition Regulation 2024).

Procurement Protest Procedures and Rights
Procurement protest procedures provide mechanisms for addressing alleged violations of procurement laws, regulations, or procedures that may affect contract award decisions. Protest procedures protect businesses' rights while ensuring that federal procurement is conducted fairly and in accordance with applicable requirements (Government Accountability Office 2024).

Protest grounds include various alleged violations such as solicitation defects, evaluation errors, improper award decisions, or procedural violations that may have affected procurement outcomes. Valid protest grounds require demonstration of prejudice resulting from alleged violations while providing bases for corrective action or award reconsideration.

Protest timing requirements specify deadlines for filing protests based on when protestors knew or should have known about the bases for their protests. Timing requirements ensure that protests are filed promptly while protecting procurement schedules and awarded contractors' interests. Missing protest deadlines typically precludes protest consideration.

Protest venues include agency-level protests filed with contracting agencies, Government Accountability Office (GAO) protests, and Court of Federal Claims protests, each with different procedures, standards, and remedies. Venue selection affects protest procedures and potential outcomes while requiring strategic consideration of protest objectives and circumstances.

Protest procedures include detailed requirements for protest filing, agency or GAO consideration, response procedures, and decision timelines that govern protest processing and resolution. Understanding procedures is essential for effective protest participation while ensuring that protest rights are preserved and exercised appropriately.

Automatic stay provisions typically suspend contract performance when protests are filed before contract performance begins, protecting protestors' interests while preventing irreparable harm during protest consideration. Stay provisions balance protest rights with procurement efficiency while protecting all parties' interests.

Protest remedies can include corrective action by procuring agencies, recommendation for award reconsideration, or other relief that addresses proven violations while protecting protestors' interests. Remedies depend on protest circumstances while providing mechanisms for addressing procurement violations and protecting competition.

The strategic value of understanding protest procedures includes protection of business interests in federal procurement, ensuring fair competition and proper procurement procedures, development of knowledge about procurement requirements and standards, and demonstration of business sophistication and commitment to proper procurement practices.

Contract Dispute Resolution and Claims Procedures

Contract dispute resolution procedures provide mechanisms for addressing disagreements about contract performance, payment, modifications, or termination that may arise during contract performance. Effective dispute resolution protects business interests while maintaining customer relationships and contract performance (Federal Acquisition Regulation 2024).

Claims procedures enable contractors to seek additional compensation, time extensions, or other relief for contract performance issues that may result from government actions, changed conditions, or other circumstances beyond contractors' control. Claims procedures provide formal mechanisms for addressing performance issues while protecting contractors' financial interests.

Certification requirements for claims over specific dollar thresholds require contractors to certify that claims are made in good faith and are supported by credible evidence. Certification requirements ensure claims integrity while protecting against frivolous or fraudulent claims that could abuse the process.

Contracting officer decisions represent initial administrative decisions on contractor claims, providing formal government responses that either grant or deny relief sought by contractors. Contracting officer decisions establish formal positions while providing bases for further dispute resolution if disagreements persist.

Appeals procedures enable contractors to challenge adverse contracting officer decisions through agency boards of contract appeals or the Court of Federal Claims, providing independent review of claim decisions. Appeals procedures ensure due process while providing mechanisms for resolving disputes that cannot be resolved through direct negotiation.

Alternative dispute resolution mechanisms include mediation, arbitration, and other procedures that can provide faster and less expensive dispute resolution compared to formal appeals processes. Alternative procedures can preserve business relationships while achieving mutually acceptable resolutions.

Dispute timing and deadlines specify requirements for filing claims, appealing decisions, and pursuing dispute resolution within established timeframes. Timing requirements ensure prompt dispute resolution while protecting all parties' interests in efficient contract performance and administration.

The strategic importance of understanding dispute resolution includes protection of contractor rights and financial interests, maintenance of positive customer relationships through professional dispute handling, demonstration of business sophistication and contract management capability, and development of expertise in contract administration and performance management.

Maintaining Positive Relationships During Disputes

Successful dispute resolution requires attention to relationship management and professional conduct that protects business interests while maintaining long-term customer relationships and market positioning. Effective relationship management during disputes can preserve business opportunities while achieving fair resolutions (Harvard Project on American Indian Economic Development 2024).

Professional communication maintains respectful and constructive dialogue with customers and dispute resolution authorities while advocating effectively for business interests. Professional communication demonstrates business maturity while supporting productive dispute resolution processes.

Good faith negotiation involves genuine efforts to understand different perspectives and find mutually acceptable solutions before resorting to formal dispute resolution procedures. Good faith efforts often resolve disputes more efficiently while preserving business relationships and avoiding formal proceedings.

Documentation and record-keeping provide evidence necessary for supporting claims and dispute positions while demonstrating professional contract management and performance. Strong documentation protects business interests while providing credible evidence for dispute resolution processes.

Performance continuation during disputes demonstrates contractor commitment to contract performance and customer service while maintaining positive relationships despite disagreements. Continued performance often supports dispute resolution while demonstrating contractor reliability and professionalism.

Legal and professional representation ensures that contractors receive appropriate guidance and advocacy during dispute resolution while avoiding procedural errors that could prejudice their interests. Professional representation provides expertise while supporting effective dispute resolution.

Reputation management during disputes involves maintaining professional conduct and communication that preserves business reputation and market positioning despite disagreements with customers. Reputation management protects long-term business interests while supporting continued market access and customer relationships.

The strategic importance of relationship management during disputes includes preservation of customer relationships and future business opportunities, demonstration of business professionalism and maturity, maintenance of positive market reputation and competitive positioning, and development of dispute resolution expertise that supports ongoing contract management and business operations.

Strategic Implementation and Coordination

Successful utilization of federal contracting opportunities requires strategic planning that integrates contracting activities with broader tribal business development and economic development objectives while building organizational capacity for sustained contracting success. The complexity and competitiveness of federal contracting create opportunities for significant business development while requiring sophisticated business capabilities and strategic management (Harvard Project on American Indian Economic Development 2024).

Comprehensive Contracting Strategy Development

Federal contracting strategies work most effectively when integrated into comprehensive business development plans that consider market opportunities, capability development, competitive positioning, and organizational capacity building within the context of broader tribal economic development objectives. Strategic planning enables tribal businesses to maximize contracting opportunities while building sustainable competitive advantages (National Center for American Indian Enterprise Development 2024).

Market analysis and opportunity identification should assess federal procurement trends, agency spending patterns, competitive landscapes, and emerging opportunities that align with tribal business capabilities and development objectives. Market analysis provides foundations for strategic planning while identifying opportunities that offer the best prospects for business development and growth.

Capability assessment and development planning should evaluate current business capabilities, identify capability gaps, and develop strategies for building expertise, resources, and competitive advantages that support contracting success. Capability development often requires substantial investment in personnel, systems, and infrastructure that build long-term competitive positioning.

Competitive positioning strategies should consider how tribal businesses can differentiate themselves from competitors while leveraging unique advantages such as cultural knowledge, geographic location, specialized expertise, or community relationships. Competitive positioning creates sustainable advantages while supporting business development and market access.

Certification and program participation strategies should evaluate various federal contracting programs and certification opportunities to determine which provide the best alignment with business capabilities and development objectives. Program participation requires strategic consideration of eligibility requirements, benefits, and obligations associated with different opportunities.

Growth and diversification planning should consider how federal contracting success can support broader business development objectives including commercial market development, service expansion, geographic growth, and capacity building that creates sustainable business development beyond government contracting.

Risk management and business sustainability planning should address the risks associated with government contracting dependence while developing strategies for business diversification, market expansion, and capability development that create sustainable competitive advantages and business viability.

The strategic value of comprehensive contracting strategy development includes maximization of contracting opportunities and success rates, development of sustainable competitive advantages and business capabilities, integration of contracting activities with broader business development objectives, and creation of frameworks for ongoing strategic planning and business development.

Building Tribal Contracting Capacity and Expertise
Successful federal contracting requires sophisticated business capabilities that many tribal businesses may need to develop through systematic capacity building and expertise development initiatives. Building contracting capacity represents a strategic investment in long-term business competitiveness and tribal economic development (National Center for American Indian Enterprise Development 2024).

Technical and professional expertise development should address specialized knowledge and skills required for successful contract performance, including technical capabilities, project management, quality control, and customer relationship management. Expertise development often requires substantial investment in training, recruitment, and systems that build organizational capabilities.

Business development and marketing capabilities should address proposal development, customer relationship management, market intelligence, and business development activities that support contracting success. Business development capabilities enable businesses to identify opportunities, develop competitive proposals, and build customer relationships that support sustained contracting success.

Financial management and administrative systems should address accounting, cost control, compliance monitoring, and administrative capabilities required for successful contract performance and business management. Strong financial and administrative systems provide foundations for business success while ensuring compliance with complex federal requirements.

Quality control and performance management systems should address project management, performance monitoring, quality assurance, and customer satisfaction activities that ensure successful contract performance and customer relationships. Performance management capabilities distinguish successful contractors while building reputations that support ongoing business development.

Legal and regulatory compliance expertise should address contract law, federal regulations, employment law, and other legal requirements that affect federal contracting. Compliance expertise protects business interests while ensuring successful contract performance and avoiding legal issues that could affect business operations.

Organizational development and infrastructure should address systems, procedures, and organizational structures that support effective business operations and contract performance. Organizational development creates foundations for business growth while building capacity for managing larger and more complex contracting opportunities.

The strategic importance of capacity building includes enhancement of business competitiveness and success rates, development of sustainable competitive advantages and market positioning, creation of foundations for business growth and diversification, and contribution to broader tribal economic development through business capability development.

Coordinating with Broader Tribal Economic Development

Federal contracting activities achieve maximum effectiveness when coordinated with broader tribal economic development initiatives, creating synergistic effects that enhance both individual business success and community economic development outcomes. Coordination enables tribal businesses to leverage contracting success for broader development impact while building sustainable economic development capacity (White House Office of Intergovernmental Affairs 2024).

Workforce development coordination should align federal contracting opportunities with tribal workforce development initiatives to create employment opportunities for tribal members while building skills and expertise that support both contracting success and broader economic development. Workforce coordination can create pathways for tribal member career development while building tribal human capital.

Business development ecosystem coordination should integrate successful federal contractors with tribal business development initiatives, mentoring programs, and entrepreneurship support systems to create comprehensive business development networks that support multiple businesses and entrepreneurs. Ecosystem coordination builds sustainable development infrastructure while leveraging successful businesses for broader development impact.

Infrastructure and economic development coordination should align federal contracting success with tribal infrastructure development, economic diversification, and community development initiatives to create comprehensive approaches that address multiple development needs simultaneously. Infrastructure coordination can leverage contracting revenues for broader development investment while building comprehensive development capacity.

Cultural preservation and community development coordination should align federal contracting activities with tribal cultural preservation, language revitalization, and community development priorities to ensure that business success supports rather than undermines broader tribal values and objectives. Cultural coordination preserves traditional values while building modern economic development capacity.

Policy and advocacy coordination should leverage federal contracting success to support tribal policy development, federal program advocacy, and intergovernmental relationship building that advances broader tribal interests and development objectives. Policy coordination builds political capital while supporting broader tribal interests and self-determination.

Partnership and network development should leverage federal contracting relationships to build partnerships with federal agencies, private sector organizations, and other tribal governments that support broader economic development and governance objectives. Partnership development creates social capital while building collaborative capacity for ongoing development activities.

The strategic importance of coordination includes maximization of contracting impact on broader tribal development, creation of synergistic effects that enhance both business and community development outcomes, demonstration of tribal capacity for comprehensive development management, and development of models for integrating business development with broader community development objectives that can guide future development planning and implementation.

The coordination frameworks and strategic planning approaches discussed in Chapter 7 provide valuable guidance for integrating federal contracting activities with broader tribal development strategies while ensuring that business success contributes to rather than detracts from broader tribal economic development and self-determination objectives.

Supplement N: Strategic Selection and Coordination Framework

Introduction to Strategic Program Selection

The diversity and complexity of federal financing programs available to tribal governments and enterprises create both substantial opportunities and significant challenges in program selection and coordination. Strategic program selection requires systematic evaluation of tribal development priorities, organizational capacity, program requirements, and coordination opportunities to maximize the effectiveness of federal investments while building sustainable development capacity (National Congress of American Indians, *Tribal Nations Policy Guide*, 2024, 45-52).

Effective program selection goes beyond simple matching of needs with available resources to encompass comprehensive strategic planning that considers timing, sequencing, coordination potential, and long-term development objectives. The most successful tribal development initiatives typically involve coordinated utilization of multiple federal programs that create synergistic effects while building organizational capacity for sustained development activities (Harvard Project on American Indian Economic Development, *Strategic Tribal Development*, 2024, 112-125).

The strategic importance of program selection and coordination extends beyond immediate project success to include demonstration of tribal capacity for complex development management, relationship building with multiple federal agencies, and creation of development momentum that attracts additional investment and partnership opportunities. Strategic coordination often distinguishes successful tribal development initiatives from those that achieve limited impact despite substantial resource investment (Government Accountability Office, *Tribal Program Coordination*, GAO-24-203415, 2024).

Understanding strategic program selection requires recognition of the interconnected nature of tribal development challenges and opportunities, where infrastructure limitations constrain business development, workforce challenges limit economic diversification, and financial access barriers affect comprehensive development planning. Effective program coordination addresses these interconnections while building comprehensive development capacity that supports sustained economic growth and community development.

The comprehensive planning and strategic coordination approaches discussed in Chapter 7 provide essential frameworks for optimizing federal program utilization within broader tribal development strategies.

Program Assessment and Prioritization Matrix

Strategic program selection requires systematic assessment and prioritization frameworks that enable tribal governments to evaluate program opportunities against their development priorities, organizational capacity, and strategic objectives. A comprehensive assessment matrix provides structure for complex decision-making while ensuring that program selections align with community priorities and development goals (Economic Development Administration, *Strategic Planning Guidelines*, 2024, 23-31).

Development Priority Alignment Analysis

Program assessment begins with clear articulation of tribal development priorities and strategic objectives that provide frameworks for evaluating program opportunities and potential outcomes. Priority alignment analysis ensures that program selections support rather than distract from core development objectives while building toward comprehensive development strategies (National Congress of American Indians, *Tribal Nations Policy Guide*, 2024, 45-52).

Community development priorities should be clearly defined through comprehensive planning processes that engage tribal members, leadership, and stakeholders in identifying development needs, opportunities, and preferred development directions. Priority identification provides foundations for program evaluation while ensuring that development activities reflect community values and aspirations.

Economic development objectives should specify desired outcomes including employment creation, business development, revenue generation, and economic diversification that guide program selection and coordination decisions. Economic objectives provide measurable targets while ensuring that program activities contribute to sustainable economic development and community prosperity.

Infrastructure development needs should be systematically assessed to identify critical infrastructure gaps that constrain development while prioritizing infrastructure investments that enable broader development activities. Infrastructure assessment provides foundations for co-ordinated development that addresses prerequisite needs while building platforms for sustained growth.

Workforce development requirements should be evaluated to identify skill gaps, training needs, and education priorities that affect development potential while ensuring that workforce development aligns with economic development and business development strategies. Workforce assessment ensures that development activities build human capital while addressing community employment and career development needs.

Cultural preservation and community development considerations should be integrated into priority assessment to ensure that development activities support rather than undermine tribal cultural values, traditional practices, and community cohesion. Cultural consideration ensures that development serves community values while preserving essential elements of tribal identity and governance.

The strategic value of priority alignment analysis includes creation of clear frameworks for program evaluation and selection, ensuring that program activities support rather than conflict with community priorities, building community support for development activities through transparent priority setting, and establishing accountability frameworks that measure development success against community objectives.

Resource Requirements and Capacity Assessment

Effective program selection requires realistic assessment of resource requirements and organizational capacity to ensure that program commitments can be successfully managed while building rather than overwhelming tribal institutional capacity. Capacity assessment provides foundations for sustainable program participation and successful development outcomes (Government Accountability Office, *Tribal Program Coordination*, GAO-24-203415, 2024).

Financial capacity assessment should evaluate tribal financial resources, debt capacity, matching fund requirements, and cash flow implications of program participation to ensure that financial commitments are manageable within tribal budgetary constraints. Financial assessment protects tribal fiscal health while ensuring realistic program planning and implementation.

Organizational capacity evaluation should assess staffing, expertise, systems, and infrastructure necessary for successful program management while identifying capacity building needs and development opportunities. Organizational assessment ensures that program commitments align with management capabilities while building sustainable institutional capacity.

Technical expertise requirements should be evaluated to identify specialized knowledge, skills, and experience necessary for successful program implementation while assessing availability of internal expertise or need for external technical assistance. Technical assessment ensures that programs can be implemented effectively while building internal capability and knowledge.

Administrative and compliance capacity should be assessed to ensure that tribal organizations can meet complex federal requirements while maintaining accountability and program effectiveness. Administrative assessment protects program integrity while ensuring that compliance requirements are manageable within organizational capacity.

Partnership and coordination requirements should be evaluated to assess tribal capacity for managing complex multi-agency or multi-partner initiatives while building collaborative relationships that support program success. Partnership assessment ensures effective collaboration while building sustainable relationship management capacity.

Community engagement and support capacity should be evaluated to ensure that programs can maintain community involvement and support throughout implementation while building community ownership and sustainability. Community assessment ensures that programs serve community interests while building local capacity for ongoing development activities.

The strategic importance of capacity assessment includes protection of tribal institutional health and effectiveness, ensuring sustainable program participation and successful outcomes, identification of capacity building needs and development opportunities, and creation of realistic program planning and implementation strategies that build rather than overwhelm organizational capabilities.

Risk Assessment and Mitigation Planning

Comprehensive program assessment requires systematic risk evaluation and mitigation planning that identifies potential challenges and develops strategies for addressing risks while protecting tribal interests and development objectives. Risk assessment provides foundations for informed decision-making and successful program implementation (Urban Institute, *Performance Measurement and Evaluation in Tribal Government Programs*, 2024).

Financial risk assessment should identify potential financial exposure, cash flow challenges, cost overruns, and other financial risks that could affect tribal fiscal health or program success. Financial risk assessment protects tribal assets while ensuring realistic financial planning and sustainable program participation.

Operational risk evaluation should assess potential implementation challenges, performance requirements, technical difficulties, and other operational risks that could affect program success or community benefit. Operational risk assessment ensures realistic implementation planning while identifying mitigation strategies and contingency planning needs.

Regulatory and compliance risk assessment should identify complex regulatory requirements, compliance monitoring obligations, audit requirements, and other regulatory risks that could affect program participation or tribal operations. Regulatory risk assessment protects against compliance failures while ensuring appropriate preparation for program requirements.

Political and relationship risk evaluation should assess potential impacts on tribal sovereignty, intergovernmental relationships, community support, and other political considerations that could affect program success or tribal interests. Political risk assessment protects tribal governance while ensuring that program activities support rather than undermine tribal self-determination.

Market and economic risk assessment should evaluate market conditions, economic trends, competitive factors, and other external risks that could affect program outcomes or development objectives. Market risk assessment ensures realistic program planning while identifying factors that could influence program success.

Reputation and credibility risk evaluation should assess potential impacts on tribal reputation, federal relationships, and future program access that could result from program participation or performance. Reputation risk assessment protects tribal interests while ensuring that program activities enhance rather than diminish tribal credibility and relationship capital.

The strategic importance of risk assessment includes protection of tribal interests and institutional capacity, enhancement of program success rates through proactive risk management, development of contingency planning and mitigation strategies that address potential challenges, and creation of informed decision-making frameworks that balance opportunities with risks and constraints.

Multi-Agency Coordination Strategies

Effective utilization of federal programs requires sophisticated coordination strategies that align multiple agency programs, requirements, and timelines to create comprehensive development approaches that achieve greater impact than individual programs could provide independently. Multi-agency coordination represents both a significant opportunity and a complex management challenge that requires strategic planning and systematic implementation (White House 2024).

Identifying Coordination Opportunities and Synergies

Strategic coordination begins with systematic identification of programs and agencies that can work together to address tribal development priorities while creating synergistic effects that enhance overall development impact. Coordination opportunity identification requires understanding of program structures, requirements, and potential complementarities (Economic Development Administration, *Strategic Planning Guidelines*, 2024, 23-31).

Infrastructure and economic development coordination can combine infrastructure investments from multiple agencies to create comprehensive development platforms that support business development, workforce development, and community development simultaneously. Infrastructure coordination creates foundations for sustained development while maximizing federal investment efficiency and effectiveness.

Business development and workforce coordination can align business development support with workforce training and education programs to create comprehensive approaches that address both business development needs and workforce preparation requirements. Business-workforce coordination ensures that development activities create sustainable employment while building human capital for ongoing economic development.

Housing and community development coordination can integrate housing development with infrastructure, economic development, and community services to create comprehensive community development approaches that address multiple needs while building sustainable communities. Housing coordination creates platforms for comprehensive development while addressing fundamental community needs.

Financial resources and technical assistance coordination can combine financing programs with business development support, technical assistance, and capacity building resources to create comprehensive support systems that address both capital access and capability development needs. Financial coordination maximizes resource effectiveness while building sustainable development capacity.

Environmental and cultural preservation coordination can align environmental protection and cultural preservation with economic development to create approaches that support both development objectives and environmental stewardship while preserving cultural values and traditional practices. Environmental-cultural coordination ensures sustainable development while preserving essential community values.

Regulatory and compliance coordination can streamline regulatory requirements and compliance obligations across multiple programs to reduce administrative burden while maintaining program integrity and accountability. Regulatory coordination enhances program efficiency while reducing administrative complexity and costs.

The strategic value of coordination opportunity identification includes maximization of federal resource effectiveness and efficiency, creation of comprehensive development approaches that address multiple needs simultaneously, reduction of administrative burden and complexity through coordinated planning and implementation, and development of synergistic effects that enhance overall development impact beyond individual program contributions.

Timing and Sequencing Considerations

Successful multi-agency coordination requires careful attention to timing and sequencing that aligns program schedules, application deadlines, implementation timelines, and performance requirements to create coherent development strategies while avoiding conflicts and coordination challenges (Government Accountability Office, *Tribal Program Coordination*, GAO-24-203415, 2024).

Program application and award timing should be coordinated to ensure that complementary programs can be pursued simultaneously while avoiding conflicts between application requirements or award timelines that could affect coordination effectiveness. Timing coordination ensures that programs can work together rather than competing for resources or attention.

Implementation sequencing should prioritize programs and activities that create foundations for subsequent programs while building capacity and momentum for comprehensive development approaches. Sequencing coordination ensures that development activities build upon each other rather than proceeding independently without coordination benefits.

Performance milestone coordination should align program performance requirements and reporting obligations to create coherent performance management systems while avoiding duplicative or conflicting requirements that could complicate program administration. Performance coordination enhances accountability while reducing administrative burden and complexity.

Funding cycle coordination should align program funding cycles and expenditure requirements to create coherent financial management while ensuring that cash flow and matching fund requirements can be managed effectively across multiple programs. Funding coordination protects financial sustainability while maximizing resource utilization and effectiveness.

Compliance and reporting coordination should align compliance requirements and reporting obligations across multiple programs to create efficient administrative systems while maintaining accountability and program integrity. Compliance coordination reduces administrative burden while ensuring effective program management and oversight.

Project completion and transition coordination should align program completion timelines and transition requirements to ensure that development activities create sustainable outcomes while building capacity for ongoing development activities. Completion coordination ensures that development investments create lasting benefits while building platforms for continued development.

The strategic importance of timing and sequencing coordination includes enhancement of program effectiveness through coordinated implementation, reduction of administrative burden and complexity through systematic planning and coordination, creation of development momentum through strategic sequencing and milestone coordination, and protection of program sustainability through effective timing and resource management.

Building Interagency Relationships and Communication
Effective multi-agency coordination requires development of strong working relationships and communication systems among federal agencies, tribal governments, and implementation partners that support collaborative planning and problem-solving while maintaining accountability and program effectiveness (Inter-Tribal Council of Arizona, *Best Practices in Multi-Agency Program Coordination*, 2024).

Federal agency relationship development should establish clear communication channels, coordination protocols, and problem-solving mechanisms that enable effective collaboration while respecting agency authorities and program requirements. Agency relationship development creates foundations for ongoing coordination while building institutional capacity for complex program management.

Tribal-federal relationship building should establish government-to-government communication and coordination frameworks that respect tribal sovereignty while enabling effective program coordination and implementation. Tribal-federal relationships provide foundations for successful program implementation while building long-term partnership capacity.

Inter-tribal collaboration development should create opportunities for coordination and resource sharing among tribal governments while building collective capacity for complex program implementation and advocacy. Inter-tribal collaboration enhances resource effectiveness while building regional development capacity and political influence.

Technical assistance and support coordination should align technical assistance resources across multiple agencies and programs to create comprehensive support systems while avoiding duplication and resource conflicts. Technical assistance coordination maximizes support effectiveness while building sustainable capacity development.

Performance monitoring and evaluation coordination should create shared monitoring and evaluation systems that track progress across multiple programs while providing information necessary for program management and improvement. Monitoring coordination enhances accountability while supporting continuous improvement and strategic planning.

Communication and information sharing systems should create regular communication protocols, information sharing mechanisms, and coordination meetings that support ongoing relationship management and problem-solving. Communication systems ensure effective coordination while building institutional capacity for collaborative program management.

The strategic importance of interagency relationship building includes creation of sustainable coordination capacity and institutional infrastructure, enhancement of program effectiveness through improved communication and collaboration, development of problem-solving capacity that addresses coordination challenges and conflicts, and building of long-term partnership capacity that supports ongoing development activities and program access.

Sequencing and Timing Considerations

Strategic program implementation requires sophisticated understanding of sequencing and timing that maximizes program effectiveness while building development capacity and momentum. Effective sequencing creates platforms for sustained development while ensuring that early programs build capacity for subsequent activities rather than overwhelming organizational capabilities (Harvard Project on American Indian Economic Development 2024, 18–22).

Prerequisites and Foundation Building
Successful development initiatives typically require systematic attention to prerequisites and foundation building that create conditions for subsequent development success while building organizational capacity and community readiness for complex development activities. Foundation building represents strategic investment in development infrastructure and capacity (National Congress of American Indians, *Tribal Nations Policy Guide*, 2024, 45-52).

Infrastructure foundation development should prioritize essential infrastructure that enables broader development activities while creating platforms for business development, workforce development, and community growth. Infrastructure foundations often represent critical prerequisites for successful economic development while providing employment and capacity building opportunities.

Organizational capacity foundation building should develop institutional systems, expertise, and capabilities necessary for managing complex development initiatives while building sustainable organizational infrastructure. Capacity foundations enable effective program management while creating platforms for ongoing development leadership and implementation.

Planning and strategic development foundations should establish comprehensive planning frameworks, community engagement systems, and strategic decision-making processes that guide development activities while building community ownership and support. Planning foundations ensure that development activities align with community priorities while building capacity for ongoing strategic planning and implementation.

Relationship and partnership foundations should develop key relationships with federal agencies, technical assistance providers, and other partners that support development activities while building social capital and collaborative capacity. Relationship foundations create resources for ongoing development while building sustainable partnership capacity.

Financial and administrative foundations should establish financial management systems, administrative procedures, and compliance capabilities that support complex program management while building sustainable administrative infrastructure. Financial foundations protect program integrity while building capacity for ongoing financial management and program administration.

Community engagement and support foundations should build community understanding, support, and participation in development activities while creating frameworks for ongoing community involvement and feedback. Community foundations ensure that development serves community interests while building sustainable community ownership and leadership.

The strategic value of foundation building includes creation of sustainable development infrastructure and capacity, enhancement of program success rates through systematic preparation and capacity building, development of platforms for sustained development activities and program implementation, and building of community ownership and support that ensures development sustainability and effectiveness.

Building Development Momentum and Capacity

Effective program sequencing creates development momentum through strategic selection and timing of programs that demonstrate success while building capacity and confidence for larger and more complex development initiatives. Momentum building represents strategic investment in development success and community confidence (Federal Reserve Bank of Minneapolis, *Building Development Momentum in Indian Country*, 2024).

Early success demonstration through carefully selected initial programs that have high success probability while providing visible community benefits creates momentum for ongoing development while building confidence in development processes and outcomes. Early success demonstrates development potential while building community support and federal agency confidence.

Capability development progression should sequence programs that build organizational capabilities and expertise systematically while creating platforms for increasingly complex and ambitious development initiatives. Capability progression ensures sustainable development while building institutional capacity for ongoing development leadership and implementation.

Resource mobilization sequencing should align program implementation with resource availability and development needs while building capacity for accessing and managing increasingly substantial resource commitments. Resource sequencing protects organizational sustainability while building capacity for larger and more complex development activities.

Partnership development progression should build collaborative capacity and relationship management expertise through systematic engagement with federal agencies, technical assistance providers, and other partners. Partnership progression creates sustainable collaborative capacity while building social capital for ongoing development activities.

Community engagement and ownership development should build community understanding, support, and leadership capacity through progressive involvement in development planning and implementation activities. Community development creates sustainable local ownership while building capacity for ongoing community leadership and development activities.

Market development and business capacity building should sequence business development activities to create sustainable economic foundations while building entrepreneurial capacity and market access that supports ongoing economic development and diversification.

The strategic importance of momentum and capacity building includes creation of sustainable development trajectories and institutional capacity, enhancement of development success rates through systematic capability and confidence building, demonstration of development potential that attracts additional investment and partnership opportunities, and building of community ownership and leadership that ensures development sustainability and effectiveness.

Managing Implementation Complexity and Coordination

Complex multi-program development initiatives require sophisticated management systems and coordination mechanisms that maintain program effectiveness while managing administrative complexity and coordination challenges. Implementation management represents critical capability for development success and sustainability (Government Accountability Office, *Tribal Program Coordination*, GAO-24-203415, 2024).

Program management system development should create comprehensive project management, coordination, and oversight systems that enable effective management of multiple programs simultaneously while maintaining accountability and performance effectiveness. Management systems provide infrastructure for complex development while building sustainable management capacity.

Communication and coordination protocol establishment should create systematic communication systems, coordination meetings, and problem-solving mechanisms that ensure effective collaboration among programs, agencies, and implementation partners. Coordination protocols maintain program effectiveness while building collaborative capacity and relationship management expertise.

Performance monitoring and evaluation system development should create comprehensive monitoring systems that track progress across multiple programs while providing information necessary for program management, coordination, and improvement. Monitoring systems enhance accountability while supporting continuous improvement and strategic planning.

Risk management and contingency planning should identify potential implementation challenges and develop systematic approaches for addressing problems and maintaining program effectiveness. Risk management protects program success while building problem-solving capacity and implementation resilience.

Resource management and allocation systems should create frameworks for managing financial resources, staff time, and other resources across multiple programs while maintaining efficiency and effectiveness. Resource management ensures sustainable program implementation while building capacity for complex resource management and allocation.

Quality control and performance assurance systems should establish quality standards, performance measurement, and accountability mechanisms that ensure program effectiveness while maintaining stakeholder confidence and support. Quality systems protect program integrity while building capacity for performance excellence and continuous improvement.

The strategic importance of implementation management includes protection of program effectiveness and success rates through systematic management and coordination, development of sustainable management capacity and institutional infrastructure, creation of accountability and performance assurance systems that maintain stakeholder confidence, and building of problem-solving and coordination expertise that supports ongoing development activities and program implementation.

Matching Fund Strategy and Resource Leverage

Federal programs typically require matching funds that represent both challenges and opportunities for tribal governments seeking to maximize their development investments while building sustainable financing strategies. Strategic matching fund planning and resource leverage can significantly enhance development impact while building financial management capacity and diversified funding strategies (Treasury Department, *Federal Program Matching Requirements and Resource Leverage Strategies*, 2024).

Creative Matching Fund Approaches

Federal matching requirements can be satisfied through various approaches that extend beyond direct cash contributions to include in-kind contributions, third-party matching, and innovative financing strategies that maximize resource leverage while maintaining program compliance and effectiveness (Office of Management and Budget, *Federal Grant Compliance and Reporting Requirements*, 2024).

In-kind contribution strategies can satisfy matching requirements through tribal labor, equipment, facilities, materials, and other resources that reduce cash matching requirements while leveraging existing tribal assets and capabilities. In-kind contributions can significantly reduce financial barriers to program participation while demonstrating tribal commitment and resource contribution.

Third-party matching development can engage partners, donors, foundations, and other entities to provide matching fund contributions that expand resource availability while building partnership capacity and collaborative funding strategies. Third-party matching creates additional resource access while building sustainable partnership and fundraising capacity.

Leveraged financing approaches can use federal grant funding to secure additional financing through loans, bonds, or other mechanisms that multiply resource availability while creating comprehensive financing strategies. Leveraged financing maximizes resource impact while building capacity for complex financing and resource development.

Phased implementation strategies can sequence program implementation to spread matching fund requirements over time while building resource generation capacity through early program success and revenue development. Phased implementation manages resource requirements while building capacity for sustained program implementation and resource development.

Resource sharing and collaboration can coordinate matching fund requirements across multiple programs or partners to achieve economies of scale while reducing individual matching burdens through collaborative resource development and sharing strategies. Resource collaboration enhances efficiency while building cooperative capacity and partnership development.

Revenue generation integration can align program implementation with revenue generation activities that provide matching funds while creating sustainable financing sources for ongoing development activities. Revenue integration builds sustainable financing while creating self-supporting development activities and business development.

The strategic value of creative matching approaches includes reduction of financial barriers to program participation and implementation, maximization of resource leverage and development impact, development of innovative financing and resource development capacity, and creation of sustainable financing strategies that support ongoing development activities and program implementation.

Building Sustainable Financing Capacity

Strategic resource leverage requires development of sustainable financing capacity that enables ongoing program participation and development activities while building diversified resource bases and reducing dependence on single funding sources. Sustainable financing represents essential infrastructure for long-term development success (Harvard Project on American Indian Economic Development, *Strategic Tribal Development*, 2024, 112-125).

Revenue diversification strategies should develop multiple revenue sources including business development, investment income, fee-for-service activities, and other revenue generation that provides sustainable financing for development activities while reducing dependence on federal programs and grants. Revenue diversification creates sustainable financing while building business development and entrepreneurial capacity.

Endowment and reserve fund development can create permanent financing sources through strategic investment and fund development that provides ongoing support for development activities while building financial security and independence. Endowment development creates sustainable financing while building investment management capacity and financial security.

Partnership and collaborative financing development should build relationships and financing strategies with foundations, corporations, other tribal governments, and financial institutions that provide additional resource access while creating sustainable financing partnerships. Partnership financing expands resource access while building collaborative capacity and relationship development.

Business development and enterprise financing should align business development activities with financing needs to create self-supporting development activities while building entrepreneurial capacity and market-based revenue generation. Business financing creates sustainable revenue while building economic development and business management capacity.

Federal program cycling and renewal strategies should develop systematic approaches to ongoing federal program participation and renewal that maintain access to federal resources while building expertise in program management and grant development. Program cycling maintains resource access while building sustainable grant development and program management capacity.

Investment and asset development strategies should build tribal assets and investment portfolios that provide ongoing income and financing capacity while creating financial security and independence. Asset development creates sustainable financing while building investment management and financial planning capacity.

The strategic importance of sustainable financing capacity includes creation of long-term development sustainability and financial independence, reduction of dependence on individual funding sources while building diversified resource strategies, development of financial management and investment capacity that supports ongoing development activities, and creation of financial security that enables strategic planning and risk-taking for ambitious development initiatives.

Resource Coordination and Optimization

Effective resource leverage requires systematic coordination and optimization strategies that maximize resource effectiveness while minimizing administrative burden and avoiding resource conflicts or duplication. Resource optimization represents strategic resource management that enhances development impact and sustainability (Inter-Tribal Council of Arizona, *Best Practices in Multi-Agency Program Coordination*, 2024).

Resource mapping and inventory development should create comprehensive understanding of available resources, funding sources, and development opportunities while identifying coordination opportunities and potential conflicts or duplication. Resource mapping provides foundations for strategic resource planning while ensuring comprehensive resource utilization and coordination.

Timing and cash flow coordination should align resource availability with development needs and program requirements while managing cash flow and funding cycles to maintain program effectiveness and financial sustainability. Timing coordination ensures resource availability while protecting financial sustainability and program implementation effectiveness.

Administrative and compliance coordination should streamline administrative requirements and compliance obligations across multiple funding sources while maintaining program integrity and accountability. Administrative coordination reduces burden while ensuring effective program management and resource accountability.

Performance and accountability coordination should align performance measurement and reporting requirements across multiple funding sources while creating coherent accountability systems that demonstrate development effectiveness and impact. Performance coordination enhances accountability while reducing administrative complexity and burden.

Strategic resource allocation should prioritize resource utilization based on development priorities, program effectiveness, and strategic objectives while ensuring that resource allocation supports comprehensive development strategies rather than fragmented activities. Strategic allocation maximizes resource impact while ensuring coherent development approaches and strategies.

Continuous resource development and renewal should create ongoing resource development capacity while building sustainable fundraising and grant development expertise that maintains resource access and development capacity. Continuous development ensures sustainable resource access while building institutional capacity for ongoing resource development and management.

The strategic importance of resource coordination and optimization includes maximization of resource effectiveness and development impact, reduction of administrative burden and complexity through systematic coordination and management, creation of sustainable resource management capacity and institutional infrastructure, and development of strategic resource planning and allocation expertise that supports ongoing development activities and program implementation success.

Administrative Capacity and Implementation Planning

Successful federal program implementation requires sophisticated administrative capacity and systematic implementation planning that manages complex requirements while building sustainable institutional infrastructure. Administrative capacity represents essential foundation for program success and long-term development effectiveness (Government Accountability Office, *Tribal Program Coordination*, GAO-24-203415, 2024).

Organizational Structure and Staffing Requirements

Federal program implementation requires appropriate organizational structures and staffing arrangements that provide necessary expertise while building sustainable capacity for ongoing program management and development activities. Organizational development represents strategic investment in institutional capacity and effectiveness (National Congress of American Indians, *Tribal Nations Policy Guide*, 2024, 45-52).

Program management structure development should create clear organizational arrangements that define roles, responsibilities, and authority for program implementation while building accountability and coordination systems. Management structures provide frameworks for effective program implementation while building sustainable management capacity and institutional infrastructure.

Staffing and expertise requirements should identify specialized knowledge, skills, and experience necessary for successful program implementation while developing strategies for recruiting, training, and retaining qualified personnel. Staffing development builds essential human capital while creating sustainable expertise and capacity for ongoing program implementation and management.

Organizational capacity assessment should evaluate existing organizational capabilities while identifying capacity building needs and development opportunities that support effective program implementation. Capacity assessment ensures realistic program planning while identifying strategic investments in organizational development and capacity building.

Training and professional development systems should create ongoing learning and skill development opportunities that build staff expertise while maintaining current knowledge of program requirements and best practices. Training systems build institutional capacity while ensuring effective program implementation and compliance with evolving requirements.

Succession planning and knowledge management should create systems for preserving institutional knowledge while building leadership capacity and ensuring continuity in program implementation and organizational management. Succession planning protects institutional capacity while building sustainable leadership and knowledge management systems.

Performance management and accountability systems should establish clear performance expectations, evaluation criteria, and accountability mechanisms that ensure effective program implementation while building performance excellence and continuous improvement capacity. Performance systems enhance effectiveness while building accountability and quality assurance capacity.

The strategic value of organizational structure and staffing development includes creation of sustainable institutional capacity and infrastructure, enhancement of program implementation effectiveness and success rates, development of specialized expertise and professional capacity that supports ongoing development activities, and building of accountability and performance management systems that ensure program effectiveness and stakeholder confidence.

Systems Development and Infrastructure

Effective program implementation requires sophisticated systems and infrastructure that support complex administrative requirements while building sustainable capacity for ongoing program management and organizational development. Systems development represents essential investment in institutional effectiveness and sustainability (Urban Institute, *Performance Measurement and Evaluation in Tribal Government Programs*, 2024).

Financial management system development should create comprehensive accounting, budgeting, reporting, and compliance systems that manage complex federal requirements while building sustainable financial management capacity. Financial systems protect program integrity while building institutional capacity for ongoing financial management and accountability.

Information management and database systems should create comprehensive data collection, analysis, and reporting capabilities that support program management while building institutional knowledge and performance measurement capacity. Information systems enhance decision-making while building analytical capacity and institutional memory.

Communication and coordination systems should establish internal and external communication protocols, collaboration tools, and information sharing mechanisms that support effective program implementation and partnership management. Communication systems enhance coordination while building collaborative capacity and relationship management expertise.

Quality assurance and compliance monitoring systems should create systematic approaches to ensuring program compliance while maintaining quality standards and accountability requirements. Quality systems protect program integrity while building compliance expertise and risk management capacity.

Document management and record-keeping systems should establish comprehensive documentation and record management protocols that maintain program accountability while building institutional memory and knowledge management capacity. Documentation systems protect program integrity while building knowledge management and institutional learning capacity.

Technology and automation systems should leverage technology to enhance program efficiency while reducing administrative burden and building capacity for managing complex program requirements. Technology systems enhance efficiency while building technical capacity and modernizing administrative infrastructure.

The strategic importance of systems development includes creation of sustainable administrative infrastructure and institutional capacity, enhancement of program efficiency and effectiveness through systematic management and automation, development of compliance and accountability capacity that protects program integrity and stakeholder confidence, and building of knowledge management and institutional learning systems that support ongoing development and improvement activities.

Compliance and Reporting Framework Development

Federal program participation requires comprehensive compliance and reporting frameworks that meet complex federal requirements while building sustainable accountability systems and institutional capacity. Compliance framework development represents essential infrastructure for program success and federal relationship management (Office of Management and Budget, *Federal Grant Compliance and Reporting Requirements*, 2024).

Regulatory compliance system development should create comprehensive understanding of federal requirements while establishing systematic approaches to ensuring compliance with complex regulations and program guidelines. Compliance systems protect program integrity while building regulatory expertise and risk management capacity.

Financial compliance and audit preparation should establish financial management and reporting systems that meet federal requirements while preparing for ongoing audit and oversight activities. Financial compliance protects program integrity while building financial management expertise and accountability systems.

Performance reporting and evaluation systems should create comprehensive performance measurement and reporting capabilities that demonstrate program effectiveness while meeting federal reporting requirements. Performance systems enhance accountability while building evaluation capacity and continuous improvement infrastructure.

Documentation and record-keeping compliance should establish systematic approaches to documentation and record management that meet federal requirements while building institutional memory and knowledge management capacity. Documentation compliance protects program integrity while building knowledge management and institutional learning systems.

Monitoring and evaluation framework development should create ongoing monitoring and evaluation systems that track program progress while providing information necessary for program improvement and federal reporting. Monitoring frameworks enhance program effectiveness while building evaluation capacity and strategic planning infrastructure.

Risk management and internal control systems should establish systematic approaches to identifying and managing compliance risks while building internal control and risk management capacity. Risk management protects program integrity while building institutional capacity for ongoing risk assessment and management.

The strategic importance of compliance and reporting framework development includes protection of program integrity and federal relationships through systematic compliance management, enhancement of program effectiveness and accountability through comprehensive monitoring and evaluation systems, development of institutional capacity and expertise in regulatory compliance and federal program management, and creation of sustainable accountability and quality assurance systems that support ongoing program implementation and federal partnership development.

Performance Measurement and Evaluation Framework

Effective federal program implementation requires comprehensive performance measurement and evaluation frameworks that demonstrate program effectiveness while supporting continuous improvement and strategic planning. Performance measurement represents essential infrastructure for accountability, learning, and development optimization (Urban Institute, *Performance Measurement and Evaluation in Tribal Government Programs*, 2024).

Developing Comprehensive Performance Indicators

Performance measurement systems must balance federal reporting requirements with tribal development priorities while creating meaningful indicators that support both accountability and strategic decision-making. Comprehensive indicator development provides foundations for effective program management and continuous improvement (Government Accountability Office, *Tribal Program Coordination*, GAO-24-203415, 2024).

Output indicators should measure direct program activities and deliverables including services provided, infrastructure developed, businesses assisted, and other tangible program outputs that demonstrate implementation progress and activity levels. Output measurement provides accountability while tracking program implementation and resource utilization effectiveness.

Outcome indicators should measure program results and impacts including employment created, incomes increased, businesses developed, infrastructure improved, and other program outcomes that demonstrate effectiveness and community benefit. Outcome measurement provides accountability while demonstrating program value and development impact.

Community development indicators should measure broader community impacts including quality of life improvements, community capacity development, infrastructure enhancement, and other community-level outcomes that demonstrate comprehensive development impact. Community indicators ensure that programs serve broader development objectives while building sustainable community development.

Economic development indicators should measure economic impacts including business development, revenue generation, employment creation, income enhancement, and economic diversification that demonstrate program contribution to tribal economic development objectives. Economic indicators provide accountability while demonstrating development effectiveness and sustainability.

Cultural and social indicators should measure program impacts on cultural preservation, community cohesion, traditional practices, and social development that ensure programs support rather than undermine tribal values and community development. Cultural indicators ensure that development serves community values while preserving essential elements of tribal identity and governance.

Sustainability and institutional development indicators should measure organizational capacity building, institutional development, sustainability planning, and other factors that ensure programs create lasting benefits while building capacity for ongoing development activities. Sustainability indicators ensure that programs create lasting value while building institutional capacity and development infrastructure.

The strategic value of comprehensive performance indicators includes creation of accountability and transparency systems that demonstrate program effectiveness, development of information systems that support strategic planning and continuous improvement, establishment of evaluation frameworks that balance federal requirements with tribal priorities, and building of institutional capacity for performance management and evaluation that supports ongoing development activities and program implementation.

Data Collection and Analysis Systems
Effective performance measurement requires sophisticated data collection and analysis systems that provide reliable information while building institutional capacity for ongoing evaluation and strategic planning. Data systems represent essential infrastructure for evidence-based decision-making and program improvement (Federal Reserve Bank of Minneapolis, *Building Development Momentum in Indian Country*, 2024).

Data collection system design should create systematic approaches to gathering performance information while minimizing administrative burden and building sustainable data collection capacity. Data collection systems provide foundations for evaluation while building institutional capacity for ongoing information management and analysis.

Data quality assurance and validation should establish protocols for ensuring data accuracy, completeness, and reliability while building institutional capacity for quality control and data management. Quality assurance protects evaluation integrity while building analytical capacity and institutional credibility.

Data analysis and interpretation capacity should develop analytical expertise and systems that transform data into useful information for program management and strategic planning while building institutional capacity for evidence-based decision-making. Analysis capacity enhances program effectiveness while building strategic planning and evaluation expertise.

Reporting and communication systems should create mechanisms for sharing evaluation results with stakeholders while building transparency and accountability that supports program improvement and stakeholder engagement. Reporting systems enhance accountability while building communication and stakeholder engagement capacity.

Technology and database management should leverage technology to enhance data collection and analysis efficiency while building institutional capacity for information management and technological innovation. Technology systems enhance efficiency while building technical capacity and modernizing evaluation infrastructure.

External evaluation and validation should engage independent evaluators and validation processes that provide objective assessment while building institutional learning and credibility with stakeholders and federal partners. External evaluation enhances credibility while building institutional learning and evaluation capacity.

The strategic value of data collection and analysis systems includes creation of reliable information systems that support evidence-based decision-making and program improvement, development of institutional capacity for ongoing evaluation and strategic planning, establishment of accountability and transparency systems that maintain stakeholder confidence and federal partnership relationships, and building of analytical and technological capacity that supports ongoing development activities and program implementation effectiveness.

Continuous Improvement and Strategic Planning Integration

Performance measurement achieves maximum value when integrated with continuous improvement and strategic planning processes that use evaluation results to enhance program effectiveness while building institutional learning and development capacity. Integration represents strategic approach to organizational learning and development optimization (Harvard Project on American Indian Economic Development, *Strategic Tribal Development*, 2024, 112-125).

Program improvement process development should create systematic approaches to using evaluation results for program enhancement while building institutional capacity for continuous improvement and learning. Improvement processes enhance program effectiveness while building learning capacity and institutional development.

Strategic planning integration should align performance measurement with strategic planning processes to ensure that evaluation results inform strategic decision-making while building capacity for evidence-based planning and strategy development. Strategic integration enhances planning effectiveness while building analytical capacity and strategic management expertise.

Stakeholder feedback and engagement should create mechanisms for incorporating community input and stakeholder perspectives into program evaluation and improvement while building community ownership and support for development activities. Stakeholder engagement enhances program relevance while building community participation and support for ongoing development activities.

Best practice identification and replication should use evaluation results to identify successful approaches while building capacity for scaling and replicating effective practices across programs and activities. Best practice development enhances program effectiveness while building institutional learning and knowledge management capacity.

Innovation and adaptation processes should create capacity for program innovation and adaptation based on evaluation results while building institutional flexibility and responsiveness to changing conditions and opportunities. Innovation capacity enhances program effectiveness while building adaptive capacity and institutional resilience.

Knowledge management and institutional learning should create systems for preserving and sharing evaluation results and lessons learned while building institutional memory and knowledge management capacity. Knowledge management enhances institutional learning while building capacity for ongoing development and program improvement.

The strategic importance of continuous improvement and strategic planning integration includes enhancement of program effectiveness and development impact through systematic learning and improvement, development of institutional capacity for evidence-based decision-making and strategic management, creation of adaptive and responsive program management capacity that addresses changing conditions and opportunities, and building of knowledge management and institutional learning systems that support ongoing development activities and organizational effectiveness.

Risk Management and Compliance Coordination

Complex federal program implementation involves substantial risks and compliance requirements that must be systematically managed to protect tribal interests while ensuring program success and federal relationship maintenance. Risk management and compliance coordination represent essential capabilities for sustainable program implementation and institutional protection (Government Accountability Office, *Tribal Program Coordination*, GAO-24-203415, 2024).

Identifying and Assessing Program Risks

Comprehensive risk management requires systematic identification and assessment of potential risks that could affect program implementation, tribal interests, or institutional capacity. Risk identification provides foundations for proactive management while building institutional capacity for risk assessment and mitigation planning (United States Department of Justice 2022, 2–12).

Financial risk assessment should identify potential financial exposure, cash flow challenges, cost overruns, matching fund difficulties, and other financial risks that could affect tribal fiscal health or program sustainability. Financial risk assessment protects tribal assets while ensuring realistic financial planning and sustainable resource management.

Operational risk evaluation should assess implementation challenges, performance requirements, technical difficulties, staffing constraints, and other operational risks that could affect program success or institutional capacity. Operational risk assessment ensures realistic implementation planning while building capacity for problem-solving and contingency management.

Regulatory and compliance risk assessment should identify complex regulatory requirements, compliance monitoring obligations, audit risks, and other regulatory challenges that could affect program implementation or tribal operations. Regulatory risk assessment protects against compliance failures while building expertise in federal regulatory management and compliance systems.

Political and relationship risk evaluation should assess potential impacts on tribal sovereignty, intergovernmental relationships, community support, federal partnerships, and other political considerations that could affect program success or tribal interests. Political risk assessment protects tribal governance while ensuring that programs support rather than undermine tribal self-determination and sovereignty.

Reputation and credibility risk assessment should evaluate potential impacts on tribal reputation, federal relationships, program access, and stakeholder confidence that could result from program implementation or performance challenges. Reputation risk assessment protects tribal interests while building capacity for reputation management and stakeholder relationship maintenance.

Technology and information risk evaluation should assess cybersecurity threats, data protection requirements, system failures, and other technology risks that could affect program operations or sensitive information protection. Technology risk assessment protects information security while building capacity for technology management and cybersecurity protection.

The strategic value of comprehensive risk identification and assessment includes protection of tribal interests and institutional capacity through proactive risk management, enhancement of program success rates through systematic risk mitigation and contingency planning, development of institutional capacity for ongoing risk assessment and management, and creation of informed decision-making frameworks that balance development opportunities with risk management and institutional protection.

Developing Risk Mitigation and Contingency Plans
Effective risk management requires systematic development of mitigation strategies and contingency plans that address identified risks while building institutional resilience and adaptive capacity. Risk mitigation planning represents strategic investment in program sustainability and institutional protection (National Congress of American Indians, *Tribal Nations Policy Guide*, 2024, 45-52).

Financial risk mitigation should develop strategies for managing financial exposure including diversified funding sources, reserve fund development, contingency financing arrangements, and financial monitoring systems that protect tribal fiscal health while maintaining program sustainability. Financial mitigation protects institutional sustainability while building financial management and planning capacity.

Operational risk mitigation should create contingency plans for addressing implementation challenges including backup systems, alternative approaches, technical assistance resources, and problem-solving protocols that maintain program effectiveness while building operational resilience and adaptive capacity. Operational mitigation ensures program continuity while building capacity for complex program management and problem-solving.

Regulatory compliance mitigation should establish compliance monitoring systems, legal support arrangements, audit preparation protocols, and regulatory relationship management that protect against compliance failures while building expertise in federal regulatory management. Compliance mitigation protects program integrity while building regulatory expertise and federal relationship management capacity.

Political and relationship risk mitigation should develop communication strategies, stakeholder engagement protocols, conflict resolution mechanisms, and relationship management systems that protect tribal interests while maintaining positive federal and community relationships. Political mitigation protects tribal sovereignty while building capacity for intergovernmental relationship management and political leadership.

Reputation management and crisis communication should create communication protocols, stakeholder engagement strategies, media relations procedures, and crisis response systems that protect tribal reputation while maintaining stakeholder confidence and support. Reputation mitigation protects tribal interests while building capacity for communication and stakeholder relationship management.

Technology and cybersecurity mitigation should establish security protocols, backup systems, data protection procedures, and incident response plans that protect information and technology systems while building capacity for technology management and cybersecurity protection. Technology mitigation protects information security while building technological capacity and security expertise.

The strategic importance of risk mitigation and contingency planning includes protection of program sustainability and institutional capacity through proactive risk management, development of institutional resilience and adaptive capacity that supports ongoing development activities, creation of systematic approaches to problem-solving and crisis management, and building of expertise in risk management and contingency planning that supports ongoing program implementation and institutional development.

Compliance Monitoring and Quality Assurance
Federal program implementation requires comprehensive compliance monitoring and quality assurance systems that ensure adherence to complex requirements while building institutional capacity for ongoing compliance management and program excellence. Compliance monitoring represents essential infrastructure for program integrity and federal relationship maintenance (Office of Management and Budget, *Federal Grant Compliance and Reporting Requirements*, 2024).

Regulatory compliance monitoring should create systematic approaches to tracking compliance with federal regulations, program guidelines, and legal requirements while building institutional expertise in regulatory management and compliance systems. Compliance monitoring protects program integrity while building regulatory expertise and federal relationship management capacity.

Financial compliance and audit readiness should establish financial monitoring systems, internal controls, audit preparation protocols, and financial reporting procedures that ensure compliance with federal financial management requirements while building financial management and accountability capacity. Financial compliance protects program integrity while building financial management expertise and accountability systems.

Performance compliance monitoring should track adherence to performance requirements, reporting obligations, and program objectives while building capacity for performance management and continuous improvement. Performance monitoring ensures program effectiveness while building evaluation capacity and strategic planning infrastructure.

Documentation and record-keeping compliance should establish systematic documentation procedures, record management systems, and information preservation protocols that meet federal requirements while building institutional memory and knowledge management capacity. Documentation compliance protects program integrity while building knowledge management and institutional learning systems.

Quality control and assurance systems should create ongoing quality monitoring, performance evaluation, and improvement processes that maintain program excellence while building institutional capacity for quality management and continuous improvement. Quality assurance enhances program effectiveness while building performance excellence and accountability capacity.

Internal audit and evaluation systems should establish independent review and evaluation processes that ensure compliance while building institutional capacity for self-assessment and continuous improvement. Internal evaluation enhances accountability while building evaluation expertise and institutional learning capacity.

The strategic importance of compliance monitoring and quality assurance includes protection of program integrity and federal relationships through systematic compliance management, enhancement of program effectiveness and accountability through comprehensive monitoring and evaluation systems, development of institutional capacity and expertise in regulatory compliance and quality management, and creation of sustainable accountability and performance excellence systems that support ongoing program implementation and federal partnership development.

Stakeholder Engagement and Community Integration

Successful federal program implementation requires comprehensive stakeholder engagement and community integration strategies that build support, ensure relevance, and create sustainable community ownership of development activities (White House Office of Intergovernmental Affairs 2024). Stakeholder engagement represents essential foundation for program success and community development effectiveness (National Congress of American Indians, *Tribal Nations Policy Guide*, 2024, 45-52).

Community Engagement and Participation Strategies

Effective federal program implementation requires meaningful community engagement that respects tribal governance while building community understanding, support, and ownership of development activities. Community engagement strategies must balance technical program requirements with community values and participation preferences (Harvard Project on American Indian Economic Development, *Strategic Tribal Development*, 2024, 112-125).

Community consultation and input processes should create meaningful opportunities for community members to understand program opportunities while providing input on priorities, approaches, and implementation strategies that ensure programs serve community interests and values. Consultation processes respect community governance while building informed community support and participation.

Cultural integration and traditional knowledge incorporation should ensure that federal programs accommodate tribal cultural values, traditional practices, and community preferences while building on traditional knowledge and community strengths. Cultural integration preserves community identity while enhancing program relevance and effectiveness.

Transparent communication and information sharing should provide community members with clear, accessible information about program opportunities, requirements, benefits, and implementation progress while building community understanding and support for development activities. Transparent communication builds trust while ensuring informed community participation and decision-making.

Participatory planning and decision-making should engage community members in program planning, priority setting, and implementation decisions while respecting tribal governance structures and community decision-making traditions. Participatory planning ensures community relevance while building community ownership and support for development activities.

Capacity building and leadership development should provide community members with opportunities to develop skills, knowledge, and leadership capacity that supports program implementation while building sustainable community capacity for ongoing development activities. Capacity building creates community infrastructure while building local expertise and leadership for sustained development.

Feedback and evaluation mechanisms should create ongoing opportunities for community input on program effectiveness while building community participation in program improvement and strategic planning activities. Feedback mechanisms enhance program relevance while building community engagement and continuous improvement capacity.

The strategic value of community engagement and participation includes creation of sustainable community support and ownership that ensures program sustainability, enhancement of program relevance and effectiveness through community input and participation, development of community capacity and leadership that supports ongoing development activities, and building of social capital and community cohesion that supports broader community development objectives.

Building Partnerships and Collaborative Networks

Federal program success often depends on effective partnerships and collaborative networks that leverage diverse resources and expertise while building sustainable capacity for ongoing development activities. Partnership development represents strategic investment in relationship capital and collaborative capacity (White House Office of Intergovernmental Affairs, *Multi-Agency Coordination for Tribal Development Programs*, 2024).

Inter-tribal collaboration and resource sharing should create opportunities for coordination and partnership among tribal governments while building collective capacity for complex program implementation and advocacy. Inter-tribal collaboration enhances resource effectiveness while building regional development capacity and political influence.

Federal agency partnership development should establish strong working relationships with federal agencies while building capacity for ongoing collaboration and program access. Federal partnerships provide resource access while building institutional capacity for federal relationship management and program implementation.

Private sector partnership and business development should engage private sector partners in development activities while building business networks and market access that support economic development and business growth. Private partnerships enhance resource access while building business development capacity and market connections.

Nonprofit and foundation partnership development should build relationships with nonprofit organizations and foundations that provide additional resources and expertise while building collaborative capacity and grant development expertise. Nonprofit partnerships expand resource access while building capacity for collaborative program implementation and resource development.

Educational institution partnerships should engage universities, colleges, and research institutions in development activities while building capacity for education, research, and technical assistance that supports program implementation and community development. Educational partnerships provide expertise while building institutional capacity and knowledge development resources.

Professional service and technical assistance partnerships should build relationships with consulting firms, professional service providers, and technical assistance organizations that provide specialized expertise while building institutional capacity for accessing and managing professional services. Professional partnerships provide expertise while building capacity for complex program implementation and technical assistance management.

The strategic value of partnership and collaborative network development includes enhanced access to resources and expertise that supports program implementation and community development, creation of sustainable collaborative capacity and relationship management expertise, development of social capital and network resources that support ongoing development activities, and building of advocacy and political capacity that supports tribal interests and development objectives.

Communication and Outreach Framework

Effective stakeholder engagement requires comprehensive communication and outreach frameworks that ensure information accessibility while building understanding and support for development activities. Communication frameworks represent essential infrastructure for stakeholder relationship management and community engagement (Inter-Tribal Council of Arizona, *Best Practices in Multi-Agency Program Coordination*, 2024).

Multi-channel communication strategies should use diverse communication methods including meetings, newsletters, websites, social media, and other channels that reach different community segments while accommodating diverse communication preferences and access capabilities. Multi-channel approaches ensure broad reach while building comprehensive communication capacity.

Culturally appropriate communication approaches should respect tribal communication traditions, language preferences, and cultural protocols while ensuring that information is accessible and meaningful to community members. Cultural appropriateness enhances communication effectiveness while preserving community values and traditions.

Regular reporting and progress updates should provide stakeholders with ongoing information about program implementation, achievements, challenges, and future plans while building transparency and accountability that maintains stakeholder confidence and support. Regular reporting builds trust while ensuring informed stakeholder engagement and participation.

Crisis communication and problem-solving protocols should establish procedures for addressing challenges, conflicts, or concerns that may arise during program implementation while maintaining stakeholder relationships and program support. Crisis communication protects relationships while building capacity for conflict resolution and problem-solving.

Educational and capacity building communication should provide stakeholders with information and training that enhances their understanding of development opportunities while building community capacity for participation in development activities. Educational communication builds capacity while enhancing community engagement and participation effectiveness.

Feedback and dialogue facilitation should create opportunities for two-way communication that enables stakeholder input while building collaborative relationships and shared understanding of development challenges and opportunities. Dialogue facilitation enhances collaboration while building relationship management and communication capacity.

The strategic importance of communication and outreach framework development includes creation of sustainable stakeholder relationship management capacity, enhancement of community understanding and support for development activities, development of transparency and accountability systems that maintain stakeholder confidence, and building of communication and relationship management expertise that supports ongoing development activities and community engagement.

Sustainability and Long-Term Planning Integration

Federal program implementation must consider long-term sustainability and strategic planning integration that ensures program investments create lasting benefits while building capacity for ongoing development activities. Sustainability planning represents essential framework for maximizing federal investment value while building tribal self-determination and development capacity (Harvard Project on American Indian Economic Development, *Strategic Tribal Development*, 2024, 112-125).

Financial Sustainability and Revenue Development
Long-term program sustainability requires comprehensive financial planning that develops sustainable revenue sources while building financial management capacity and reducing dependence on federal programs. Financial sustainability represents strategic investment in tribal economic independence and development capacity (Treasury Department, *Federal Program Matching Requirements and Resource Leverage Strategies*, 2024).

Revenue diversification strategies should develop multiple income sources including business development, investment returns, fee-for-service activities, and other revenue generation that provides sustainable financing for ongoing development activities while reducing dependence on federal programs. Revenue diversification creates financial independence while building entrepreneurial capacity and business development expertise.

Endowment and investment fund development should create permanent financing sources through strategic investment and fund management that provides ongoing support for development activities while building financial security and institutional sustainability. Endowment development creates sustainable financing while building investment management capacity and financial planning expertise.

Business development and enterprise sustainability should align business development activities with long-term financing needs while creating self-supporting enterprises that generate revenue for ongoing development activities. Business sustainability creates economic independence while building entrepreneurial capacity and market development expertise.

Cost recovery and efficiency improvement should develop strategies for reducing program costs while improving efficiency through technology adoption, process improvement, and resource optimization that enhances program sustainability and effectiveness. Efficiency improvement enhances sustainability while building management capacity and operational excellence.

Grant development and fundraising capacity should build institutional expertise in accessing diverse funding sources while creating sustainable resource development capacity that maintains access to federal programs and other funding opportunities. Grant development builds resource access while creating institutional capacity for ongoing resource development and management.

Financial planning and management system development should create comprehensive financial planning, budgeting, and management systems that support sustainable program implementation while building financial management expertise and accountability systems. Financial planning enhances sustainability while building financial management capacity and institutional infrastructure.

The strategic value of financial sustainability and revenue development includes creation of long-term financial independence and institutional sustainability, reduction of dependence on federal programs while building diversified financing capacity, development of business and entrepreneurial capacity that supports economic development, and building of financial management expertise that supports ongoing development activities and institutional effectiveness.

Organizational Development and Capacity Building

Sustainable program implementation requires ongoing organizational development and capacity building that creates institutional infrastructure while building expertise and leadership capacity for ongoing development activities. Organizational development represents strategic investment in institutional sustainability and effectiveness (National Congress of American Indians, *Tribal Nations Policy Guide*, 2024, 45-52).

Leadership development and succession planning should create ongoing leadership training and development opportunities while building succession planning systems that ensure continuity in program implementation and organizational management. Leadership development builds human capital while ensuring institutional sustainability and continuity.

Staff development and professional capacity building should provide ongoing training and professional development opportunities that build staff expertise while creating career advancement pathways that retain institutional knowledge and capacity. Staff development builds institutional capacity while creating professional development opportunities that enhance retention and performance.

Institutional knowledge management and preservation should create systems for documenting and preserving institutional knowledge while building knowledge management capacity that supports ongoing learning and development activities. Knowledge management protects institutional memory while building learning capacity and institutional effectiveness.

Technology adoption and modernization should leverage technology to enhance organizational effectiveness while building technological capacity and modernizing institutional infrastructure that supports ongoing development activities. Technology adoption enhances efficiency while building technological capacity and institutional modernization.

Quality management and continuous improvement systems should establish ongoing quality improvement processes while building institutional capacity for performance excellence and continuous learning that enhances program effectiveness and sustainability. Quality management builds excellence while creating continuous improvement capacity and institutional learning systems.

Strategic planning and evaluation capacity should develop institutional expertise in strategic planning and evaluation while building capacity for ongoing strategic management and development planning that supports institutional effectiveness and sustainability. Strategic planning builds management capacity while creating planning expertise and institutional strategic management capability.

The strategic value of organizational development and capacity building includes creation of sustainable institutional infrastructure and human capital, enhancement of institutional effectiveness and program implementation capacity, development of leadership and management expertise that supports ongoing development activities, and building of institutional learning and adaptation.

Supplement O: Tribal General Welfare Exclusion (GWE): Key Concepts

The Tribal General Welfare Exclusion represents one of the most significant developments in federal tax policy affecting tribal governments and their members since the establishment of tribal tax exemption principles. Understanding how GWE payments operate, particularly regarding support for business start-up and development, provides tribal governments with powerful tools for supporting economic development while maintaining favorable tax treatment for program beneficiaries. The intersection of GWE policies with tribal business structures creates both opportunities and limitations that require careful analysis and strategic implementation.

The evolution of GWE policy reflects broader federal recognition of tribal sovereignty and self-determination in economic development programming. Unlike many federal tax provisions that apply uniformly across governmental entities, GWE regulations specifically acknowledge tribal governmental authority to design and implement programs that serve tribal community needs while preserving beneficial tax treatment for recipients (Treasury Department 2024).

Understanding the Tribal General Welfare Exclusion Framework

Legislative Foundation and Statutory Authority

The Tribal General Welfare Exclusion Act of 2014 codified longstanding administrative practice by establishing Internal Revenue Code Section 139E, which specifically authorizes tribal government programs to provide benefits that are excluded from recipients' gross income when they meet defined criteria (26 U.S.C. § 139E). This legislation addressed decades of uncertainty regarding the tax treatment of tribal governmental benefit programs and provided tribes with clear statutory authority to design comprehensive support programs without creating adverse tax consequences for beneficiaries (Holland & Knight 2024).

The statutory framework builds upon the broader general welfare exclusion doctrine that allows certain government-provided benefits—including housing assistance, educational support, and health programs—to be excluded from recipients' gross income for federal tax purposes. The tribal-specific provisions recognize the unique governmental status of tribes and their particular responsibility for supporting tribal member welfare through culturally appropriate programming (Federal Register 2024).

The legislative history of the 2014 Act demonstrates congressional recognition that tribal governments often provide more comprehensive social services than other governmental entities due to the federal trust responsibility and the concentrated nature of tribal communities. This recognition enabled Congress to create specific provisions that accommodate tribal governmental approaches while maintaining appropriate safeguards against program abuse (Washington State Bar Association 2024).

Proposed Regulatory Framework

The proposed GWE regulations issued September 17, 2024, by the Internal Revenue Service and Treasury Department represent a significant advancement in implementing the 2014 statutory framework, providing detailed guidance that affirms tribal flexibility in program design while establishing clear criteria for tax-exempt treatment (Internal Revenue Service 2024). These proposed regulations reflect extensive tribal consultation and demonstrate federal recognition of tribal sovereignty in designing benefit programs that serve community needs.

The regulatory framework establishes several key principles that enhance tribal program flexibility while maintaining appropriate oversight mechanisms. Most significantly, the proposed regulations affirm that the IRS will defer to tribal determinations about whether specific benefits promote general welfare within their communities, providing tribes with substantial autonomy in program design and implementation (Treasury Department 2024).

Eligibility Criteria and Program Design Requirements

The proposed regulations establish four fundamental criteria that tribal GWE programs must satisfy to qualify for tax-exempt treatment. Benefits must be available based on published guidelines that ensure transparent and consistent program administration, demonstrate non-discriminatory application that serves legitimate governmental purposes, maintain reasonable benefit levels that are not lavish or extravagant, and ensure that payments do not constitute compensation for services rendered to the tribal government (Internal Revenue Service 2024).

The requirement for published guidelines serves multiple purposes, including ensuring program transparency, establishing consistent eligibility criteria, providing documentation for IRS review, and enabling tribal members to understand available benefits and application processes. These guidelines must be written and publicly available, though tribes maintain flexibility in determining appropriate distribution mechanisms and eligibility criteria based on community needs (Bureau of Indian Affairs 2024).

The non-discriminatory application requirement recognizes that tribal governments may appropriately limit certain benefits to tribal members or specific community segments based on legitimate governmental purposes, including cultural preservation, economic development priorities, or resource limitations. This flexibility enables tribes to design targeted programs that address specific community needs while maintaining compliance with federal tax requirements (Federal Register 2024).

Presumption of Compliance and Administrative Procedures

One of the most significant features of the proposed regulations is the establishment of a presumption that benefits provided under written guidelines are not lavish or extravagant, substantially reducing the administrative burden on tribes to justify individual benefit determinations (Bureau of Indian Affairs 2024). This presumption recognizes tribal governmental authority and reduces the potential for intrusive federal oversight of tribal program administration.

The presumption operates by placing the burden on the IRS to demonstrate that specific benefits exceed reasonable limits rather than requiring tribes to justify each payment decision. This approach aligns with federal Indian law principles that favor tribal self-determination and recognize tribal governments as capable of managing their own affairs without excessive federal micromanagement (Holland & Knight 2024).

To maintain this presumption, tribal programs must maintain adequate documentation demonstrating compliance with published guidelines, including records of eligibility determinations, benefit calculations, and program administration procedures. The documentation requirements are designed to be reasonable and consistent with standard governmental record-keeping practices rather than imposing unusual administrative burdens (Internal Revenue Service 2024).

Funding Source Flexibility

The proposed regulations provide tribes with complete flexibility regarding funding sources for GWE programs, explicitly confirming that tribes may use any available revenue sources, including net gaming revenues, federal appropriations, tribal governmental revenues, or other lawful income sources (Bureau of Indian Affairs 2024). This funding flexibility represents a significant advantage for tribal governments that often manage diverse revenue portfolios and need administrative flexibility to optimize program effectiveness.

The ability to use gaming revenues for GWE programs is particularly significant given that gaming represents a major revenue source for many tribal governments and that gaming revenues are often subject to specific regulatory requirements under the Indian Gaming Regulatory Act. The GWE regulations confirm that appropriately structured benefit programs funded with gaming revenues can qualify for tax-exempt treatment, enabling tribes to leverage gaming success for broader community benefit (Federal Register 2024).

The funding flexibility also enables tribes to coordinate GWE programs with other federal programs and funding sources, creating comprehensive support systems that maximize available resources while maintaining appropriate segregation of funds for accountability purposes. This coordination capability is essential for tribal governments that often manage multiple federal programs with varying requirements and restrictions (Holland & Knight 2024).

Business Development Applications and Limitations
Individual vs. Business Entity Distinctions

The fundamental limitation of GWE regulations is that they apply exclusively to individual recipients and cannot provide tax-exempt treatment for payments made directly to business entities, including corporations, limited liability companies, partnerships, or other business structures (Internal Revenue Service 2024). This limitation reflects broader federal tax policy that treats business entities as separate taxpayers responsible for their own tax obligations, regardless of their ownership or control relationships.

The individual limitation means that tribal governments cannot utilize GWE provisions to provide direct grants, loans, or other financial assistance to tribal business entities, even when those entities are wholly owned by the tribe or serve important community development objectives. This restriction applies regardless of the business entity structure, including Section 17 corporations, tribally chartered entities, and state-chartered corporations discussed throughout this manuscript (Federal Register 2024).

However, the individual focus creates opportunities for tribal governments to structure business development support through programs that benefit individual tribal members who may then utilize those benefits for business development purposes. This approach requires careful program design to ensure compliance with both GWE requirements and business development objectives while maintaining appropriate documentation and oversight (Washington State Bar Association 2024).

Revenue Ruling 77-77 and Historical Precedent

Revenue Ruling 77-77, issued in 1977, provides a limited but important exception to general taxation principles by allowing non-reimbursable grants to individual tribal members for expanding or recovering Indian-owned businesses located near reservations to be excluded from gross income under the administrative general welfare doctrine (Internal Revenue Service 1977). This ruling predates the 2014 statutory framework but remains valid and provides an alternative pathway for tax-exempt business development assistance.

The 1977 ruling applies specifically to grants provided to individual tribal members rather than business entities, requires that grants be non-reimbursable rather than loans or other repayable assistance, focuses on business expansion or recovery rather than general business operations, and limits geographic scope to businesses located near reservations rather than extending to all tribal member businesses (Federal Register 2024).

While Revenue Ruling 77-77 provides important precedent for business-related GWE applications, its narrow scope and specific requirements limit its applicability to comprehensive tribal business development strategies. Most significantly, the ruling's focus on business recovery and expansion may not encompass business start-up assistance or other forms of entrepreneurship support that many tribes seek to provide (Holland & Knight 2024).

Strategic Approaches to Business Development Support
Despite the limitations on direct business entity support, tribal governments can design GWE programs that provide substantial support for individual tribal members pursuing business development opportunities. These programs must be structured to provide benefits to individuals rather than business entities while serving legitimate general welfare purposes and maintaining compliance with regulatory requirements.

Educational and training programs represent one of the most straightforward applications of GWE principles to business development, as tribes can provide comprehensive business education, entrepreneurship training, and professional development assistance to individual tribal members under general welfare principles. These programs can include tuition assistance for business education, training program costs, professional certification expenses, and related educational support that enhances individual capacity for business success (Bureau of Indian Affairs 2024).

Direct financial assistance to individuals for business-related purposes requires more careful structuring but can be accomplished through programs that provide general welfare support that recipients may utilize for business development purposes. For example, tribes might provide housing assistance, transportation support, childcare assistance, or other general welfare benefits that enable individuals to pursue business opportunities while maintaining compliance with GWE requirements (Internal Revenue Service 2024).

Coordination with Tribal Business Structures
The relationship between GWE programs and tribal business structures requires careful analysis to optimize both individual support and business development objectives. Tribal governments must consider how individual benefits interact with business entity operations and ensure that program design achieves intended outcomes while maintaining regulatory compliance.

For tribal members operating sole proprietorships or other individual business structures, GWE benefits may provide direct support for business activities when structured appropriately. However, tribal governments must ensure that benefits serve general welfare purposes rather than constituting compensation for business services or creating inappropriate business subsidies that could compromise tax-exempt treatment (Federal Register 2024).

When tribal members operate businesses through corporate entities, including Section 17 corporations, tribally chartered corporations, or state-chartered entities, the separation between individual benefits and business operations becomes more complex. GWE benefits provided to individuals cannot be passed through to business entities without potentially compromising tax-exempt treatment, requiring careful attention to program design and administration (Holland & Knight 2024).

The coordination between GWE programs and tribal business development initiatives should consider both immediate individual support needs and longer-term business development objectives, ensuring that programs complement rather than conflict with broader tribal economic development strategies. This coordination may involve collaboration between tribal social services, economic development, and business development departments to create comprehensive support systems (Washington State Bar Association 2024).

Implementation Strategies and Best Practices

Program Design and Documentation Requirements

Successful GWE program implementation requires comprehensive program design that addresses eligibility criteria, benefit determination procedures, application processes, and ongoing administration while maintaining appropriate documentation for IRS compliance purposes. The program design process should involve collaboration between tribal governmental departments, legal counsel, and financial management to ensure regulatory compliance and operational effectiveness.

Written program guidelines must establish clear eligibility criteria that define beneficiary populations, specify benefit types and amounts, outline application and approval procedures, and include appropriate oversight and accountability mechanisms. These guidelines should be sufficiently detailed to enable consistent program administration while maintaining appropriate flexibility for individual circumstances and changing community needs (Bureau of Indian Affairs 2024).

Documentation requirements include maintaining records of program guidelines and updates, eligibility determinations and supporting documentation, benefit payments and recipient information, program administration procedures and staff training, and periodic program evaluation and compliance monitoring. The documentation should be sufficient to demonstrate regulatory compliance without creating excessive administrative burdens that compromise program effectiveness (Internal Revenue Service 2024).

Administrative Procedures and Oversight

The proposed regulations include a temporary suspension of IRS audits on GWE issues until completion of training programs for both IRS agents and tribal finance officers, recognizing the complexity of GWE regulations and the need for adequate education before enforcement activities commence (Holland & Knight 2024). This audit suspension provides tribes with implementation time while ensuring that federal oversight reflects adequate understanding of tribal governmental operations and GWE regulatory requirements.

During the audit suspension period, tribal governments should focus on implementing comprehensive GWE programs, developing appropriate documentation systems, training staff on regulatory requirements and program administration, and establishing coordination mechanisms with other tribal programs and federal agencies. This preparation period enables tribes to optimize program effectiveness while ensuring regulatory compliance when normal oversight activities resume.

The training requirements for IRS agents reflect federal recognition that tribal governmental operations often differ significantly from other governmental entities and that effective oversight requires understanding of tribal sovereignty, governmental structures, and cultural considerations. Similarly, training for tribal finance officers ensures that tribal staff understand federal requirements and can maintain appropriate compliance systems (Federal Register 2024).

Coordination with Federal Programs and Agencies

GWE programs must be coordinated with other federal programs and agencies to ensure compliance with multiple regulatory frameworks while optimizing program effectiveness and avoiding conflicts or duplicative oversight. This coordination is particularly important for tribal governments that manage numerous federal programs with varying requirements and reporting obligations.

Coordination with federal agencies should address program eligibility and benefit determination procedures, reporting and accountability requirements, funding source documentation and segregation, and dispute resolution and appeals processes. Effective coordination enables tribal governments to leverage multiple federal programs while maintaining compliance with specific program requirements and avoiding administrative conflicts (Washington State Bar Association 2024).

The coordination process should also consider how GWE programs interact with tribal governmental operations, including budget development and financial management, policy development and tribal council oversight, staff training and capacity building, and community engagement and member communication. This comprehensive approach ensures that GWE programs serve broader tribal governmental objectives while maintaining appropriate oversight and accountability (Bureau of Indian Affairs 2024).

Strategic Considerations for Tribal Governments
Integration with Economic Development Planning
GWE programs should be integrated into broader tribal economic development planning to ensure that individual support programs complement business development initiatives, workforce development activities, and community development objectives. This integration requires systematic planning that considers both immediate individual needs and longer-term community development goals.

The integration process should evaluate how individual support programs can enhance tribal member capacity for business development, including education and training programs that build entrepreneurship skills, financial assistance that enables business start-up activities, and support services that address barriers to business development. This comprehensive approach maximizes the community development impact of GWE programs while maintaining regulatory compliance (Holland & Knight 2024).

Economic development integration should also consider how GWE programs can support broader tribal business development strategies, including workforce development for tribal enterprises, entrepreneurship development that complements existing tribal businesses, and community development that enhances the business environment. This strategic approach ensures that individual support programs contribute to comprehensive community development rather than operating in isolation (Federal Register 2024).

Cultural and Community Considerations
GWE program design should reflect tribal cultural values and community priorities while maintaining compliance with federal regulatory requirements. This balance requires careful attention to traditional tribal values, contemporary community needs, and federal compliance obligations to create programs that serve authentic community development purposes.

Cultural considerations may include incorporating traditional values into program design and administration, ensuring that programs support cultural preservation and language maintenance, addressing community-specific needs that reflect tribal governmental responsibilities, and maintaining appropriate respect for tribal sovereignty and self-determination. These considerations ensure that GWE programs serve genuine tribal governmental purposes rather than simply accessing federal tax benefits (Washington State Bar Association 2024).

Community engagement in program design and implementation ensures that GWE programs address actual community needs and receive appropriate community support. This engagement should include tribal member input on program priorities and design, ongoing communication about program availability and requirements, feedback mechanisms for program improvement, and appropriate oversight to ensure program effectiveness and accountability (Bureau of Indian Affairs 2024).

Future Developments and Policy Considerations
Pending Regulatory Finalization
At the time of this writing the proposed GWE regulations remain subject to public comment and potential modification before final publication, creating opportunities for tribal governments and practitioners to influence final regulatory language through the administrative process. The public comment period enables tribes to address specific concerns, suggest improvements, and advocate for enhanced flexibility in program design and implementation.

Key areas for potential advocacy include expansion of business development applications, clarification of coordination with other federal programs, enhancement of administrative flexibility and reduced documentation requirements, and improvement of dispute resolution and appeals processes. Tribal advocacy during the comment period can influence final regulations to better serve tribal governmental needs and community development objectives (Holland & Knight 2024).

The finalization timeline for GWE regulations will affect tribal planning and implementation activities, requiring tribal governments to monitor regulatory developments and adjust program design based on final regulatory requirements. This monitoring process should include legal counsel consultation, policy development coordination, and staff training updates to ensure compliance with final regulations (Internal Revenue Service 2024).

Potential Legislative and Policy Developments

Future legislative developments may expand GWE applications to business development activities, particularly in response to tribal advocacy for enhanced business development support capabilities. The Treasury Tribal Advisory Committee (TTAC) and tribal commenters have advocated for including grants to Indian-owned enterprises under GWE provisions, suggesting potential future policy developments that could enhance tribal business development capabilities (Federal Register 2024).

Policy developments may also address coordination between GWE programs and other federal economic development initiatives, including Small Business Administration programs, Economic Development Administration activities, and Treasury Department financing programs. Enhanced coordination could create comprehensive support systems that leverage multiple federal programs while maintaining appropriate oversight and accountability (Washington State Bar Association 2024).

The evolution of federal Indian policy toward enhanced tribal self-determination and economic development may create additional opportunities for expanding GWE applications and improving program flexibility. Tribal governments should monitor policy developments and engage in advocacy activities that promote enhanced tribal governmental authority and program flexibility while maintaining appropriate federal oversight and accountability mechanisms.

Conclusion

The Tribal General Welfare Exclusion represents a significant tool for tribal governments seeking to support individual tribal members while maintaining favorable tax treatment for program beneficiaries. While current regulations limit direct support for business entities, careful program design can enable substantial support for individual business development activities while maintaining regulatory compliance and serving broader community development objectives.

Successful GWE implementation requires comprehensive program design, appropriate documentation and oversight, coordination with other tribal programs and federal agencies, and ongoing attention to regulatory developments and policy changes. Tribal governments that invest in appropriate planning and implementation can utilize GWE programs to enhance individual opportunity while contributing to broader economic development and community building objectives.

The intersection of GWE programs with tribal business structures creates both opportunities and limitations that require careful navigation and professional guidance. As regulatory frameworks continue to evolve and tribal advocacy efforts continue, GWE programs may become even more valuable tools for supporting tribal economic development while preserving the unique advantages that distinguish tribal governmental operations from other economic development approaches.

References

American Indian Law Deskbook. 2021. American Indian Law Deskbook. Conference of Western Attorneys General. Thomson Reuters.

Atkinson, Brian, and Mark Nilles. 2008. Federal Taxation of Native American Tribes and Tribal Entities.

Bureau of Indian Affairs. 2015. Section 17 Corporation Guidance.

Bureau of Indian Affairs. 2015. Section 17 Corporation Handbook.

Bureau of Indian Affairs. 2023. Section 17 Corporation Handbook. U.S. Department of the Interior, Bureau of Indian Affairs.

Bureau of Indian Affairs. 2024. Buy Indian Act Implementation Guidance.

Bureau of Indian Affairs. 2024. Tribal Set-Aside Contracting Procedures.

Bureau of Indian Affairs. 2024. Guidelines on Tribal General Welfare Programs.

Buy Indian Act, 25 U.S.C. 47. 2025.

Cherokee Nation v. Georgia, 30 U.S. (5 Pet.) 1 (1831).

Cherokee Nation v. Nash, Civil Action No. 13-01313 (D.D.C. Aug. 30, 2017) (Hogan, J.).

Cohen, Felix S. 2012. Cohen's Handbook of Federal Indian Law. Newark: LexisNexis.

CNN. 2021. Cherokee Nation Removes Anti-Black Language from Its Constitution. February 24.

CNN. 2021. The Cherokee Nation acknowledges that descendants of people once enslaved by the tribe are citizens. February 25.

Community Development Financial Institutions Fund. 2023. CDFI Program Annual Report.

Cornell, Stephen, and Joseph P. Kalt. 2003. Reloading the Dice: Improving the Chances for Economic Development on American Indian Reservations. Joint Occasional Papers on Native Affairs No. 2003-02. Tucson: Harvard Project on American Indian Economic Development and Native Nations Institute for Leadership, Management, and Policy, University of Arizona.

Debo, Angie. 1940. And Still the Waters Run: The Betrayal of the Five Civilized Tribes. Princeton: Princeton University Press.

Desiderio, Dante. 2016. Tribal Economic Policy During Federal Stimulus.

Economic Development Administration. 2023. EDA Programs for Tribal Economic Development. U.S. Department of Commerce.

Economic Development Administration. 2023. Innovation and Entrepreneurship Initiatives. U.S. Department of Commerce.

Economic Development Administration. 2023. Multi-Tribal Project Eligibility in EDA Programs. U.S. Department of Commerce.

Economic Development Administration. 2023. Revolving Loan Fund Guidelines. U.S. Department of Commerce.

Economic Innovation Group. 2025. Policy Analysis: Tribal Opportunity Zones and Federal Tax Incentives. July 14.

Economic Innovation Group. 2025. Proposed Regulations Provide Clarity on Tax Treatment of Entities Wholly Owned by Tribal Governments. January 9.

Ehle, John. 1988. Trail of Tears: The Rise and Fall of the Cherokee Nation. New York: Anchor Books.

Federal Acquisition Regulation. 2025. Part 19: Small Business Programs.

Federal Register. 2024. "Proposed Regulations: Tribal General Welfare Exclusion." Federal Register 89, no. 182 (Sept. 17).

Federal Register. 2024. "Proposed Regulations Regarding Tribal General Welfare Exclusion." Federal Register 89, no. 194 (Oct. 9): 81871–81880.

Fields, Harold. 2024. Tribal Taxation in Context. Journal of Federal Indian Law 19(2): 45–69.

General Welfare Exclusion Act, Pub. L. No. 113-168, codified at 26 U.S.C. § 139E (2014).

Government Accountability Office. 2023. Cross-Agency Coordination in Federal Tribal Programs.

Government Accountability Office. 2023. Economic Development Administration: Flexibility in Tribal Programs. U.S. Accountability Office.

Government Accountability Office. 2023. USDA Rural Development Program Structure and Tribal Eligibility.

Harvard Project on American Indian Economic Development. 2021. Policy Brief.

Harvard Project on American Indian Economic Development. 2024. Self-Government, Taxation, and Tribal Development: The Critical Role of American Indian Nation Business Enterprises. Cambridge, MA: Harvard Kennedy School, 18–22.

Holland & Knight LLP. 2024. General Welfare Exclusion and Tribal Tax Issues.

Holland & Knight LLP. 2024. Analysis of Tribal GWE Regulations and Business Entity Restrictions.

HUD Office of Native American Programs. 2023. Section 184 Indian Housing Loan Guarantee Program.

HUD ONAP. 2022. Indian Community Development Block Grant Program Guidance.

Internal Revenue Service. 1977. Revenue Ruling 77-77.

Internal Revenue Service. 2015. Notice 2015-54: Supplemental Guidance with Respect to the General Welfare Exclusion, August 14.

Internal Revenue Service. 2022. Historic Preservation Tax Credit Guidance for Indian Country.

Internal Revenue Service. 2024. "Treasury and IRS Issue Proposed Regulations Providing Clarity Regarding the Federal Tax Classification of Entities Entirely Owned by Tribal Governments." October 6.

Internal Revenue Service. 2024. "Treasury and IRS Issue Proposed Regulations Providing Clarity Regarding the Federal Tax Classification of Entities Entirely Owned by Tribal Governments." News Release IR-2024-261, October 7.

Internal Revenue Service. 2024. "Entities Wholly Owned by Indian Tribal Governments." Federal Register 89, no. 194 (Oct. 9): 81871–81880.

Internal Revenue Service. 2024. "Is an incorporated business owned by a tribe subject to federal income tax?" Updated October 10.

Internal Revenue Service. 2024. Proposed Regulations for Tribal General Welfare Exclusion. September 17.

Morton v. Mancari, 417 U.S. 535 (1974).

NAFOA. 2025. Navigating the One Big Beautiful Bill: What It Means for Indian Country. July 20.

National Congress of American Indians. 2018. Policy Platform: Self-Determination and Governance.

National Congress of American Indians. 2019. Tribal Self-Governance Report.

National Congress of American Indians. 2024. Annual Report—Federal Program Coordination.

National Park Service. 2023. Historic Preservation Tax Credits and Tribal Communities.

National Trust for Historic Preservation. 2023. Preservation Success Stories in Indian Country.

NPR. 2017. Judge Rules That Cherokee Freedmen Have Right To Tribal Citizenship. August 30.

Perdue, Theda. 2008. Mixed Blood Indians: Racial Construction in the Early South. Athens: University of Georgia Press.

Prucha, Francis Paul. 1986. The Great Father: The United States Government and the American Indians. Lincoln: University of Nebraska Press.

Small Business Administration. 2023. SBA Tribal Programs Guide.

Small Business Administration. 2025. HUBZone Program Eligibility and Guidance.

Treasury Department. 2024. Fact Sheet: Tax Status of Wholly Owned Tribal Entities. October 6.

Treasury Department. 2024. Fact Sheet: Tribal General Welfare Exclusion Regulatory Update.

U.S. Constitution, Article I, Section 8, Clause 3.

U.S. Department of Agriculture. 2024. Beginning Farmer and Rancher Development Program.

U.S. Department of Agriculture. 2024. Business and Industry Loan Guarantee Program.

U.S. Department of Agriculture. 2024. Rural Development Technical Assistance Programs.

U.S. Department of Agriculture. 2024. Rural Development Tribal Programs Overview.

U.S. Department of Agriculture. 2024. Rural Utilities Service Water and Sewer Program for Tribal Areas.

U.S. Department of Agriculture. 2024. Value-Added Producer Grant Program.

U.S. Department of Energy. 2023. Indian Energy Policy and Programs Annual Report.

U.S. Department of Health and Human Services, Indian Health Service. 2025. IHS Procurement and Contracting Manual.

U.S. Department of Treasury. 2025. Fact Sheet: Tribal Tax Law Updates 2025.

U.S. Department of Treasury. 2025. Tribal Opportunity Zones Final Regulations.

United States Department of Justice. 2022. Risk Management Tribal Consultation Final Report. March. Office of Tribal Justice.

United States v. Lara, 541 U.S. 193 (2004).

USDA Rural Development. 2023. Tribal Rural Development Programs.

Washington State Bar Association. 2024. General Welfare Exclusion in Tribal Program Design.

Washington State Bar Association. 2024. Tribal General Welfare Exclusion: Legal Perspectives.

White House Office of Intergovernmental Affairs. 2024. Best Practices for Tribal Partnership Projects.

White House Office of Intergovernmental Affairs. 2024. Stakeholder Engagement for Tribal Projects.

White House. 2024. Fact Sheet: Biden-Harris Administration Announces New Actions and Historic Progress Supporting Tribal Nations and Native Communities Ahead of Fourth Annual White House Tribal Nations Summit. December 8.

Worcester v. Georgia, 31 U.S. (6 Pet.) 515 (1832).

Bibliography

Advisory Council on Historic Preservation. 2022. "Federal Historic Preservation Tax Incentive Projects Certified by National Park Service Generated $7 Billion in GDP, 122,000 Jobs in 2022." National Park Service Office of Communications. https://www.nps.gov/orgs/1207/federal-historic-preservation-tax-incentive-projects-certified-by-national-park-service-generated-$7-billion-in-gdp-122-000-jobs-in-2022.htm

British Library. 2025. "Catawba Deerskin Map (circa 1721)." Colonial America Manuscript Collection. Accessed July 22, 2025. https://www.bl.uk/collection-items/catawba-deerskin-map

Brown, Marley. 2019. "Catawba Map." In Mapping the Past. Archaeology, May-June 2019. https://archaeology.org/issues/may-june-2019/collection/maps-south-carolina-catawba-map/mapping-the-past/

Bureau of Indian Affairs. 2025. "Choosing a Tribal Business Structure." Indian Affairs. Accessed June 24, 2025. https://www.bia.gov/service/starting-business/choosing-tribal-business-structure

Candid. 2025. "Oklahoma Indian Welfare Act of 1936." Native Philanthropy. Accessed June 24, 2025. https://nativephilanthropy.candid.org/events/oklahoma-indian-welfare-act-of-1936/

Citizen Potawatomi Nation. 2025. "Citizen Potawatomi Community Development Corporation." Accessed August 2, 2025. https://www.potawatomi.org/blog/enterprise/citizen-potawatomi-community-development-corporation/

Community Development Financial Institutions Fund. 2023. "New Markets Tax Credit Program." Accessed December 2024. https://www.cdfifund.gov/programs-training/programs/new-markets-tax-credit

Community Development Financial Institutions Fund. 2024. CDFI Fund FY 2023 Annual Report. Washington, DC: U.S. Department of Treasury. https://www.cdfifund.gov/sites/cdfi/files/2024-05/CDFI_Fund_FY_2023_Annual_Report_FINAL_508c.pdf

Dorsey & Whitney LLP. 2004. "Doing Business In Indian Country." News & Resources, July 2004. https://www.dorsey.com/newsresources/publications/2004/07/doing-business-in-indian-country

EBSCO. 2025. "Oklahoma Welfare Act (1936)." Research Starters: Politics and Government. Accessed June 24, 2025. https://www.ebsco.com/research-starters/politics-and-government/oklahoma-welfare-act-1936

Economic Innovation Group. 2025. "Opportunity Zones 2.0: Where Things Stand After the One Big Beautiful Bill Act." July 11, 2025. https://eig.org/opportunity-zones-2-0-where-things-stand/

Federal Indian Law: Cases and Materials. 2011. 6th Edition. West Academic Publishing.

Five Civilized Tribes. 2025. "Chapter Six." Accessed June 24, 2025. https://www.fivecivilizedtribes.org/Chapter-Six.html

Haas, Theodore H. 2025. "Ten Years of Government under I.R.A." Accessed June 24, 2025. https://thorpe.law.ou.edu/IRA/IRAbook/tribal-govtp1-12.htm

Harvard Project on American Indian Economic Development. 2006. "Citizen Potawatomi Community Development Corporation." Harvard Kennedy School. https://hwpi.harvard.edu/files/hpaied/files/citizen_potawatomi_comm_dev_corp.pdf

Holland & Knight LLP. 2025. "Proposed Regulations Provide Clarity on Tax Treatment of Entities Wholly Owned by Tribal Governments." Insights, January 2025. https://www.hklaw.com/en/insights/publications/2025/01/proposed-regulations-provide-clarity-on-tax-treatment-of-entities

Internal Revenue Service. 2022. "About Form 8874, New Markets Credit." U.S. Department of Treasury. https://www.irs.gov/forms-pubs/about-form-8874

Internal Revenue Service. 2025a. "FAQs for Indian tribal governments regarding employee plans and exempt organization issues." Accessed June 24, 2025. https://www.irs.gov/government-entities/indian-tribal-governments/faqs-for-indian-tribal-governments-regarding-employee-plans-and-exempt-organization-issues

Internal Revenue Service. 2025b. "Treasury and IRS issue proposed regulations providing clarity regarding the federal tax classification of entities entirely owned by tribal governments." IRS Newsroom. Accessed June 24, 2025. https://www.irs.gov/newsroom/treasury-and-irs-issue-proposed-regulations-providing-clarity-regarding-the-federal-tax-classification-of-entities-entirely-owned-by-tribal-governments

Library of Congress. Geography and Map Division. 2025. "Catawba Deerskin Map, ca. 1721." Accessed July 22, 2025. https://www.loc.gov/resource/g3860.ct000734/

McClanahan v. Arizona State Tax Commission. 1973. 411 U.S. 164 (1973).

Mescalero Apache Tribe v. Jones. 1973. 411 U.S. 145 (1973).

Michigan v. Bay Mills Indian Community. 2014. 572 U.S. 782 (2014).

Moyer, Richard. 2021. Tribal Business Law Developments. American Bar Association, 12-15.

National Congress of American Indians. 2024. Tribal Nations and the United States: An Introduction. NCAI Publications.

National Park Service. 2023. "Historic Preservation Tax Incentives." Technical Preservation Services. Accessed December 2024. https://www.nps.gov/subjects/taxincentives/index.htm

National Trust for Historic Preservation. 2023. "Federal Historic Preservation Tax Incentives Program." National Park Service. https://www.nps.gov/tps/tax-incentives.htm

Native American Finance Officers Association. 2023. Tribal Financial Management Best Practices.

Native CDFI Network. 2022. "Interview 25: Cindy Logsdon, Citizen Potawatomi Community Development Corporation." September 20, 2022. https://nativecdfi.net/blog/2022/09/20/interview-25-cindy-logsdon-citizen-potawatomi-community-development-corporation/

The Neshoba Democrat. 2025. "Multi-Tribal Hotel Development Partnership Announcement."

Nilles, Scott. 2016. Tribal Employment Rights and Economic Development. University of New Mexico Law Review, 22-25.

NPR. 2017. "Judge Rules That Cherokee Freedmen Have Right To Tribal Citizenship." The Two-Way, August 31, 2017. https://www.npr.org/sections/thetwo-way/2017/08/31/547705829/judge-rules-that-cherokee-freedmen-have-right-to-tribal-citizenship

Oklahoma Historical Society. 2025. "Oklahoma Indian Welfare Act." The Encyclopedia of Oklahoma History and Culture. Accessed June 24, 2025. https://www.okhistory.org/publications/enc/entry?entry=OK059

People v. Miami Nation Enterprises. 2016. 2 Cal. 5th 222 (2016).

Sequoyah National Research Center. 2025. "Change in Indian Affairs is proposed by Senator Thomas." UA Little Rock. Accessed June 24, 2025. https://ualr.edu/sequoyah/thisday/change-indian-affairs-proposed-senator-thomas/

Tribal Business News. 2025. Annual Economic Impact Report: Native American Business Development.

Tribal Economic Development: Law, Policy, and Practice. 2018. Carolina Academic Press.

U.S. Department of Energy. 2023. "Current Funding Opportunities." Office of Indian Energy Policy and Programs. Accessed December 2024. https://www.energy.gov/indianenergy/current-funding-opportunities

U.S. Department of the Interior. 2025. "HR 4002 - 3.27.14." Office of Congressional and Legislative Affairs. Accessed June 24, 2025. https:// www.doi.gov/ocl/hearings/113/hr4002_032714

U.S. Department of the Interior, Bureau of Indian Affairs. 2023. "Indian Entities Recognized by and Eligible to Receive Services From the United States Bureau of Indian Affairs." Federal Register....

U.S. Department of Treasury. 2024. "U.S. Department of the Treasury, IRS Announce New Milestone in Implementation of Key Provisions to Expand the Reach of Clean Energy Tax Credits." Press Release. March 19, 2024. https://home.treasury.gov/news/press-releases/jy2190

U.S. Department of Treasury. 2025. "Enhanced Federal Tax Benefits from Recent Legislation: One Big Beautiful Bill Act Implementation Guide." Washington, DC: U.S. Department of Treasury.

U.S. Department of Treasury. 2025a. "How did the One Big Beautiful Bill Act change Opportunity Zones?" Brookings Institution. July 9, 2025. https://www.brookings.edu/articles/how-did-the-one-big-beautiful-bill-act-change-opportunity-zones/

U.S. Department of Treasury. 2025b. "Tax Status of Tribally Chartered Corporations Consultation Summary." Accessed June 24, 2025. https:// home.treasury.gov/system/files/136/Tax-Status-of-Tribally-Char-tered-Corporations-Consultation-Summary.pdf

U.S. Government Accountability Office. 2022. Tribal Business Structures and Federal Tax Treatment. GAO-22-104503, 23-25, 45-48.

U.S. House of Representatives. 2025. "25 USC Ch. 45A: Oklahoma Indian Welfare." U.S. Code. Accessed June 24, 2025. https://uscode.house.gov/view.xhtml?path=/prelim@title25/chapter45A&edition=prelim

UK National Archives. 2025. "Catawba Map, Colonial Office Series CO 700/NAC 6/1." Colonial Office Maps and Plans. Accessed July 22, 2025. https://discovery.nationalarchives.gov.uk/details/r/C3042112

Wikimedia Commons. 2025. "Catawba Map 1721." Accessed July 22, 2025. http://upload.wikimedia.org/wikipedia/commons/1/15/Catawba-Map1721.jpg

Wikipedia. 2025. "Oklahoma Indian Welfare Act." Accessed June 24, 2025. https://en.wikipedia.org/wiki/Oklahoma_Indian_Welfare_Act

Williams, Robert A. 2012. Like a Loaded Weapon: The Rehnquist Court, Indian Rights, and the Legal History of Racism in America. University of Minnesota Press.

www.ingramcontent.com/pod-product-compliance
Lightning Source LLC
Chambersburg PA
CBHW022134020426
42334CB00015B/897